Electric Animal

T0204539

Electric | Animal

Toward a Rhetoric of Wildlife

AKIRA MIZUTA LIPPIT

University of Minnesota Press Minneapolis London

The University of Minnesota Press gratefully acknowledges the
assistance provided for the publication of this book by the McKnight
Foundation.

Earlier versions of two chapters appeared as "Afterthoughts on the Animal
World" in *Modern Language Notes* 109 (1994): 786–830 and "Magnetic
Animal: Derrida, Wildlife, *Animetaphor*" in *Modern Language Notes* 113
(1998): 1111–1125. Copyright 1994 and 1998 by The Johns Hopkins
University Press.

"A Photograph" from *Nervous Horses* by Vicki Hearne. Copyright 1980;
reproduced by permission of the University of Texas Press.

Published by the University of Minnesota Press
111 Third Avenue South, Suite 290
Minneapolis, MN 55401-2520
http://www.upress.umn.edu

Printed in the United States of America on acid-free paper

The University of Minnesota is an equal-opportunity educator and
employer.

Library of Congress Cataloging-in-Publication Data:

Lippit, Akira Mizuta.
    Electric animal : toward a rhetoric of wildlife / Akira Mizuta Lippit.
        p. cm.
    Includes bibliographical references (p.   ) and index.
    ISBN 978-0-8166-3486-6 (pb : alk. paper)
    1. Animals (Philosophy)   I. Title.
  B105.A55 L56   2000
  179'.3—dc21   99-086532

15 14 13 12 11 10 09 08   10 9 8 7 6 5 4 3 2 1

Contents

Acknowledgments

Michael Fried and Richard Macksey have guided this book from its inception to its current evolution. I wish to express my deepest gratitude to them for their wisdom and patience at every stage of the process. I am indebted to Jacques Derrida and Werner Hamacher for providing their invaluable insight and generous support.

Miya Lippit, Seiji Lippit, Albert Liu, and Willis Regier read the manuscript meticulously, suggesting critical revisions as well as clarifications. Judith Butler, Milad Doueihi, and Felicia Miller read portions of the manuscript. I have benefited from their criticisms and thank them all for their contributions to the book.

Most of the revisions to this manuscript were completed in the collegial environments of the Department of English at the University of Nebraska–Lincoln and the Department of Cinema at San Francisco State University. I wish to thank my colleagues for their support.

Finally, I would like to thank Jennifer Moore of the University of Minnesota Press, and Paula Dragosh, who copyedited this manuscript.

Introduction | Remembering Animals

> *. . . and already the knowing animals are*
> *aware that we are not really at home in our*
> *interpreted world.*
>
> —RAINER MARIA RILKE, "DUINO ELEGIES"

"EVERYWHERE ANIMALS DISAPPEAR," writes John Berger.[1] Or perhaps, everywhere one looks one is surrounded by the absence of animals. No longer a sign of nature's abundance, animals now inspire a sense of panic for the earth's dwindling resources. Spectral animals recede into the shadows of human consumption and environmental destruction. With the prosperity of human civilization and global colonization, ecospheres are vanishing, species are moving toward extinction, and the environment is sinking, one is told, into a state of uninhabitability. Arguably, modernity has cost existence its diversity, has strained the earth's capacity to maintain life. It is a cliché of modernity: human advancement always coincides with a recession of nature and its figures—wildlife, wilderness, human nature, and so forth. Modernity sustains, in the brief compass of this text, the disappearance of animals as a constant state. That is, through a curious configuration to be analyzed in what follows, animals never *entirely* vanish. Rather, they exist in a state of *perpetual vanishing*. Animals enter a new economy of being during the modern period, one that is no longer sacrificial in the traditional sense of the term but, considering modern technological media generally and the cinema more specifically, *spectral*. In supernatural terms, modernity finds animals lingering in the world *undead*.[2]

1

During the late nineteenth and early twentieth centuries, the cultural and epistemological disciplines, as well as various literary and artistic practices, became preoccupied with the transmission of ideas from one body to another, one forum to another, one consciousness to another. In many disciplines, animals—the figure of the animal—played a crucial role in the articulation of new forms of communication, transmission, and exchange. With the Darwinian revolution, Freudian psychoanalysis, and the advances of the optical and technological media, animals symbolized not only new structures of thought but also the process by which those new thoughts were transported. Animals—and their capacity for instinctive, almost telepathic communication—put into question the primacy of human language and consciousness as optimal modes of communication. This investigation seeks to gauge the effects of animal discourses on select philosophical and psychoanalytic texts, the history of ideas, various creative ventures, and theses on technology of this period.

Beginning with the classical oppositions that distinguish humanity from nature, technology from being, this study argues that such polarities may be read as harboring insights into the structures of scientific thought and artistic representation. Roaming between the two extremes, animals establish a third term with its own realm of being, knowledge, and communication. Animals form an essential epistemological category.

Despite the constancy with which animals have hovered at the fringes of humanity, principally as sacrifices to maintain its limit, the notion of animal being changed dramatically during the nineteenth and twentieth centuries. This is perhaps especially true of the modern period, which can be said to begin with late-eighteenth- and early-nineteenth-century technological advances and conclude in the devastation of World War II. Modernity can be defined by the disappearance of wildlife from humanity's habitat and by the reappearance of the same in humanity's reflections on itself: in philosophy, psychoanalysis, and technological media such as the telephone, film, and radio. During this period, the status of the animal itself began to change—at the very point that animals began to vanish from the empirical world. "Public zoos came into existence," Berger writes, "at the beginning of the period which was to see the disappearance of animals from daily life. The zoo to which people go to meet animals, to observe them, to see them, is, in fact, a monument to their disappearance."[3] In its specular, zoological world, the modern animal evolved into a lost object that could then, in turn, be mourned. A new breed of animals now surrounds the human populace—a genus of vanishing animals, whose very being is constituted by that state of disappearing. The modern animal became, to borrow Jacques Derrida's expression, "a memory of the present."[4]

Animal Phenomenology

IN SEPTEMBER 1992, researchers at Johns Hopkins diagnosed "a rare neurological illness known as paraneoplastic encephalopathy." The disease afflicted the patient's cognitive function and "was marked by a slight but very specific disruption in one category of information: she could not name or describe the physical attributes of animals."[5] Over several months of observation, the patient could neither remember nor describe the visual appearance of animals: she could not conjure up their colors, shapes, sizes, or dimensions. She was, however, capable of describing these same attributes when they modified objects or ideas other than those of an animal nature, leading the researchers to believe that the phenomenality of animals designated—at least in this instance—an altogether unique repository of knowledge, one wholly distinct from that containing other kinds of information.

Aware of the deficiency in her knowledge, the patient actively sought to overcome it by expanding the framework of her consciousness—to suture the gaps in her knowledge by increasing her awareness of them. Sensing that her archives had been erased by the illness, the patient tried to reinscribe the attributes of animals in her memory and reproduce them later. Despite her attempts to memorize the features of animals, the patient could not recall any descriptions of specific animals without the aid of some visual cue. The damage was apparently permanent and irreversible, and her efforts only resulted in a heightened state of distress.

Although the appearance of the animal figure in this case may have been a mere contingency, its intrusion underscores the uncanny effect of animals on human thought and imagination. At once familiar and distant, animals have traditionally illuminated human existence. As David Clark notes: "If the thought of 'the animal' is in question, so too, inevitably, is the thought of 'the human' with which it has always been inextricably bound."[6] Paraneoplastic encephalopathy, appearing in the form of animal phenomenology, had forced the patient to accept the limits of her psyche: against the figure of the animal, she encountered the threshold of her consciousness.[7] Unable to think beyond the limit established by the animal, the patient could only project her consciousness. The aporia had provided her with a view of the outside of her consciousness, a glimpse of the unknowable.

To the extent that the patient was diagnosed with a neurological disorder, the case raises fundamental questions concerning knowledge and consciousness, impelling one to view the patient's struggle, at least in part, as brain against mind. As the medical examination progressed, the disparity between the workings of the brain and the desires of the mind came into sharper focus: the apparent inability of the mind to reach into certain areas of mnemic, cerebral, and sensual data became increasingly clearer in the brain's adamant blockage of the animal. From the standpoint of biology, the brain represents the material center of intelligent life. An animal's intelligence is frequently measured by the capacities of its brain, which exists in the body as an organ. The mind belongs exclusively to human beings and establishes the unique subjectivity of each human organism: it is an abstraction and, like the soul, cannot be found within the human anatomy. The brain regulates a number of neurological and bodily functions, whereas the mind attends to only one: consciousness. That difference, according to Johns Hopkins neuroscientist Dr. John Hart Jr., greatly affects how human beings conceive knowledge. Hart, who also supervised and analyzed the aforementioned medical case, states: "There are separate systems in the brain to deal with different categories of knowledge. . . . The brain is not necessarily built the way your mind thinks it is."[8] In other words, while the brain works, the mind reflects: while the brain disperses knowledge (sensations, warnings, and other signals) throughout the body, the mind organizes that movement into subjectivity. Accordingly, the distinction between brain and mind rests ultimately in the question of agency: the brain possesses no agency for imagining itself as coherent, whereas the mind cannot conceive its own fragmentation, the areas beyond its reach. The long-standing dichotomy between the conceptual and biomechanical modes of cognition has influenced not only psychological and philosophical discourses on the mind but also, as this case confirms, approaches to neurobiology, psychobiology, and other sciences of the brain.

Hegel summarizes the mind's desire to usurp the function of human determination and articulates the challenge that this imposed subjectivity presents to science:

It belongs to the nature of the mind to cognize its Notion. Consequently, the summons to the Greeks of the

Delphic Apollo, *Know thyself,* does not have the meaning of a law imposed on the human mind by an alien power; on the contrary, the god who impels to self-knowledge is none other than the absolute law of mind itself. Mind is, therefore, in its every act only apprehending itself, and the aim of all genuine science is just this, that the mind shall recognize itself in everything in heaven and on earth. An out-and-out Other simply does not exist for the mind.[9]

The very attempt to situate the mind as not only the highest law of science but also one that originates from within being, as the very condition of being, which is to say as subjectivity, exposes the underlying anxiety that the mind may not, in fact, originate within being: that consciousness may rather be the effect of some profoundly alien thought—a thought of the other, in the sense elaborated in recent philosophy. In the case of paraneoplastic encephalopathy described above, the possibility of knowing oneself as a unified self—of excluding any possibility of an other—was jeopardized by the appearance of an other. The animal other, despite its erasure, made its presence known as an unknowable other, known only as unknowable to the mind.

The case itself may indicate that a third term or agent might be required to supplement the traditional mind/brain duality: something beyond the neurological/conceptual opposition, something precipitated by or resulting in the figure of the animal. It is not by accident, however, that the figure of the animal fulfills the function of such a third term: the animal is particularly suited to that task. Animals are exemplary vehicles with which to mediate between the corporeality of the brain and the ideality of the mind. Traditionally, they are held to be neither nonconscious like stones or plants, nor self-conscious like human beings. Animals, it is said, can act without reason, can exist without language. In this sense, animal being might best be described as *un*conscious, that is, as existing somewhere other than in the manifest realms of consciousness. Animal being can be understood as determining the place of an alien thought.

Animals are linked to humanity through mythic, fabulous, allegorical, and symbolic associations, but not through the shared possession of language as such. Without language one cannot participate in the world of human beings. For the patient in question, animals inhabit a separate world within the universe of human knowledge—a world that in the case of paraneoplastic encephalopathy is susceptible to permanent displacement. Rachel Wilder describes the disorder:

> Tests over a period of several months showed that she [the patient] could, for example, talk in great detail about where animals live or whether they were pets, but she could not say what they look like.
>
> Her impairment was only verbal and only in the category of the physical attributes of animals, in which she could not correctly answer questions about size, number of legs or colors of animals. Thus she could say that celery is green, but not that a frog or turtle is green.
>
> She could, however, accurately discuss the physical attributes of any other object, and correctly identify an animal's attributes when the information was presented visually in pictures. For example, while she could say that the color of an animal was wrong in a picture, she had trouble naming its correct color.[10]

Evidently, the patient was aware of discrepancies and inaccuracies in the representation of animals but could not rectify them through language. Such disruptions in the patient's discursive capacities suggest that although human beings can readily "perceive" the existence of animals, they are not always able to translate that perception into the linguistic registers that constitute human understanding. Animals seem to necessitate some form of mediation or allegorization—some initial transposition to language—before they can be absorbed into and dispersed throughout the flow of everyday psychology. The mechanism for such conversions between the animal and verbal worlds had collapsed in the stricken subject. During her illness, the patient lost the ability to realign and integrate nonverbal animal data into the virtual world of language. From the vantage point of the animals (although, in the absence of a verifiable subjectivity, the possibility of such a vantage point must also be carefully questioned), they were now suspended in a spectral beyond; they were destined to reside in the interstice between mind and matter, unable to migrate into consciousness. The patient died without ever regaining "consciousness of animals."

The case of paraneoplastic encephalopathy offers a useful entry point for this discussion, since it explores a phantom world that has haunted, throughout its long history, the domain of human subjectivity. Despite the distance of animal being from the human world, the uncanny proximity of animals to human beings necessarily involves them in any attempt to define a human essence. The effort to define the human being has usually required a preliminary gesture of exclusion: a rhetorical animal sacrifice. The presence of the animal must first be extinguished for the human being to appear. Although the determination of human autonomy in contrast to animality is not an especially unusual notion, the *return of the animal,* despite strenuous efforts to exclude it, is worthy of attention. The Johns Hopkins case suggests that some "unconscious" agency may be at work rigorously segregating animals from language and knowledge, and that those excluded animals nevertheless manage to return in the guise of a profound negativity. Temple Grandin, a scientist who grew up autistic, argues that autism, which is also a neurological disorder, can sometimes compel a person to "think in pictures" like an animal. According to Grandin, the oversensitivity that accompanies autism can result in a shift from the abstraction of linguistic signs to the precision of images: "I think in pictures. Words are like a second language to me. I translate both spoken and written words into full-color movies, complete with sound, which run like a VCR tape in my head. When somebody speaks to me, his words are immediately translated into pictures."[11] Grandin links this capacity to animal thought, claiming that "it is very likely that animals think in pictures and memories of smell, light, and sound patterns. In fact, my visual thinking patterns probably resemble animal thinking more closely than those of verbal thinkers."[12] If, as Grandin suggests, the capacity to think in pictures is a feature of animal consciousness, then the paraneoplastic encephalopath may have been undergoing, like Kafka's Gregor Samsa, a kind of metamorphosis, a becoming-animal.

The paraneoplastic encephalopath's systemic annihilation of animal traces from her field of consciousness, although remarkable in its specificity, reveals something about the history of human self-constitution: animals have often functioned as an ambiguous excess upon whose elimination human identity consolidates itself. For example, the doctrine of "universal" love that founds the Christian community, Marc Shell explains, does not extend to animals but rather is limited to the infinitude and universality said to exist within humanity's being. Tracing the exclusion of animals to early Christian rhetoric and its demarcation of sibling human beings from nonsibling (nonhuman) others, Shell writes: "Christians often conflated species with family. . . . so it is not surprising that the argument that we should tolerate others' religious views because they are our kin, or 'brother,' should take sometimes the form of a claim that we should tolerate their views because they are our kind, or 'human beings.' "[13] In this vein, Max Horkheimer and Theodor Adorno assert that Western humanist culture depends on the exclusion of animals, and that its historical progression culminates logically in the justification of mass murder. The National Socialist state, they argue, excused the elimination of Jews from the "German" populace by transforming them first into nonhuman or animal others, "to the condition of a species."[14] The atrocities of World War II derive from the anthropological foundation that separates humanity from animals.

> The idea of man in European history is expressed in the way in which he is distinguished from the animal. Animal irrationality is adduced as proof of human dignity. This contrast has been reiterated with such persistence and unanimity by all the predecessors of bourgeois thought —by the ancient Jews, Stoics, Fathers of the Church, and then throughout the Middle Ages down to modern times —that few ideas have taken such a hold on Western anthropology.[15]

As Adorno and Horkheimer insist, the idea of human superiority has been restated so frequently that it has become an unqualified truth. Although the discourse on humanity features the rhetorical exclusion of animal beings from the Lebenswelt of human ontology, within the broader range of epistemological disciplines and artistic practices animals have played a prominent role in the articulation of human identity.

Animality

The birth of this extreme emotion, which we designate under the name eroticism and which separates man from animals, is without doubt an essential dimension of what prehistoric research can contribute to knowledge.

—GEORGES BATAILLE, "THE TEARS OF EROS"

THE FAMOUS PAINTING from the Lascaux cave, discovered in 1940 and dating from around 13,500 B.C., depicts humanity's entry along with the animal into the world of representation: it is, ironically, a death scene. Among the elements of the painting is a dying man wearing what appears to be a bird's head or mask and several other dying animals. Bataille describes the scene at length:

> . . . [A] man with a bird's face, who asserts his being with an erect penis, but who is falling down. This man is lying in front of a wounded bison. The bison is about to die, but facing the man, it spills its entrails horrifically.
>
> Something obscure, strange, sets apart this pathetic scene, to which nothing in our time can be compared. Above this fallen man, a bird drawn in a single stroke, on the end of a stick, contrives to distract our thoughts.
>
> Further away, toward the left, a rhinoceros is moving away, but it is surely not linked to the scene where the bison and the man-bird appear, united in the face of death.
>
> As the Abbé Breuil has suggested, the rhinoceros might be moving slowly away from the dying figure after having torn open the stomach of the bison. But clearly the composition of the image attributes the origin of the wound to the man, to the spear that the hand of the dying figure could have thrown. The rhinoceros, on the contrary, seems

independent of the principal scene, which might remain forever unexplained.[16]

"What can one say about this striking evocation," Bataille asks, "buried for thousands of years in these lost, and so to speak, inaccessible depths?"[17] In the end, Bataille concurs with the anthropological interpretation of that scene as one of expiation in which a shaman is seen atoning for the murder of the bison,[18] adding that the Lascaux cave painting also marks the birth of "eroticism."[19] The birth of eros, the aspect of human existence that Bataille links elsewhere to mortality, entails the sacrifice of animals and an interchangeable relation between human and animal forms. The motifs of animal death, metamorphosis, and palingenesis have dominated ancient religious concepts from Greco-Roman sacrifice to Hindu reincarnation.[20]

The killing of animals, however, is not restricted to religion. Experiments on animal bodies for the purpose of anatomical comparison and medical knowledge date back to Aristotle (384–322 B.C.) and Galen (A.D. 129–199), although the first documented vivisections did not take place until the sixteenth century.[21] The use of animals to advance knowledge has often aroused feelings of antipathy and discomfort in the human world, and today such practices continue to unsettle the social conscience. Still, the dissection of animals for biological and medical purposes derived a considerable measure of acceptance from the paradigmatic work of Aristotle, whose projects in zoology perhaps first validated—in a nonreligious context—the enterprise of animal sacrifice. A brief glance at Aristotle's work reveals the importance given to the study of animals, and that emphasis has been retained throughout much of the Western philosophical canon. Richard J. Bernstein speculates that "an entire history of philosophy could be written simply by tracking what philosophers have said about animals."[22]

Another classical figure, Aesop, employs animal surrogates to expose the moral mechanisms of the human world. Aesop's fables, which are generally considered a precursor of the literary genres of fiction and pedagogical writing, rely heavily upon the satirical posturings of animals to depict various aspects of human nature.[23] In this connection, one might also note the frequent recourse to animal beings in fairy tales. As with fables, fairy tales also tend to utilize animals for editorial or allegorical purposes. Regarding the similar, that is, instructional role of animal models in the social sciences, Donna J. Haraway writes:

> Animals have continued to have a special status as natural objects that can show people their origin, and therefore their pre-rational, pre-management, pre-cultural essence. That is, animals have been ominously ambiguous in their place in the doctrine of autonomy of the human and natural sciences. So, despite the claims of anthropology to be able to understand human beings solely with the concept of culture, and of sociology to need nothing but the idea of the human social group, animal societies have been extensively employed in rationalization and naturalization of the oppressive orders of domination in the human body politic. They have provided the point of union of the physiological and political for modern liberal theorists while they continue to accept the ideology of the split between nature and culture.[24]

Through the figure of the animal, Haraway analyzes the development of gender politics and the exclusion of women (as well as aliens, cyborgs, animals, and other minority beings) on the grounds of ontology.[25] In the related field of sociobiology, perhaps the most significant discussions of animal and human evolution are Charles Darwin's *On the Origin of Species* (1859) and *The Descent of Man* (1871). Taken together, Darwin's interventions radically altered the place occupied by animals in the biohistory of the earth, preparing the way for Freudian psychoanalysis and Mendel's genetics.

Language

ARGUABLY THE MOST sensitive arena in which human subjectivity struggles for dominance is that of language in general, and speech in particular. Most surveys of Western philosophical thought affirm (with a few very important exceptions) the consensus that although animals undoubtedly communicate with one another, only human beings convey their subjectivity in speech. That is, human speech exceeds its function as communication and actually performs, with each utterance, the subject.[26]

Although proponents of structuralism in linguistic and literary theory moved the emphasis of subjectivity from human speech to the "text," the logic of the subject remained intact. Derrida, the most prominent critic of the structuralist assumption that textuality—the system of semiological signs grounded in language—institutes the place of the subject, argues that the text produces an entirely other discursive site, the trace *(trait)* of an other's discourse that can never be reduced to the subject.[27] The figure of the animal frequently stands, for Derrida, in the place of such alterity.

The philosophy of Jacques Derrida remains, throughout this work, crucial to the discussion of animal being. Beginning with his theses on language, Derrida's deconstructions of Western metaphysics have contributed many key philosophical concepts that will be used throughout this study. In the opening remarks to his presentation at Cerisy-la-Salle in 1997, where he spoke to the subject of the "autobiographical animal," Derrida claims that although he has not addressed, in his work to date, the question of the animal as such, he has nonetheless been talking about nothing but animals.[28] Inevitably, Derrida has turned his attention toward the question of the animal. Beyond his own thoughts on animal being and the metaphysical disruption it causes, Derrida has introduced the philosophemes that make an investigation of the animal as such possible. This study pursues many of Derrida's themes—*différance*, supplement, trace, frame, graft, parasite, and dissemination, to name only a few— as it tracks the figure of the animal through the terrain mapped by conceptions of language. It seeks to uncover the traces of animality that are embedded in language, arguing that the animals that Descartes vehemently censured as irrational machines or speechless "automata" nonetheless remain inextricably linked to the discourse on human language. Although lacking the capacity for human speech, animals remain essential to its constitution.[29]

The important role of animals in the metaphysics of speech is also an antithetical one. The economy of human subjectivity and speech is restricted: only human beings are capable of speech, which, in turn, founds the human subject. Animals enter that tautology as a phantasmatic counterpoint to human language. The animal voice establishes an imaginary place of being beyond the threshold of human discourse. It is in the vehicle of speech, the "*system* of speech, or the *system* of truth," Derrida explains, that humanity founds the transcendental principles of its own existence above and in contradistinction to that of animals.[30] Derrida describes the connection between language and humanism, language and the subject, and offers a line of escape from the seemingly closed economy in which those terms are bound:

> The idea according to which man is the only speaking being, in its traditional form or in its Heideggerian form, seems to me at once undisplaceable and highly problematic.

Of course, if one defines language in such a way that it is reserved for what we call man, what is there to say? But if one reinscribes language in a network of possibilities that do not merely encompass it but mark it irreducibly from the inside, everything changes. I am thinking in particular of the mark in general, of the trace, of iterability, of *différance*. These possibilities or necessities, without which there would be no language, *are themselves not only human.* It is not a question of covering up ruptures and heterogeneities. I would simply contest that they give rise to a single linear, indivisible, oppositional limit, to a binary opposition between the human and the infra-human. And what I am proposing here should allow us to take into account scientific knowledge about the complexity of "animal languages," genetic coding, all forms of marking within which so-called human language, as original as it might be, does not allow us to "cut" once and for all where we would in general like to cut. . . . And this also means that we never know, and never have known, how to *cut up* a subject.[31]

For Derrida, the sacrificial *cut* that implements subjectivity cannot be placed unproblematically between humanity and animal, between beings that do and do not have language in the traditional sense. The locus of animality itself functions as a cut that lacerates the discourse of the subject. The field of animal being cannot be severed from that of the subject because neither field is constituted apart from one another.

Umwelt (Environment)

As scientific understanding has grown, so our world has become dehumanized. Man feels himself no longer involved in nature and has lost his emotional "unconscious identity" with natural phenomena. . . . No voices now speak to man from stones, plants, and animals, nor does he speak to them believing they can hear.
— CARL JUNG, "APPROACHING THE UNCONSCIOUS"

IT IS INTERESTING that Jung should choose in 1961 the term *dehumanized* to describe humanity's elimination of animals from the immediate environment. Jung's lament for the displacement of animals through scientific progress is itself a commonplace sentiment, yet the idea that the disappearance of animals effects a dehumanization of "our world" is a reversal of the sacrificial structure discussed earlier. According to Jung, the dislocation of animal being lessens the fullness of *our* world and not the animal's. The absence of animal being weakens the humanity of the human world. Jung's statement reverses the terms of animal sacrifice: it is now the human world that suffers from the exclusion of animals, whereas before, it was precisely the removal of animals that allowed human beings to establish their autonomy. In the modern era, human beings miss the animals that no longer make themselves heard in the world. Jung's logic points toward a crucial feature of modernity, mourning.

Sigmund Freud's explanation of the causes that lead to mourning (and also to melancholia, an "incomplete" form of mourning) help chart the movement of humanity away from the animal and interpret the symptoms of mourning that such separations produce.[32] A common anthropological myth seeks to explain the development of animals and human beings as distinct entities. To the extent that human beings once considered animals to be intrinsic to their environment and existence, the two forms of being—animal and human—were undifferentiated. Human beings did not yet exist apart from animals.

As the burden of survival lessened, human beings began to develop an awareness of themselves and to recognize the animal as a foreign being. Humanity began to constitute itself within a world of human differences, and subsequently, the animal was metamorphosed into an other creature. In turn, the animal came to inhabit a new topology of its own, and humanity was left to mourn the loss of its former self. The mourning is for the self—a self that had become dehumanized in the very process of humanity's becoming-human.

The anthropological narrative is similar to the one that Freud presents in relation to individual human development. In Freud's account, the place of the animal in the anthropological version is taken by the narcissistic object, or the preformed ego in the infantile state. As the infant begins to recognize the differences that separate its body from other things and beings, it makes a crucial distinction between self and other. The other forms from the residues of a self that emerges by excising what is other. The self recognizes the traces of a former correspondence with the other. Both stories conclude with a loss of the former self and the implementation of a phase of mourning. Taken to its extreme, Freud explains, the normative process of mourning can degenerate into a pathology, melancholia. In that case, the lost object—the former, pre-egoical self—is treated with an ambivalence that frequently takes the form of hostility. For Freud, "The melancholic's erotic cathexis in regard to his object has thus undergone a double vicissitude: part of it has regressed to identification, but the other part, under the influence of the conflict due to ambivalence, has been carried back to the stage of sadism, which is nearer to that conflict."[33] Seen in this light, one can view the origin of animal sacrifice as a melancholic ritual, replete with sadism and ambivalence, which repeats the origin of humanity. It serves to affirm and renounce humanity's primal identification with animals, and the need to overcome it.

This is not to say, however, that such an origin coincides with that of humanism, or what Michel Foucault in *The Order of Things* calls "the human sciences."[34] "Before the end of the eighteenth century, *man* did not exist . . . there was no epistemological consciousness of man as such."[35] For the present purposes, it is interesting to note that the invention of the idea of humanity, its appearance in the human sciences, was accompanied by an intensive investigation of the animal in those very sciences. At precisely the moment when the bond between humanity and animal came to be seen as broken, humanity became a subject and the animal its reflection. According to Jung, but also to a wide array of modernist writers to be discussed shortly, the sacrificial economy by which animals were negated entered a new phase during the modern era—a phase marked by melancholia. Jung writes of an abandoned humanity in the age of scientific or technological advance: "[Its] contact with nature has gone, and with it has gone the profound emotional energy that this symbolic connection supplied."[36] The animal, the representative subject of nature, no longer calls to humanity. It is this sequence of events—the appearance of a dehumanized human being and the disappearance of the animal—that will frame and focus the following text.

A world in which the connection between humanity and nature has been severed does not, however, necessarily result in a nonhuman world. On the antithesis to humanism, Jean-François Lyotard writes: "Dehumanized still implies human—a dead human, but conceivable: because dead in human terms, still capable of being sublated in thought."[37] A semirevolution then: humanity is no longer at the center of a world that remains nonetheless human. By displacing animals from the phenomenal world, humanity disrupts the delicate balance between human beings and animals (among other forms of nature such as plants, insects, raw materials, land and water formations, diurnal and nocturnal dynamics, atmospheric conditions, and so on)—a balance that had, in fact, constituted the very humanness of the human world. But, as Lyotard, following Hegel, insists, the human world can survive dialectically the absence of humanized beings. Dehumanized beings, human beings that have broken their primordial link to nature, are an ironic legacy of humanism. As for the animals, their disappearance does not release them from their bond with human beings in a human world. Even as absent beings, animals accompany the crisis in human ontology. Even in a dehumanized world, animals survive—although in a manner altogether different from that of human beings.

The human world, according to Giorgio Agamben, is "irreparable" in the sense of being "thus" and "not otherwise."[38] Following Spinoza, Agamben defines this deictic term: "The Irreparable is that things are just as they are, in this or that mode, consigned without remedy to their way of being."[39] The human world is thus irreparable. In contrast, the world of animals can never be "thus," or as such, remaining rather in flux, reparable, adjustable, and generally resistant to the *thusness* of the human world. It follows that the elimination of animals from the human atmosphere is irreparable from the perspective of modern humanity. Thus animals disappear; it is thus that animals disappear; it is inevitable that animals disappear. From the elusive vantage point of the animal, however, one cannot say it is "thus"—animals cannot say (for more than one reason) that they have disappeared.

Would we say of an animal that its world is thus-and-thus? Even if we could exactly describe the animal's world, representing it as the animal sees it (as in the color illustrations of Uexküll's books that depict the world of the bee, the hermit crab, and the fly), certainly that world would still not contain the *thus;* it would not be *thus* for the animal: It would not be irreparable.[40]

In this sense, the paraneoplastic encephalopath's erasure of the animal is interesting as a symptom of an irreparable world. It can be seen as the manifestation of an animal ontology to which human beings have no access—the irreparable loss of a once possible relation to animal worlds. Animals once contributed to the constitution of human ontology; now their absence contributes to a dehumanized ontology. Put another way, although animals have always haunted the topology of human subjectivity, the nature of the animal has shifted in the modern era from a metaphysic to a phantasm; from a body to an image; from a living voice to a technical echo.

What is unique to and thus problematic of the bestial paradigm resides in its parasitic relation to the two rival empires, humanity and nature. The sacrificial economy by which animals are linked to human beings has already been mentioned. In contrast, the relation of animals to nature is not unlike that of technology to humanity. Animals are often seen as *grafts* that help organize the *body* onto which they have been appended; they complete or realize the idea of nature. To employ Derrida's logic of the frame or "parergonality," animals at once establish and yet are excluded from the plenitude of nature. Furthermore, because they exist as the manifestations of a voiceless but omnipresent nature, animals emerge in this context as instruments of dissemination. As figures of nature that lack the capacity for speech and thus (self-) reflection and (self-) conception, animals are incapable of determining or regulating the discourse they put forth: they simply transmit. Animals are unable to withhold the outflow of signals and significations with which they are endowed. In Derrida's paraphrase, although animals may hold a huge responsibility in the discourse of the other (here, of nature), they cannot represent the consciousness of their representations. That is, even as exemplary wild beings, animals cannot respond to the call of the wild "as such." Derrida explains: "Animals are incapable of keeping or even having a secret, because they cannot *represent as such,* as an *object* before consciousness, something that they would then forbid themselves from showing."[41] Given the openness of animals, what Lyotard refers to as their "passivity," one must ask whether human beings have learned to read or decipher such animal disclosures.[42] And to the extent that animals are incapable of maintaining secrets, mustn't one question not only the nature of their expression but also its figurative modalities, its expressive form? For if animals are indeed incapable of language, as most traditional philosophers argue (with the notable exceptions of Montaigne and Nietzsche), then mustn't one be attentive to the possibility that another communicative medium may in fact be operative in nature's animal provocations?

The present study examines these questions as they arise in philosophy, psychoanalysis, critical theory, and the technological media. In each instance, the book surveys the position of the animal and analyzes how it participates in that particular discourse or discipline. The first two chapters assemble a history of animal being in the fields of traditional philosophy, from Aristotle to Heidegger. The third and fourth chapters look at the ideas on animality that emerged from evolutionary theory and the advent of psychoanalysis, from the Darwinian to Freudian revolutions, and at contemporary critical theory. The text concludes with a brief analysis of photography and cinema, and the animal ghosts that haunt not only the inception of cinema (the protoanimations of Eadweard James Muybridge and Etienne-Jules Marey) but also its subsequent theorization and practice. En route to the photographic media, the fifth chapter looks at the work of Lewis Carroll, Franz Kafka, and Akutagawa Ryunosuke—three authors representing three separate cultures, sets of conceptual problems, and literary projects—who can be seen as having played crucial roles in facilitating the transition to modernism by thematizing the animal.

The purpose in addressing these authors is to show how (1) the theme of animality plays an important role in their fiction, and (2) their work, in many ways, prefigures a move to (in the case of Carroll) and acts as a response to (in the cases of Kafka and Akutagawa) cinema. As a transition to the cinematic body, this section addresses the movement through three thematic regions that relate to animality and literature: language in Carroll, corporeality in Kafka, and madness in Akutagawa. The glimpse into modern literature concludes by addressing the special relationship between animals and literature (compared with that of philosophy and animals, psychoanalysis and animals, and critical theory and animals, respectively). Here, the text proposes that literature has always maintained a privileged relation to the nonliterary referent or to nonlinguistic writing, to media that problematize the notion of writing. The figure of the animal in literature makes such contact between the literary and nonliterary worlds visible. It is the rapport between language and animals in modernist literature that perhaps best points to the emergence of the cinema and its cryptic relation to the animal.

The final chapter presents a speculative reading of the history of modernism through the lenses of photography and film. Beginning with an interpretation of Muybridge's photographs of animals in motion, the conclusion argues that the elimination of animals from the immediate environment coincided with accelerated industrialization in the late nineteenth and early twentieth centuries and the rise of the technological media. Not only were animals thematized, they were also appropriated by the technological media for the symbolic and actual powers they represented—"horsepower" in engines, electrocuted animals in direct current, animated animals in early cinema. In fact, cinema perhaps best embodied the transfer of animals from nature to technology. In the writings of Soviet filmmaker and theorist Sergei Eisenstein, for example, the process of editing, or montage, is frequently likened to a genetic code in which dominant as well as recessive links are made between convergent strings of information. Eisenstein, along with other early film theorists such as Germaine Dulac, often discusses the filmic process in biological and organic terms, strengthening the impression that the cinema was somehow expected to replace or supplant a rapidly declining animal presence. Animals were particularly useful in the development of technical media because they seemed to figure a pace of communication that was both more rapid and more efficient than that of language.

During the discussion of animal being and the technological media, the text addresses a number of psychoanalytic writings on photography and film. From the phenomenological speculations of André Bazin to the structural analyses of Jean-Louis Baudry and Christian Metz, the application of Freudian and Lacanian psychoanalysis to filmic structures has provided a compelling examination of an otherwise insufficiently addressed medium. Particularly helpful in those theorizations is the attention paid to the relationship between the apparatus and the spectator/subject, between the editing process and human psychology. In the registers of psychoanalysis, a similarity between cinematic processes and those of the mind begins to take shape. Apart from the important role that condensation and displacement play in both the psychoanalytic and cinematic discourses, the structure of transference perhaps best confirms the rapport between film and the unconscious, between cinematic communication and animal being. Through readings of essential psychoanalytic texts on transference from Sandor Ferenczi to Lyotard, the text concludes that transference is precisely the modality in which language is circumvented for a more expedient connection between drives, points, thoughts, or instincts. It is, in fact, the mode of communication that philosophy accords the animal.

With the process of transference at its base, cinema is no longer a machine like other machines. Transference allows films to communicate. The transferential dynamic, according to Dziga Vertov and Eisenstein, establishes something like an unconscious in the topology of cinema. In that sense, cinema can be seen as a technological supplement of the subject. As such, cinema comes to resemble its counterpart in nature, the animal supplement. The alliance between animals and cinema brings together two poles of a traditional opposition, animals and technology. Not surprisingly, then, early cinema frequently thematizes animals. And thus while animals were disappearing from the immediate world, they were reappearing in the mediated world of technological reproduction. Undying, animals seemed to fuel the phantom thermodynamic engines that would run perpetually. Animals and their figures had come full circle in the modern era, from philosophy to technology. Animals had found a proper habitat or world in the recording devices of the technological media. The capacities of the technological media in general and the photographic media in particular to record and recall served as a mnemic supplement that allowed modern culture to preserve animals.

In conclusion, the text re-presents the thesis that animals have remained a compelling figure in the discursive structures of philosophy, critical theory, literature, and cinema, despite their secondary or supplementary role. Especially during the modern era, animals were transposed into the discursive and figurative arenas precisely because they offered a rhetorical "line of escape," as Deleuze and Guattari phrase it, from a history saturated with immutable linguistic and methodological modes of conception—a history, as it were, in crisis. And because they had been denied the status of conscious subjects, animals were now sought as the ideal figures of a destabilized subjectivity. Not only can the animal be seen as a crucial figure for the reading of that history, but the animal also serves as the very figure of modernity itself. The animal can be seen, in fact, as the figure of modern subjectivity. Neither a regressive nor primitive figure, animal being founds the site of an excess, a place of being that exceeds the subject. In this sense, the paraneoplastic encephalopath can be seen as the last subject of a recent history; the task of this text is to recover the traces of animality, to remember animals.

1 | Philosophy and the Animal World

Even inarticulate noises (of beasts, for instance) do
indeed reveal something, yet none of them is a name.
—ARISTOTLE, "DE INTERPRETATIONE"

THE SCENE OF the crime is the fourth story of a house in Paris. The occupants have been brutally slain and the Parisian police are scrambling for answers. Under the heading "Extraordinary Murders," the *Gazette des Tribunaux* gives notice of the affair: a widow and her daughter, Madame and Mademoiselle L'Espanaye, have been found bludgeoned, mutilated, and partially dismembered—the daughter forced into the chimney, the mother thrown from the window. The domestic assault appears to have extended even to the house itself: "The apartment was in the wildest disorder—the furniture broken and thrown about in all directions."[1] "To this horrible mystery there is not as yet," the newspaper reports, "the slightest clue."[2] Still missing are a perpetrator and motive, an explanation of the crime. The *Gazette* concludes: "A murder so mysterious, and so perplexing in all its particulars, was never before committed in Paris—if indeed a murder has been committed at all."[3]

Edgar Allan Poe's 1841 story "The Murders in the Rue Morgue" brings to the surface a quintessentially modern catastrophe: the domicile of humanity has been assailed from the outside, indeed *by* the outside. The social and architectural structures that protect the human world appear to have weakened, exposing those inside, like the L'Espanayes, to the dangers of the wild side. Poe's crisis begins with an emergency, a cry reverberating with the call of the wild. The protagonist, C. Auguste Dupin, the first figure of modern detection, undertakes the task of trailing a murderer whose identity, as the narrative progresses, appears to exceed the realm of the human. At stake in his pursuit is the delineation of the criminal being and of the world within which criminal acts take place, and as it proceeds his investigation of the "in-human" murder reveals the forms of animality that begin to coalesce in the exteriorities of the wild.

The crime has been committed by an orangutan. But can an orangutan or any other animal be considered a criminal, can it be forced to take responsibility for its actions in the human world? Perhaps there has been no crime at the house on Rue Morgue, after all—only death. Animals are, according to Aristotle, lacking in *logos* and are therefore incapable of ethical behavior and thus of crime.[4] "It is a characteristic of man that he alone has any sense of good and evil."[5] Animals do not inhabit the philosophical world projected and animated by human beings. Accordingly, as the case unfolds, the crime itself disappears. The criminal trespass dissolves into a series of accidental encounters between two women and an ape—an arbitrary slaying of two human beings by an animal. Despite the suggestion of a perverse psychopathology at work in the grotesque killings, Poe's death scene reverts back into the flow of "everyday life," everyday savagery—there are, in the end, no monsters, only animals.

Reexamining the premises of this case, however, one finds that the extraordinary elements resist being reduced to the or-dinary. The distinction between extraordinary and ordinary states appears to have collapsed: one can no longer distinguish between them, their difference shifted to a more subtle dis-tinction between the ordinary-in-the-extraordinary and the extraordinary-in-the-ordinary. Even as "Rue Morgue" depicts the "savage" transgression of human society, indeed humanity, by an orangutan, Poe's narrative recounts the framing of human paradigms around animal acts. The oscillation between the mundane and the fantastic helps establish the compelling uncertainty that sustains Poe's narrative. Throughout the newspaper reports and eyewitness accounts, Dupin remarks, the assassin's nationality and gender—key points in the constitution of an identity—remain unascertainable. Retracing his hypothesis, Dupin poses the following speculation to his accomplice, the narrator: "an agility astounding, a strength superhuman, a ferocity brutal, a butchery without motive, a *grotesquerie* in horror *absolutely alien from humanity,* and a voice foreign in tone to the ears of men of many nations, and devoid of all distinct or intelligible syllabification. What result, then, has ensued? What impression have I made upon your fancy?"[6] Dupin's reasoning launches the reader into an unintelligible world in which the familiar indices of language and gender recede beyond the grasp of comprehension, or even recognition. Among the facts gathered by the police, the evidence remains defiantly foreign. Each witness spoke of the killer's voice "as that of a foreigner. Each is sure that it was not the voice of one of his own countrymen. . . . No words—no sounds resembling words—were by any witness mentioned as distinguishable."[7] In this instance, language and the demand upon the faculty of recognition that it imposes actively impede the crime's solution.

The witnesses to the Rue Morgue atrocities have misconstrued the startled, panicked cries of the orangutan for those of a human being. From the indistinguishable noises of the struggle, each witness thought that he or she was able to discern (without understanding) the alien tongue of a foreigner. Each auditor was able to project the language and identity of a foreign being into the open spaces of animal noise.

In general, voices tend to provoke such misidentifications. Rousseau, for example, attempting to introduce his study of the origin of language, quickly loses control of his rhetoric when he reaches the thresholds of speech. Slipping into philological abstraction and a phonetic dilemma, he writes:

> Speech distinguishes man among the animals; language distinguishes nations from each other; one does not know where a man comes from until he has spoken. Out of usage and necessity, each learns the language of his own country. But what determines that this language is that of his country and not of another? In order to tell, it is necessary to go back to some principle that belongs to the locality itself and antedates its customs, for speech, being the first social institution, owes its form to natural causes alone.[8]

As Poe's story illustrates, animals may also be mistaken for human beings when one confuses rhythmical sounds (grunts of exertion, for example) for semantic structure (an unfamiliar but distinctly foreign language). Although animals are without language, they are nonetheless equipped with a semiotic capacity. Animals are able to transmit the cries that signal their presence without possessing the means of referring to absent objects or abstract concepts. Derrida has suggested, reversing the usual distinction between humanity and the animals, that what is characteristically animal is the *inability* to refrain from self-exhibition; that language may best be considered to follow from the capacity for silence—restraint—rather than as the function of self-determination and expression.[9]

What, then, is the nature of the animal's disclosure? What does the animal, "which can neither choose to keep silent, nor keep a secret," so irrepressibly reveal?[10] Without the semiosis that transforms sounds into words, animal utterances, like the *nonsense* of foreigners, can only portray the dynamic of affects and bodily states. Philosophical thought has often maintained the distinction between races and species, language and signals. Aristotle, for example, argues that although all animals possess the capacity to signal pleasure and pain, only human beings can form words from those signals: "And whereas mere voice is but an indication of pleasure or pain, and is therefore found in other animals (for their nature attains to the perception of pleasure and pain and the intimation of them to one another, and no further), the power of speech is intended to set forth the expedient and inexpedient, and therefore likewise the just and the unjust."[11] Animals form, in Aristotle's account, finite sentimental communities—their communications express sensations, the reach of which remains within the immediate horde. Apparently, not only does the expressive range of human speech exceed that of the animal's cry (which is limited to the two poles of affect, pleasure and pain), but speech establishes a larger realm of communication. Whereas animals convey their affects only "to one another," Aristotle suggests that the effects of speech reach a wider audience and carry greater implications, permitting, for instance, the foundation of justice.

The animal, signified by its cry, supplements the classical opposition between word and sound. Derrida explains the separation of speech from the cry, and the problematic of language that it introduces:

[Speech's] system requires that it be heard and understood immediately by whoever emits it. It produces a signifier which seems not to fall into the world, outside the ideality of the signified, but to remain sheltered—even at the moment that it attains the audiophonic system of the other—within the pure interiority of auto-affection. It does not fall into the exteriority of space, into what one calls the world, which is nothing but the outside of speech. Within so-called "living" speech, the spatial exteriority of the signifier seems absolutely reduced. It is in the context of this possibility that one must pose the problem of the cry—of that which one has always excluded, pushing it into the area of animality or of madness, like the myth of the inarticulate cry—and the problem of speech (voice) within the history of life.[12]

Problematizing the fall of speech out of the world, Derrida exposes the proximity of all speech to the inarticulate cries of animals and opens to scrutiny a long history of tension between the figure of the animal and the limits of discourse. Indeed, while *logos* enjoys a singular privilege in the philosophical hierarchy, *zoon* always supplements that privilege, undermining its autonomy. For example, in Plato's *Sophist,* Derrida explains, "*Logos* is a *zoon*":

> An animal that is born, grows, belongs to *phusis.* Linguistics, logic, dialectics, and zoology are all in the same camp.
>
> In describing *logos* as *zoon,* Plato is following certain rhetors and sophists before him who, as a contrast to the cadaverous rigidity of writing, had held up the living spoken word, which infallibly conforms to the necessities of the situation at hand, to the expectations and demands of the interlocutors present, and which *sniffs out* the spots where it ought to produce itself, feigning to bend and adapt at the moment it is actually achieving maximum persuasiveness and control.
>
> *Logos,* a living, animate creature, is thus also an organism that has been engendered. An *organism:* a differentiated body *proper,* with a center and extremities, joints, a head, and feet. In order to be "proper," a written discourse *ought* to submit to the laws of life just as a living discourse does. Logographical necessity *(anangke logographike)* ought to be analogous to biological, or rather zoological necessity.[13]

By tracing *logos* back to its origin as *zoon,* Derrida exposes the early attempts in Greek metaphysics to unite the living body with the "logographical" text: an attempt to secure the proximity of *logos* to vitality. The phantasm of a primordial unity continues to haunt the dialectics of *logos* and *zoon,* writing and speech, human and animal being, even as the proximity of speech to its other, the affective cry of the animal, establishes the spaces and temporalities that regulate the opening of worlds — the human and animal worlds that form apart from one another.

Cogito and Monad: René Descartes (1596–1650) and Gottfried Wilhelm Leibniz (1646–1716)

PERHAPS THE MOST notorious of the dualist thinkers, Descartes has come to stand for the insistent segregation of the human and animal worlds in philosophy. Likening animals to automata, Descartes argues in his 1637 *Discourse on the Method* that not only "do the beasts have less reason than men, but they have no reason at all."[14] Although he conceded in private that the animal possesses not only an "âme organique ou végétale" but also an "âme sensible," Descartes warns that one should not "think, like some of the ancients that the beasts speak, although we do not understand their language. For if that were true, then since they have many organs that correspond to ours, they could make themselves understood by us as well as by their fellows."[15] Since animals are endowed with the capacity for movement, Descartes continues, they are in this regard like human beings and machines. Unable to engage in genuine speech, however, animals remain, along with machines, simple mimics. "We must not confuse speech with the natural movements which express passions and which can be imitated by machines as well as by animals."[16] It is Descartes who most deeply instilled in the philosophical tradition the idea that the capacity for reason and consciousness determines the ontological universe. As the greatest vehicle for such reflection, human beings occupy the center of the universe that they themselves have conjured. Across the Cartesian plane of being, only human beings establish an authentic site: all other beings reflect the *eidos* of humanity's productions. In this schema, animals, like automata, simply reflect the priority of humanity's presence, its cogito.[17]

Challenging the Cartesian view of animals, Leibniz approaches the question of animal being from the perspective of monadic composition. Animals, or "divine machines," are incapable of death, but only because the monads that compose them are reorganized into new beings rather than extinguished at the end of life. To this extent they resemble souls, which are likewise immortal. Leibniz explains:

> Thus, not only souls, but also animals cannot be generated and cannot perish. They are only unfolded, enfolded, reclothed, unclothed, and transformed; souls never entirely leave their body, and do not pass from one body into another that is entirely new to them. There is therefore no *metempsychosis,* but there is *metamorphosis.* Animals change, but they acquire and leave behind only parts. In nutrition this happens a little at a time and by small insensible particles, though continually, but it happens suddenly, visibly, but rarely, in conception or in death, which causes animals to acquire or lose a great deal all at once.[18]

Leibniz has here linked conception with death. By attaching the question of appearance to that of being, Leibniz extends the rift between human and animal existence to include the limits of appearance as well as disappearance, the finitude of beginning as well as ending. In the anonymously published "New System of Nature" (1695), Leibniz aligns his theory of the "conservation" of animal matter with those of classical naturalists Democritus and Hippocrates. Claiming to follow in their paths, Leibniz asserts that it is "natural that an animal, having always been alive and organized . . . always remains so," and that "animals are not born and do not die. . . . [the] things we believe to begin and perish merely appear and disappear."[19] According to Leibniz's physics, what he calls in 1714 the "Monadology," only the souls of rational creatures are prone to creation and destruction, whereas the souls and bodies of "brutes" form a limitless continuum, an expanse of life and matter that neither begins nor ends, but rather transforms itself into further material figurations. Thus Jean-Luc Nancy writes in *The Inoperative Community:* "Since Leibniz there has been no death in our universe: in one way or another an absolute circulation of meaning (of values, of ends, of History) fills or reabsorbs all finite negativity, draws from each finite singular destiny a surplus value of humanity or an infinite superhumanity."[20]

Despite his departure from the rigid metaphysics of Descartes, and despite the radical contributions he brings to the philosophies of composition and formation, Leibniz nonetheless reinscribes the distinction between "beasts" and "rational animals." He locates the gulf between two modes of cognition, "perception" and "apperception," arguing that "it is good to distinguish between *perception,* which is the internal state of the monad representing external things, and *apperception,* which is *consciousness,* or the reflective knowledge of the internal state, something not given to all souls, nor at all times to a given soul."[21] Thus all animals and souls are imperishable, but only "rational animals" are equipped with the apperceptive faculties that are required to experience or anticipate death. In Leibniz's discourse, death assumes the properties of "necessary or eternal truths, such as those of logic, numbers, and geometry, which bring about an indubitable connection of ideas and *infallible consequences.*"[22] And because the "interconnection" of perceptions in animals is founded "in the memory of *facts* or effects, and not at all in the knowledge of *causes,*" animals "do not fully perish in what we call *death*."[23] According to Leibniz, death requires a certain calculation toward finitude, toward "infallible consequences," and without such reflective faculties animals remain in the world undying. Animals, like souls, are those creatures thus destined to survive, or at least to remain: their apparent lack of language commits them to a perpetual and protean evolution toward eternity.

Palingenesis: Arthur Schopenhauer (1788–1860)

LEIBNIZ'S BELIEF IN the perpetuation of being through existing monadic compositions returns much later in Schopenhauer's articulation of "palingenesis," or the survival of the will. Like Leibniz, Schopenhauer insists that although "consciousness is destroyed in death, . . . that which has been producing it is by no means destroyed."[24] Schopenhauer, a key precursor of evolutionary theory, argues that consciousness is in fact a mere component of corporeality and has little bearing on what is essential in being. Consciousness is "something secondary, as a result of the life-process, it is also secondary psychologically, in antithesis to will, which alone is primary and everywhere the original element."[25] Leaning increasingly close to Lamarck's preliminary evolutionism—in which interior orthogenetic forces "will" the organism to adapt—Schopenhauer claims that consciousness, which is in truth a consciousness of life and whose sole content is the desire to remain alive, is shared by all living creatures. Consciousness is thus an effect of being alive rather than of being. "That which cries 'I, I, I want to exist' is not you alone; it is everything, absolutely everything that has the slightest trace of consciousness. So that this desire in you is precisely that which is not individual but common to everything without exception."[26] Regarding the loss of consciousness in death, Schopenhauer writes that what dies in death (consciousness) is common but what survives is "the being's intrinsic state":

But cheer up!—for what kind of consciousness is it? A cerebral, an animal, a somewhat more highly charged bestial consciousness, in as far as we have it in all essentials in common with the whole animal world, even if it does reach its peak in us. This consciousness is, in its origin and aim, merely an expedient for helping the animal to get what it needs. The state to which death restores us on the other hand, is our original state, i.e. is the being's intrinsic state, the moving principle of which appears in the production and maintenance of the life which is now coming to an end: it is the state of the thing in itself, in antithesis to the world of appearance.[27]

All consciousness is animal consciousness, according to Schopenhauer, and disappears in death. In death, however, the individual is born: death separates intrinsic being from animal being. Schopenhauer's description of the transcendence of the individual in death to an authentic state of being connects this morbid philosophy to the doctrines already observed. Still, it is important to note that Schopenhauer concedes a form of consciousness to "the whole animal world."

What distinguishes humanity from the animal then is not the ability to be conscious, but rather, once again, the ability to perish, to lose consciousness. For Schopenhauer, the unconsciousness effected by death, or put more precisely the "*cognitionless* primal state," restores being to its originary state as "will." Furthermore, the metaphysical will defies "the world of appearance," its representation as phenomenon or consciousness.[28] "One can thus regard every human being from two opposed viewpoints. From the one he is the fleeting individual, burdened with error and sorrow and with a beginning and end in time; from the other he is the indestructible primal being which is objectified in everything that exists."[29] The distinction is important. The fleeting individual, marked by finitude in space and time, takes place in the world, whereas the "indestructible primal being," although "objectified in everything that exists," cannot be objectified "as such." Although maintaining the metaphysical structure, Schopenhauer here reverses the terms of the opposition between humanity and nature by granting animals a measure of consciousness and individuality. In Schopenhauer's world only the individual can signify, that is, appear in the phenomenal world. The individual, however, does not signify individuality but commonality. Individuality in Schopenhauer's discourse is derived from the generality of life, of living beings, and does not accord any direct access to the "primal state." Thus what the individual consciousness signifies is essentially common. Like his description of a consciousness "common to everything," Schopenhauer consigns individuality to a secondary and derivative category that is superseded by a transcendental and unrepresentable singularity, the will. Therefore animals, which are constituted primarily by the multitude, as hordes, are purely phenomenal— capable of individuated appearances but unable to participate in the transcendental specificity that comes from willing. In sum, immortality does not necessarily mean perpetual being: "Immortality can also be termed an indestructibility without continued existence."[30]

Schopenhauer's opposition between indestructibility and existence leads invariably toward evolutionary thought, as well as to a zoomorphic rendering of *Dasein*. It is in the earlier work of Rousseau, however, that the question of the animal's capacity to represent is seriously examined. Ultimately, these two authors raise the question of whether the phenomenality of the animal—its cry—in fact points philosophy to the existence of another world.

Imagination: Jean-Jacques Rousseau (1712–78)

ROUSSEAU, LIKE DESCARTES and Leibniz before him, also likens animals to automata, or "ingenious machines." He does, however, concede that animals possess intelligence, or at least that they have ideas: "Every animal has ideas since it has senses."[31] Sensing, in Rousseau, achieves the status of intelligence, since it comes from the source of all reason, nature. What truly distinguishes humanity from animals, according to Rousseau, lies in the "faculty of self-perfection, a faculty which, with the aid of circumstances, successively develops all the others, and resides among us as much in the species as in the individual."[32] What the animal lacks is not intelligence but imagination, which is to say, language. Imagination and language are linked, for Rousseau, in the capacity to perfect oneself. Efforts toward self-perfection, in turn, force one to consider finitude and thus death. Addressing the conception of death, Rousseau repeats the familiar axiom that the animal does not fear death because it cannot imagine death, "because an animal will never know what it is to die."[33] Rousseau concludes that the "knowledge of death and its terrors is one of the first acquisitions that man has made in withdrawing from the animal condition."[34] The inability of the animal to proceed toward death results from its inability to imagine and fear death, which, in turn, limits its capacity to perfect itself. What Rousseau has added to the human reason/animal instinct dialectic is a supplementary capacity for imagination. Derrida addresses Rousseau's supplement to reason in *Of Grammatology,* observing that

> although the concept of reason is very complex in Rousseau, it may be said that, in certain regards, reason, in as much as it is the understanding and the faculty of forming ideas, is less proper to humanity than imagination and perfectibility. We have already noticed in what sense reason may be called natural. One may also remark that from another point of view animals, although gifted with intelligence, are not perfectible. They are deprived of imagination, of that power of anticipation that exceeds the givens of the senses and takes us toward the unperceived.[35]

Animals are deprived of futures. Thus in Rousseau's contribution to the thought of animal being, the animal is confined to a perpetual presence that never advances in being or time, since the animal can never anticipate the arrival of what is unperceived, or unimagined. Derrida concludes that Rousseau's intervention in the field of animal philosophy produces a link between the powers of imagination—the ability to produce images or representations—and mortality:

> If one moves along the course of the supplementary series, he sees that imagination belongs to the same chain of significations as the anticipation of death. Imagination is at bottom the relationship with death. The image is death. A proposition that one may define or make indefinite thus: *the* image is *a* death or (*the*) death is *an* image. Imagination is the power that allows life to affect itself with its own re-presentation.[36]

According to Derrida, Rousseau positions the essence of death in the imagination, in the production of images. Only beings that imagine can die. Rousseau's theses on language are also related to the faculty of imagination and illuminate further the question of animal being.

Seeking to re-create the stages that led to the invention of language, Rousseau conjures a prehistoric time when humanity existed alongside animals. In that condition, Rousseau reasons, humanity only expressed itself, like animals, affectively. "Man's first language, the most universal, the most energetic and the only language he needed before it was necessary to persuade men assembled together, is the cry of nature."[37] The cry of nature, according to Rousseau, is a primordial, natural articulation available to all animals and precedes discourse. From this spontaneous eruption, which issues from "a kind of instinct in pressing circumstances, to beg for help in great dangers, or for relief of violent ills," human beings form societies from smaller communities and subsequently acquire a more "extensive language" through "multiplied vocal inflections . . . combined with gestures."[38] What seems to be at work in Rousseau's account is a mimetic theory of language culled from the plenitude of an unspeakable but total natural language. In other words, language, according to Rousseau, exists in nature and is derived by humanity through mimesis, through imagination. In this scenario humanity, and not the animal, emerges as the mimic. And humanity's language, its technical language, as Derrida has shown, enters into the world as a supplement to the "voice" of nature.

Mimesis: Immanuel Kant (1724–1804)

ALSO INVOKING HUMANITY'S first gesture toward language, Kant arrives at the mimetic structure that opposes, like Rousseau's, the Cartesian sequence. In a footnote to his 1786 essay "Conjectural Beginning of Human History," Kant designates a primary utterance in the sounds of animals. The animal cry is subsequently mimicked by man. "While as yet alone, man must have been moved by the urge for communication to make his existence known to other living beings, particularly to such as utter sounds. These sounds he could imitate, and they could later serve as names."[39] Here, the animal possesses a primordial capacity from which naming arises; it is a proto-nominative capacity that allows one to make one's "existence known to other living beings." Kant's "conjectural beginning" posits, in fact, an a priori ontology into which man is thrust as an existential afterthought or effect. Nature, according to Kant, exists first, but the existence of man cannot be derived from that origin. Indeed, just prior to the footnote, Kant claims of the conjectural enterprise: "Unless one is to indulge in irresponsible conjectures, one must start out with something which human reason cannot derive from prior natural causes—in the present case, the existence of man."[40] Accordingly, it would appear that it is humanity that does not inhabit the natural world and that only in imitation can humanity determine the world to which it improperly belongs.[41] Humanity enters the world through mimesis. Kant alludes here to the sequence of events as related in Genesis: "God formed every beast of the field and every bird of the air, and brought them to the man to see what he would call them; and whatever the man called every living creature, that was its name."

Hegel also reads the Genetic appropriation of animals by humanity and language as an essential act in the constitution of humanity's dialectical existence. For Hegel, the named animal is sublated into the recesses of human ideation and language.

> In the *name* its [the animal's] empirical being is removed from it, that is, it is no longer concrete, no longer a multiplicity in itself, no longer a living entity. Instead it is transformed into a pure and simple ideal. Adam's first mediating action in establishing his dominion over the animals consisted in his granting them names; thus he denied them as independent beings and he transformed them into ideals.[42]

According to Hegel, the act of naming transforms animals from independent beings into idealized beings: language, in essence, nullifies animal life. In disappearing, the animal leaves only its cry.

The Animal Cry: Edmund Burke (1729–97) and Georg Wilhelm Friedrich Hegel (1770–1831)

DERRIDA'S DESCRIPTION OF the animal cry as a moment of articulation that simultaneously pierces the world of language and the other, the alien topology of the animal can be traced to the oeuvres of Burke and Hegel. The idea of the animal cry is related to the question of death. As discussed earlier, Schopenhauer holds that in death the individual takes leave of its animal existence and passes into the transcendental, paraphenomenal realm of intrinsic being, or will. The animal thus exists in one temporality while being inhabits another: "Death announces itself frankly as the end of the individual, but in this individual lies the germ of a new being. Thus nothing that dies dies for ever. . . . The contrivance which prevents us from perceiving this is time."[43] Schopenhauer implies that being consists of two temporal dimensions whose connection, palingenesis, cannot be secured in the phenomenality of either space or time.

The animal cry signals the moment of contact between those two ontic worlds: the cry is, as Derrida explains, a signal burdened with the antidiscursive force of animality and madness. Burke's 1757 reflection on the sublime includes a section on "The Cries of Animals." For Burke, the experience of the sublime aroused by the animal's cry imposes a moment wholly outside time—an *extemporaneous* moment—in which the dynamics of reason are temporarily halted. According to Burke, this moment is registered by "astonishment," the limit response to the sublime in nature. "Astonishment is that state of the soul, in which all its motions are suspended, with some degree of horror."[44] In this state, Burke argues, human reasoning succumbs to and lags behind "the great power of the sublime," which "anticipates our reasonings, and hurries us on by an irresistible force."[45] What is most astonishing, however, is Burke's assertion that "such sounds as imitate the natural inarticulate voices of men, or any animals in pain or danger, are capable of conveying *great ideas*."[46] This suggests that the sublime experience constitutes an idea, and that the cries of animals are, to some degree, its facilitators. In fact, according to Burke, this "great idea" approximates a glimpse into the very essence of an idea-generating affect. It is a power denied to language. "It might seem that these modulations of sound carry some connection with the nature of the things they represent, and are not merely arbitrary; because the natural cries of all animals, even of those animals with whom we have not been acquainted, never fail to make themselves sufficiently understood; this cannot be said of language."[47] The inarticulate cries of animals convey—with urgency (sublime temporality always signals an *emergency*)—the sudden realization of a primary relation between the noise and its referent. This referent, however, is not something already known to the listener; rather, its existence is made manifest to the subject for the first time as a sublime incarnation. And because of its prematurity (with regard to the rational faculties) and force of necessity (its "connection with the nature of the things they represent"), the inarticulate sublime only impacts the registers of affect. In other words, the sublimity of this cry astonishes the subject with its explosive urgency and density; it hurls that subject toward the epistemic instant—the moment of an immediate knowledge—with no time to contemplate or experience its taking place.

The sublimity of Burke's animal cry also pierces the enclaves of Hegel's animal thanatology. Hegel explains: "Every animal finds a voice in its violent death; it expresses itself as a removed-self *[als aufgehobnes Selbst]*."[48] At the moment of its "violent death," every animal, in Hegel's formulation, removes itself from itself, and thus from death. It survives its own death as an inarticulate cry, as the animal voice. Giorgio Agamben reads this displaced sound as the origin of the "voice of consciousness." Inscribing that voice within the infinite negativity from which (Hegelian) language erupts, Agamben hears the voice as the return of negativity. Of the death cry Agamben writes:

> And although it is not yet meaningful speech, it already contains within itself the power of the negative and of memory. . . . In dying, the animal finds its voice, it exalts the soul in one voice, and, in this act, it expresses and preserves itself *as dead*. Thus the animal voice is the *voice of death* . . . which preserves and recalls the living as dead,

and it is, at the same time, an immediate trace and memory of death, pure negativity.[49]

According to the logic of Agamben's reading of Hegel, the Hegelian dialectic is already at work in the seemingly predialectical moment. At the moment of death, the animal tears itself away from any proper experience of death. Only the voice crosses that existential threshold. The body disappears while the voice lingers as pure negativity in the realm of the living. Thus the voice remains apart from the eventness of dying, preserving death in the living world. The animal cry erupts at the moment of death without referent, without body, without meaning: it emerges from and returns to the realm of pure negativity as "death itself." And as such, the animal never dies: it merely vanishes, leaving behind its voice as an "immediate trace and memory" upon which the second dialectical moment (the inception of language, or the "voice of consciousness") is founded. Of Hegel's supernatural transformation of the animal into memory and then language, Agamben concludes that "language has this power and it truly dwells in the realm of death only because it is the articulation of the 'vanishing trace' that is the animal voice; that is, only because already in its very voice, the animal, in violent death, had expressed itself as removed."[50] Like Burke's animal cry that invokes "great ideas" at the limits of consciousness, Hegel's animal initiates a dialectics of death from which it is nonetheless excluded. For Hegel, the animal cry erupts from outside the confines of "natural life"; it marks death but only as an event beyond the capacities of animal being. In the *Phenomenology,* Hegel explains, "Whatever is confined within the limits of a natural life cannot by its own efforts go beyond its immediate existence; but it is driven beyond it by something else, and this uprooting entails death."[51] The logic here remains impeccably Hegelian: (1) Nature cannot surpass itself by its own means; (2) death intervenes from beyond the limits of nature to push nature past itself; (3) this exteriority, in turn, gives nature its essence. Accordingly, the animal cry (the "something else"), which converges on the limits of reason and being, bursts forth from the site of an absolute exteriority. The cry comes to determine, dialectically, the animal's very being. It is, as Hegel writes, not only the expression of alterity, but of the "anti-human."

Hegel also ascribes an innate, murderous quality to all modes of conceptualization. The naming of animals, Hegel insists, turns them into ideals. And in the abstraction of the animal from essence to language, the animal dies. Kojève reads this process in Hegel:

> As long as the Meaning (or Essence, Concept, Logos, Idea, etc.) is embodied in an empirically existing entity, this Meaning or Essence, as well as the entity, *lives*. For example, as long as the Meaning (or Essence) "dog" is embodied in a sensible entity, this Meaning (Essence) *lives:* it is the real dog, the living dog which runs, drinks, and eats. But when the Meaning (Essence) "dog" passes into the *word* "dog"—that is, becomes *abstract* Concept which is *different* from the sensible reality that it reveals by its Meaning—the Meaning (Essence) *dies:* the *word* "dog" does not run, drink, and eat; in it the Meaning (Essence) *ceases* to live—that is, it *dies*. And that is why the conceptual understanding of empirical reality is equivalent to a *murder*.[52]

Connecting conceptual language to acts of murder, Kojève brings to light the temporal sequence through which language and the capacity for death are aligned. The killing takes place at the moment that language intervenes. Once murdered by abstraction, however, the animal's vitality ceases to adhere to its semantic body. Henceforth, as word, the "dog" ceases to die empirically, while, as representation, it continues to die repeatedly. Kojève continues to unravel Hegel's astonishing killings:

"Now, this dog which is annihilated at every instant is precisely the dog which endures in Time, which at every instant ceases to live or exist in the Present so as to be annihilated in the Past, or as Past."[53] Kojève pursues this thought in a footnote that follows from his reexamination of "the Past." Contrasting Aristotle's eternal dog (a dog whose identity as "dog" is dispersed across the species "Dog") with Hegel's mortal dog (a mortality that allows Hegel to repeatedly kill the dog), Kojève offers the following conclusion:

> Therefore: for Aristotle there is a concept "dog" only because there is an *eternal* real dog, namely the *species* "dog," which is always in the present; for Hegel, on the other hand, there is a concept "dog" only because the real dog is a *temporal* entity—that is, an essentially finite or "mortal" entity, an entity which is annihilated at every instant: and the Concept *is* the permanent support of this nihilation of the spatial real, while *nihilation* is itself nothing other than *Time.* For Hegel too, then, the Concept is something that is preserved ("eternally," if you will, but in the sense of: as long as time lasts). But for him, it is only the *Concept* "dog" that is preserved (the Concept—that is, the temporal nihilation of the real dog, while nihilation actually lasts as long as Time lasts, since Time *is* this nihilation as such); whereas for Aristotle, the real *dog* is what is preserved (eternally, in the strict sense, since there is *eternal* return), at least as *species.* That is why Hegel explains what Aristotle cannot explain, namely, the preservation (in and by Man) of the Concept of an animal belonging, for example, to an *extinct* species (even if there are no fossil remains).[54]

In this account, Kojève elucidates the notion of eternity as it traverses Aristotle and Hegel. The Aristotelian animal survives time, in spite of time, through *speciation* (expansion through space and time); the Hegelian animal dies a repeated death because of the murderous persistence of time. In Hegel's dialectic, only the concept survives the nihilating passage of time. It is clear in Kojève's presentation of the dialectic between being and time, that in fact the animal, in its essence, precedes both being and time. Whether in the registers of a spatialized existence or in the eternal returns of a nihilating temporality, the bestial *Dasein* has vanished before ever having entered the horizons of an ontic or ontological representation. The animal has already perished before it has had the chance to represent its death, or to represent itself *in* death. The Hegelian animal suffers an a priori death, a type of pre-extinction.

The philosophical circle continues: the animal dies at the moment it is thrust into contact with abstraction, with language. Killed by the word, the animal enters a figurative empire (of signs) in which its death is repeated endlessly. In such transmigrations, however, death itself is circumvented: no longer a "dog" but "Dog," this creature now supersedes any incidental dying of dogs. Thus the "dog" is immortalized, preserved (taxidermically) in the slaughterhouse of being, language. Still, however, following Derrida's conception of the accountability of the name—"only the name can inherit" —it is only the name of the dog that dies those multiple deaths *and* lives on in the afterlives of conception.[55] The dog "itself," the "prelinguistic" entity, has ceased to exist before either existence or time. One finds the Hegelian dog hovering, not unlike Schrödinger's cat, between the realms of life and death, suspended in the interstices of a paralyzed dialectic. In this manner, the semiotically reconfigured "dog" is denied access to the present, to self-presence, and is instead relegated to the endless returns of abstraction. Ultimately, the animal does not so much *exist* as *express:* in its cry and conceptualization, animal being is marked by expression rather than being-in-the-world.

Lyotard refers to animal expression as an instance of the "affect-phrase." "One could say that a feeling appears and disappears entirely at every instant, that it is ageless."[56] As such, feelings, or "affect-phrases," do not participate in the world of discourse, address, and reference. Rather, the affect-phrase problematizes discursive order: "The affect-phrase is untimely and unruly."[57] Not only does the affect-phrase linger in the recesses of the communicative universe, it also, according to Lyotard, disrupts the dialogic momentum. The affect-phrase is a nonlanguage (not "language-al," says Lyotard) whose appearance tears at the unity of language. In Lyotard's Aristotelian reading, the affect-phrase enters communication as an impossible moment of completion that suspends, for the duration of its expression, the activity of language. Following Aristotle's description of pleasure and pain as being always achieved entirely in the "now," Lyotard claims that the affect-phrase determines a total and finite disclosure: it produces an unrepeatable, singular utterance that disappears forever.[58] As such, the affect-phrase remains severed from both human discourse and subjectivity.

For Lyotard, the animal is a primary agent of the inarticulate affect-phrase. Endowed with a "communicability or transitivity" that is affective rather than discursive, Lyotard's animal signals its affects from a region that is "banished from human language."[59] From this banished region, however, bursts of affect reenter the world through secret channels opened up by transference, or affective communication: transference opens a line of communication that is essentially antidiscursive:

There is, however, a communicability of pleasure and pain, of *pathemata,* which is effected by the "confused voice" alone, without the mediation of *logos.* Animals, Aristotle says, "signal" their feelings "to one another."—We already know the stakes that Kant will attach to this sentimental communicability. It can be said to be mute, if it's recalled that the root *mu* connotes closed lips which suggest keeping still or talking in a muted voice. From that root comes *murmurer* (to murmur), *mugir* (to low), *mystère* (mystery) and the vulgar [low] Latin *muttum,* which yielded *mot* (word) in French. Muted communication is made up of continuous inhalations and exhalations of air: grunts, gasps and sighs.[60]

The "muted communication" comprising "grunts, gasps and sighs" brings one within earshot of the astonished (and astonishing, in Burke's sense of the term) cries of the Rue Morgue assassin. If those murmuring animals remain exiles from the "political community," then they are also exempt from any *responsibility* as such to the demands of its *logos.* For Lyotard, the animal resides in a kind of "differend," a logically irresolvable impasse.[61] The animal cannot be held accountable for its crimes because, like Oedipus, it is unaware of its actions. To this extent, Lyotard's animal implies a separate mode of being that can be best described as unconscious. Lyotard's murmuring animal communicates not consciously but unconsciously. According to Lyotard, then, the animal opens up a channel of unconscious communication that carries with it the possibility of an unconscious world, the world of the unconscious. It is thus toward the unconscious that modern philosophy inevitably edges. The figure of the animal leads, in many ways, that progression: dispossessed of language and mortality, and excluded from the philosophical community of beings, the animal recedes into what Lyotard terms a "time before *logos*": a time, that is, before the human subject.

The human subject has determined thus far much of the discussion on animal being: from Aristotelian speechlessness to Cartesian automatism and Hegelian negation, the philosophical animal has come to occupy a constant position in the shadow of human ontology. The animal has become, according to this genealogy, a trace that never fully exits the range of human awareness. Even without the fullness of world, the animal problematizes human ontology. Or rather, precisely because it appears to occupy an indeterminate world, the animal threatens the safety of world, of the world that human beings inhabit. In other words, animal being adds something to the topos of ontology that philosophical discourse does not or cannot fully absorb, sublate, or abolish. Something about animal being remains in excess of human discourse about it. Animal being opens a space between manifestation and metaphysics, between appearance and the unconscious. Stated as a formula, the animal can be pictured as a being minus being, ~~being~~, or b minus b — pure negation. In philosophical discourse, the figure of the animal often signifies such phantasms.

Lyotard contests the philosophical desire to configure the animal as a locus of negation, as a pure body: "The body, as it exists, presupposes *logos*. Logical animals alone *have* a body."[62] This is not to say that animals, who have bodies, have *logos*. Rather, it means that since body and *logos* are inextricable, the animal is either a purely phantasmatic creature with neither body nor *logos,* or it occupies in a manner yet to be elucidated the body and *logos* of the human being. Thus, despite the conceptual distances and existential barriers that human beings maintain against the threat of the wild, all human beings, like the L'Espanayes of Rue Morgue, are vulnerable to the sudden appearance of animals. Nor is humanity restricted, in its vulnerability, to bodily assault: the crises that the animal unleashes strike at the core of human existence. The strange ontology of animal being disrupts humanity's notions of consciousness, being, and world: in the presence of animals, humanity is thrust from the traditional loci of its subjectivity. Contact with animals turns human beings into others, effecting a metamorphosis. Animality is, in this sense, a kind of seduction, a magnetic force or gaze that brings humanity to the threshold of its subjectivity.

The present discussion of philosophy and the animal has been primarily concerned with modern philosophy, that is, the body of work that questions humanity's being. By contrast, some premodern philosophers, notably the group of thinkers deemed theriophilists, have explored the inherent rationality of animal being.[63] In fact, these premodern philosophers believed animals to be particularly suited to certain epistemological activities. From Chrysippus's exemplary dog to Montaigne's imaginative beasts, the premodern animal opens up vast areas of knowledge.[64] Montaigne (1533–92), for example, insists that animals are the primordial possessors of language.

> As for speech, it is certain that if it is not natural, it is not necessary. . . . And it is not credible that Nature has denied us this resource that she has given to many other animals: for what is it but speech, this faculty we see in them of complaining, rejoicing, calling to each other for help, inviting each other to love, as they do by the use of their voice? How could they not speak to one another? They certainly speak to us, and we to them.[65]

For Montaigne, who quotes freely from the ancients, especially Plutarch and Pliny, animals are not only capable of language but of reason. And it is a mere failure of the human faculties, in Montaigne's view, that this truth passes unrecognized.[66] Animals, according to the premodern philosophers, precede human beings in their claims to knowledge and the earth. In his *Natural History,* for example, Pliny the Elder suggests that human beings, who enter life with little more than the ability to cry, might be better off unborn. Comparing the innate skills of animals with the almost total absence of those in human beings, he writes: "Man, however, knows nothing unless by learning—neither how to speak nor how to walk nor how to eat; in a word, the only thing he knows instinctively is how to weep. And so there have been many people who judged that it would have been better not to have been born, or to have died as soon as possible.[67] Since human beings must work to secure their existence and, unlike animals, nothing is given a priori toward their survival, Pliny insists that "we cannot confidently say whether she [Nature] is a good parent to mankind or a harsh stepmother."[68] As Pliny's comment suggests, when compared to animals, human beings cannot but doubt their lineage, their standing in the worldly order. Despite the celebration of humanism that modernity embodies, humanity's need to work at survival has produced, Nietzsche claims, a culture of ressentiment. Humanity has come to assume the role of a resentful sovereign, of an unnatural heir or stepchild. Meanwhile, the disappearance of animal being in the discourse of modernity has also implemented a state of mourning: humanity has yet to recover, Nietzsche says, from the impossible death of the animal. Of mourning and the modern era, he writes: "Thus began the gravest and uncanniest illness, from which humanity has not yet recovered, man's suffering *of man, of himself*—the result of a forcible sundering from his animal past, as it were a leap and plunge into new surroundings and conditions of existence, a declaration of war against the old instincts upon which his strength, joy, and terribleness had rested hitherto."[69]

From a historical viewpoint, the advent of modern thought has coincided with a catastrophic break in the genealogy of animal being. Modernity represents a crucial moment in the consolidation of metaphysics during which the superiority of humanity is achieved from the lowest ranks of being. According to the dialectic of humanism, an a priori animality (thesis) is subsumed by a competing humanity (antithesis): as a result, animality ceases to occupy a proper space apart from the humanity that succeeds, appropriates, and enframes it. The animal, according to that historical rendering, no longer remains in the realm of ontology; it has been effaced. Since philosophical reason does not recognize the death of the animal, however, the negated animal never passes into an authentic state of nonexistence. In the era of modernity, therefore, the animal is relegated to the interstices of ontology. Neither present nor absent, the animal hangs in the dialectical moment that marks the beginning of human history. In this manner, the animal becomes an active phantom in what might be termed the crypt of modernity. Ineradicable, the animal continues to haunt the recesses of the modern human being, appearing only to reestablish human identity in moments of crisis. Because modern philosophy fails to eliminate entirely the residues of the animal, its texts continue to inscribe the secret history of the animal as phantom. In the philosophical world, the figure of the animal moves undying from one corpus to another, one text to another, leaving distinct though faintly perceptible tracks, signs of its migration across the field.

Perhaps the most pressing dialogue on animality, one that would echo throughout the twentieth century, occurs between Nietzsche and Heidegger, whose oeuvres have been so closely linked. Both philosophers spoke to the question of animal being, although their ultimate destinations are far apart, even radically opposed.

2 | Afterthoughts on the Animal ~~World~~: Heidegger to Nietzsche

> *Yet in the alert, warm animal there lies the pain*
> *and burden of an enormous sadness. For it too feels*
> *the presence of what often overwhelms us: a memory,*
> *as if the element we keep pressing toward was once*
> *more intimate, more true, and our communion*
> *infinitely tender. Here all is distance; there it was*
> *breath. After that first home, the second seems*
> *ambiguous and drafty.*
>
> —RAINER MARIA RILKE, "DUINO ELEGIES"

THE WORK OF Martin Heidegger thematizes the idea of a world in danger. It also signals the place of the last philosopher's last stand against the swelling tide of psychology and technology, two movements that contested the epistemological ground of philosophical discourse during the nineteenth century. Pressured by the existential crisis that the figure of the animal presents, Heidegger culminates the philosophical momentum that brought metaphysics to a violent confrontation with the twentieth century. Following the brief recapitulation of the philosophical tradition from Descartes to Hegel that led to Heidegger's intervention, the discussion now turns to the question of the animal in the Heideggerian and Nietzschean corpora. The key indexes that return throughout this dialogue involve the exclusion of the animal from the world established by language, the absence of death from the life of the animal, and, therefore, its indestructibility. Those three dimensions of animal being characterize the distance of the animal from the human world.

Heidegger's writings display a curious preoccupation with the world — the absent world — of animals. For Heidegger as for the Western philosophical tradition that he sustains, language establishes the gulf between human beings and animals. Like the Aristotelian animal that is capable of expressing only pleasure and pain, the animal in Heidegger's account is held to be incapable of developing the greater faculty possessed by humanity for language. As a condition of being, language fundamentally expands the ontological dimension of a being's being, and this expansion forms the basis for a theory of world. The concept of world, which motivates much of Heidegger's writing, denies a place for the animal, unless that place can be defined as a space of exclusion. In Heidegger's thought the animal does not have world, or is "poor" in the world, incapable at any rate of a worldly existence. In his 1935 essay "The Origin of the Work of Art," in many ways a treatise on the world-forming activities of *technē,* Heidegger presents the contours of a world envisaged by the artwork:

> The world is not the mere collection of the countable or uncountable, familiar and unfamiliar things that are just there. But neither is it a merely imagined framework added by our representation to the sum of such given things. The *world worlds,* and is more fully in being than the tangible and perceptible realm in which we believe ourselves to be at home. World is never an object that stands before us and can be seen. World is the ever-nonobjective to which we are subject as long as the paths of birth and death, blessing and curse keep us transported into Being. Wherever those decisions of our history that relate to our very being are made, are taken up and abandoned by us, go unrecognized and are rediscovered by

new inquiry, there the world worlds. *A stone is worldless. Plant and animal likewise have no world; but they belong to the covert throng of a surrounding into which they are linked.*[1]

Evidently, Heidegger's "world" is one that precedes such anthropocentric notions as subjectivity, phenomenality, and consciousness: the "world worlds," for Heidegger, even in the absence of human consciousness. World makes possible those various modes of being, without being itself one of them. The "ever-nonobjective" world secures the ground for objects, entities, and various levels of conscious and nonconscious existence. And yet human beings do "have" a world or are, at least, equipped with the capacity to have a world. Human beings possess the means— *technē*—with which to make the world appear: in artworks, for example.

"A stone is worldless," however, and plants and animals also suffer this privation. As entities, stones, plants, and animals belong to the world, are in the world, but this world is not their own: it is another's world. Stones, plants, and animals exist in the world externally. For Heidegger, the abyss that separates humanity from other forms of being resides in the worldly power of language, which is to say, language and world are inseparable. Heidegger makes this relation clear: "Language alone brings what is, as something that is, into the Open for the first time. Where there is no language, as in the being of stone, plant, and animal, there is also no openness either of that which is not and of the empty."[2] Where there is no language, there is no openness of being, nonbeing, nor absence of being. And this, in turn, is inseparable from the question of death. For world is also the place of nothing, the space in which nothing takes place. In the case of being, death signifies the presence of nothing in the world. Heidegger strengthens the connection between world and the capacity for death in "The Thing" (1950):

The mortals are human beings. They are called mortals because they can die. To die means to be capable of death as death. Only man dies. The animal perishes. It has death neither ahead of itself nor behind it. Death is the shrine of Nothing, that is, of that which in every respect is never something that merely exists, but which nevertheless presences, even as the mystery of Being itself.[3]

Without death, Heidegger argues—without the capacity to name the disappearance of being from the world—the world itself ceases to appear as the foundation that gives existence its place. Stressing the reciprocal and codependent momentum of this logic, Heidegger posits world within the faculty of language and mortality at the same time that he ascribes to world the task of preserving language and mortality (being's finitude). "Mortals are they who can experience death as death. Animals cannot do so. But animals cannot speak either. The essential relation between language and death flashes up before us, but remains still unthought."[4] Animals cannot experience death, the giving of being, of absolute singularity, to existence. And since they cannot die, conversely, animals cannot experience the death or loss of others. Unable to mourn a priori, the animal falls, according to Heidegger, beyond the existential abodes of humanity—the very situation of its worldly being falls into doubt.

Heidegger's attempts to delimit the boundaries that surround "world," *Dasein,* and the topology of the animal remain at best inconclusive. In *An Introduction to Metaphysics* (1935), he makes this claim regarding "the darkening of the world *[Entmachtung]*": "What do we mean by world when we speak of a darkening of the world? World is always world of the *spirit.* The animal has no world nor any environment *[Das Tier hat keine Welt, auch keine Umwelt].*"[5] The unequivocal tone of Heidegger's assertion is challenged by Derrida, who in *Of Spirit* offers a searching analysis of Heidegger's theses on the animal. Derrida finds that Heidegger in the *Introduction to*

Metaphysics has modified an earlier vision of the relations of three "essents" to world. He returns to Heidegger's 1929–30 world-configuration in *The Fundamental Concepts of Metaphysics:* "[1.] The stone (material object) is *worldless [weltlos];* [2.] the animal is *poor in world [weltarm];* [3.] man is *world-forming [welt-bildend]."*[6] Establishing the apparent contradictions between this early view and Heidegger's later claims, Derrida highlights the difference between the animal's poverty in the earlier work and the absence of world in the later one. It is, he says, a difference between essence and degree. The distinction is crucial, for if indeed the animal's poverty of world marks a distinct existential condition (rather than the midpoint of a descending scale of privation that spans from humanity to stone), then the animal must be said to subside *within* some world, if not the world of man or of *Dasein.* Can poverty be construed as a mode of being? Moving toward that question, Derrida rejects the question of a degree of world from Heidegger's postulation:

> The difference he is talking about between poverty and wealth is not one of degree. For precisely because of a difference in essence, the world of the animal—and if the animal is poor in the world, and therefore in spirit, one *must* be able to talk about a world of the animal, and therefore of a spiritual world—is not a species or a degree of the human world. This poverty is not an indigence, a meagreness of world. It has, without doubt, the sense of privation *(Entbehrung),* of a lack: the animal does not have enough world, to be sure. But this lack is not to be evaluated as a quantitative relation to the entities of the world. It is not that the animal has a lesser relationship, a more limited access to entities, it has an *other* relationship.[7]

The idea of an "other relationship" provides a crucial glimpse into the possibility of an animal world. Positing another way of relating the human and animal worlds, Derrida moves the question of animal world from one of its existence (does the animal have world?) to that of the relationship by which humanity might discover the animal world (can one speak of or comprehend an animal world?). This, in turn, questions the use of language as a universal mode of determining the relation of being to world. (Elsewhere, for example, Derrida poses the following questions of the animal's relation to world and to *Dasein:* "Does the animal hear the call that originates responsibility? Does it question? Moreover, can the call heard by *Dasein* come originally to or from the animal? Is there an advent of the animal?")[8] In Derrida's critique of Heidegger, the poverty of animal being presupposes, nonetheless, some mode of having, even as it drifts toward a not-having: "[The animal] is deprived of world because it *can* have a world."[9] Accordingly, animals are neither reticent inhabitants of the human world, nor are they, like stones, impassive to the environment of entities. Rather, the animal inhabits, even if in a negative manner, a world that is at the same time not a world. Although this notion of poverty seems to summon a philosophical paradox, Derrida is hesitant to concede this aporia in Heidegger's formulation, noting that for Heidegger, "The animal . . . reveals itself as a being which both *has and does not have world.*"[10]

The ambiguity that Derrida describes in Heidegger's animal world, the duplicity of a (simultaneous) having and not-having, follows from the inability of the animal to reflect upon the beings that surround it. The animal is enveloped in a "world," or environment of beings, it can perceive or sense those beings (by sight, smell, or touch, for example), but cannot appropriate them "as such"—that is, as conceptual or ideal beings. "The animal can have a world because it has access to entities, but it is deprived of a world because it does not have access to beings *as such* and in their Being."[11] In other words, the animal cannot interiorize the world through reflection: unreflected, the world remains exterior to its being. Johann Gottfried Herder had insisted upon this very point in his 1772 investigation of the origin of language, an important text for Heidegger. One cannot derive by any means the world of human language from the cries of animals. According to Herder, the faculty of reflection, which forms the foundation of language, is complete in human beings and distinguishes language essentially from the "dark language of even all animals." Prefiguring the structural difference that Heidegger inscribes between the world-forming habits of humanity and the worldly destitution of the animal, Herder asserts that "the human species stands above the animals not by stages of more or of less but in kind."[12] At the same time, since Heideggerian world is essentially one of *Dasein*, the animal's having a world suggests in some sense its capacity to exist in the world, inside the world, and in the world of expression, although the poverty of this expression must be illustrated by summoning a hypothetical language under erasure. He marks the animal world as a world under erasure.

In Heidegger's technique of "crossing through," words both written and erased represent the animal world. Thus, a lizard on a rock sees that rock as "~~rock~~," crossed through in order to signify the lizard's inability to access this rock "as entity." Derrida explains the importance of this gesture: "Erasure of the name, then, here of the name of the rock which would designate the possibility of naming the rock itself, *as such* and accessible in its being-rock. The erasing would mark in *our* language, by avoiding a word, this inability of the animal to name."[13] According to Derrida, the erasure signifies, "in *our* language," the absence of the lizard world. And yet, the lizard is not in total deprivation (the rock "is doubtless given him in *some way*," claims Heidegger): it lacks only the ability

to open itself to the *as such* of the thing. It is not of the rock as such that the lizard has experience. This is why the name of the rock must be erased when we want to designate what the lizard is stretched out upon. . . . This inability to name is not primarily or simply linguistic; it derives from the properly *phenomenological* impossibility of speaking the phenomenon whose phenomenality as such, or whose very *as such,* does not appear to the animal and does not unveil the Being of the entity.[14]

The animal "world" is thus, despite its qualification, undeniably a world, albeit a world apart: "However little we can identify with the lizard, we know that it has a relationship with the sun—and with the stone, which itself has none, neither with the sun nor with the lizard."[15] Elsewhere, Derrida recounts Heidegger's complex delineation of the animal world:

The Heideggerian discourse on the animal is violent and awkward, at times contradictory. Heidegger does not simply say "The animal is poor in the world [*weltarm*]," for, as distinct from the stone, it has a world. He says: the animal *has* a world in the mode of a *not-having*. But this not-having does not constitute in his view an indigence, the *lack* of a world that would be human. So why this negative determination? Where does it come from? There is no category of original existence for the animal: it is evidently not *Dasein,* either as *vorhandene* or *zuhandene* (Being cannot appear, be, or be questioned as such [*als*] for the animal).[16]

Animals are not entirely excluded from Heidegger's world, but they are put at a distance from the openness of being: "The animal *has* a world in the mode of *not-having*." Unwilling to relinquish the animal entirely from the topoi of being, Heidegger sets the animal forth, instead, into the recesses of worldly poverty: the animal is "poor in world," it exists without the plenitude of world and perishes without dying—without loss.

Heidegger's most conciliatory and lucid efforts to correlate the domains of mortal and animal worlds appear in his 1926 exploration of poetic destitution, "What Are Poets For?" In this reading of Hölderlin and Rilke, Heidegger offers the world to human beings, beasts, and plants alike, reserving only the "world's night," or the possibility of a worldly absence, for human "mortals." Heidegger swiftly links, in the space of his analysis, the destitution of the "present" with the failure of mortals to experience death: "The time remains destitute not only because God is dead, but because mortals are hardly aware and capable of even their own mortality. Mortals have not yet come into ownership of their own nature. Death withdraws into the enigmatic. The mystery of pain remains veiled. Love has not yet been learned. But the mortals *are*. They are, in that there is language."[17] Under the sway, perhaps, of the poetic "spirit," Heidegger departs from his usual sobriety and pursues instead the trajectory of mortality through to its convergence with love. If one follows the logic of this rhetorical overflow, then one can infer that in language mortals discover or recover being. Mortals *"are"* because language "is there" *(Dasein)*, because language takes place. Love constitutes, furthermore, a lesson to be learned, a knowledge or experience to be acquired that would, if mastered, lift the veil of pain's mystery. Not simply a pain among pains, however, the pain of which Heidegger speaks claims as its source the enigmatic abyss or "world's night" of death. Death is the place in which being arrives unto itself, becomes itself by fusing with nature: world, the world of *Dasein,* is formed in the alliance of interiority and exteriority, of nature and love, of humanity as mortal and humanity as animal. The alliance, however, is never given: it must be achieved by "venturing" forth, by risking. In having world, one is never far from the destitution of its withdrawal: and the awareness of that finitude, according to Heidegger, constitutes the risk that gives humanity its mortality, and its capacity to love.

Following Rilke, who names the ground shared by all living creatures "the Open," Heidegger grants to animals and plants the same "daring" that necessitates humanity's existence. In Rilke's poem, all creatures are exposed to the "unprotectedness" of the Open, or as Heidegger quotes it: "As Nature gives the other creatures over to the venture of their dim delight and in our soil and branchwork grants none special cover, so too our being's pristine ground settles our plight; we are no dearer to it; it ventures us."[18] Heidegger concedes, in Rilke's world-structure, the existence of a community of living beings. And to the extent that those beings are in the world, they are susceptible to death: "Plant, animal, and man—insofar as they are beings at all, that is, insofar as they are ventured—agree in this, that they are not specially protected. But since they differ nonetheless in their being, there will also be a difference in their unprotectedness."[19] This difference finds expression in Rilke's next lines: "Except that we, more eager than plant and beast, go *with* this venture, will it, adventurous more sometimes than Life itself is, more daring by a breath."[20] Humanity exposes itself further, beyond even "Life itself," to the dangers that await all living creatures in the Open. Humanity alone wills the danger, risks its whole life for the sake of being, living more so than plants and animals, "unshielded in the world." Finding confirmation elsewhere in Rilke's work, Heidegger argues that humanity's unshieldedness actually stands it "before the world":

> Plant and animal are admitted into the Open. They are "*in*" the world." The "in" means: they are included and drawn, unlightened, into the drawing of the pure draft. The relation to the Open—if indeed we may still speak here of a "to"—is the unconscious one of a merely striving-drawing ramification into the whole of what is. With the heightening of consciousness, the nature of which, for modern metaphysics, is representation, the standing and the counterstanding of objects are also heightened. *The*

higher its consciousness, the more the conscious being is ex-
cluded from the world. This is why man, in the words of
Rilke's letter, is "before the world." He is not admitted into
the Open. Man stands over against the world.[21]

Heidegger has, it would appear, reversed his position on the animal, being, and world under the influence of Rilke, or poetry,
or both. Now, plants and animals are in the world, and it is
rather humanity that stands "before the world," "not admitted
into the Open," "over against the world." And yet before rush-
ing to confirm this reversal, one must further situate the evolution of Heidegger's thought.

In Heidegger's articulation of humanity's venture into the
world, the latter stands before humanity as a world to come.
The fullest manifestation of Heidegger's world is none other
than the future: to have world is to have a future. Thus standing before the world, over against the world, humanity stands
in the world. The world is essentially a world to come, and humanity stands in it even while being denied the Open. Plants
and beasts, however, who stand in the world, remain nonetheless outside the world's presence (as future) as well as outside
and behind the present. Plant and beast remain secure in the
world while possessing neither hope nor desire:

> Plant and beast, "in the venture of their dim delight," are
> held carefree in the Open. Their bodily character does not
> perplex them. By their drives, the living creatures are
> lulled into the Open. They too remain in danger to be
> sure, but not in their nature. Plant and beast lie in the bal-
> ance in such a way that the balance always settles into the
> repose of a secureness. The balance in which plant and
> beast are ventured does not yet reach into the realm of
> what is in essence and thus constantly unstilled.[22]

The security that surrounds plants and beasts in the world
comes from their inability to reflect the world "as such." Although

providing security, that inability denies plants and animals access to the future. Animals, who, according to Aristotle, "live by appearances and memories, and have but little of connected experience," cannot bring together the "invisible of the world's inner space" with the world of objects (the outer world of objects and their representations, or language) to form the experience of being that Heidegger values[23]: "What has merely passed away is without destiny even before it has passed. The once-present being, on the contrary, partakes in destiny."[24] Heidegger differentiates the nonpresent being of animals and plants from the "once-present being" of mortals in the capacity for self-representation. "It is by the positioning [pro-positing] that belongs to representation that Nature is brought before man. . . . Plant and animal do not will because, muted in their desire, they never bring the Open before themselves as an object. They cannot go with the venture as one that is represented."[25] In this sense, representation establishes the capacity for "connected experience," the ability to bring willing and appearance together into the world—as world and future. Thus humanity, according to Heidegger, stands within the dimension of connected experience *and* before the world as the always "once-present being," whereas the animal, denied the means of a historical and world-forming *technē*—language—remains "without destiny even before it has passed." In the world, but unable to risk the venture of its loss, the animal turns its back to the future of the world. Without language, the animal remains in the memories of a merely passed world: undying, undestined, and unmourned. In "The Eighth Elegy," Rilke projects this animal world: "We know what is really out there only from the animal's gaze; for we take the very young child and force it around, so that it sees objects—not the Open which is so deep in animals' faces. Free from death. We, only, can see death; the free animal has its decline in back of it, forever."[26]

Friedrich Nietzsche (1844–1900)

*Most of those who have written about the origin of language . . .
looked for [it] in the superior articulation of the organs of speech.
As if an orangutan with precisely the same organs had invented a
language.*

—JOHANN GOTTFRIED HERDER,
"ON THE ORIGIN OF LANGUAGE"

ALTHOUGH THE CHASM that separates an impoverished animality from the world-forming surge of *Dasein* is found to be unbridgeable in Heidegger, one discovers in Nietzsche a more sympathetic relation to the worldly differences and distances that animals disclose. In contrast to the Heideggerian animal, Nietzsche's creatures display, for the most part, a joyous, even ecstatic, disposition. Of the animal's joyous nature, Nietzsche writes: "A human being may well ask an animal: 'Why do you not speak to me of your happiness but only stand and gaze at me?' And the animal would like to answer, and say: 'The reason is I always forget what I was going to say'—but then he forgot this answer too, and stayed silent: so that the human being was left wondering."[27] Here, the animal has language but lacks memory: it is constantly *forgetting* to speak.[28] For Nietzsche, the forgetting that animals do marks their impermanent relation to language: animals are not bound by language, they maintain a cordial but indifferent relation to its demands.[29] The implications of an essential forgetting—of an existence based upon the capacity to forget—are far-reaching. Unable to wield the apparatus of memory, animal being elaborates an entirely different relation to world, history, and language from that of humanity:

Then man says "I remember" and envies the animal which immediately forgets and sees each moment really die, sink back into deep night extinguished forever. In this way the animal lives *unhistorically:* for it goes into the present like a number without leaving a fraction; it does not know how to dissimulate, hides nothing, appears at every moment fully as what it is and so cannot but be honest.[30]

The animal's instinctive honesty (glossed earlier by Derrida as its inability to keep secrets) also prevents the animal from establishing an awareness of the death that overtakes beings. Without memory, without history, death loses the singularity of its finitude: for the animal there can no longer be death, only deaths. As Nietzsche indicates, in the animal world it is not the being that dies, but rather the moment that dies, passes, sinks "back into deep night extinguished forever." Unlike human beings, who believe themselves to occupy unique moments in time, to be bound by singularity, the Nietzschean animal appears rather to be inhabited by singular moments: as each moment dies and sinks back into oblivion, the animal passes into another moment, another world, another history. In this fashion the animal survives time, which is essentially human. Accordingly, the animal returns to each new world as an immortal, incapable of only dying once. It is, perhaps, with this aspect of animal immortality that Nietzsche identifies when he writes in *Ecce Homo:* "One pays dearly for immortality: one has to die several times while still alive."[31] Nietzsche repeatedly turns his philosophy toward this strenuous fatality of animals.

Even Heidegger, his adamant denial of the animal world or full animal world notwithstanding, appears to concede a privileged interaction between the Dionysian philosopher and his animals. In his lectures on Nietzsche under the heading "Zarathustra's Animals," Heidegger observes: "The animals [do] talk to Zarathustra." Heidegger sanctions this exchange by allowing for a sensuous expression on the part of the animals, an emblematic signing. He writes:

Zarathustra's animals are all the more implacable inasmuch as we hear them—not expressing certain propositions or rules or admonitions—but saying from out of their essential natures what is essential, and saying it with growing lucidity through the palpable presence of sensuous imagery. Sense-images speak only to those who possess the constructive energy to give them shape, so that they make sense. As soon as the poetic force—that is, the higher constructive energy—wanes, the emblems turn mute. They petrify, become sheer "facade" and "ornament."[32]

Surprisingly, Heidegger grants to Zarathustra and his animals a world that frames their interaction. The "constructive energy," although operative, allows the two worlds, if indeed they are two separate worlds and not two dimensions of the same world, to intersect. Furthermore, in Heidegger's account, the energy or "poetic force" that forges a passage between the human and animal worlds also creates a time for dialogue. In this sense, the poetic force is also a temporal force: it founds a temporality. As time passes, the energy wanes and the animals return to their former, emblematic muteness. During the time of the poetic force, however, what is invariably transmitted between the species remains on the highest order of the essential, in this case the eternal return: "Zarathustra's animals speak to him about what they themselves symbolize: they speak of eternal return."[33] Zarathustra's animal transgression carries, however, a price. The effect of the exchange is, according to Heidegger, a profound solitude: "When Zarathustra's loneliness speaks, it is his animals who are speaking."[34] (Another figure marked by loneliness, Orpheus, also spoke to the animals in their language and also sought to cross the barriers that enclose humanity and its finite temporality.) In this sense, the voices of Zarathustra's eagle and serpent signal an impossible communion and bring Zarathustra closer to the abyss of a collapsing subjectivity. Heidegger adds:

These two animals define for the first time the loneliest loneliness, and it is something different from what the usual view takes it to be. In the usual view, solitude is what liberates us, frees us from all things. Solitude, according to this view, is what happens after you post the "Do Not Disturb" sign. Yet in our loneliest loneliness the most hair-raising and hazardous things are loosed upon us and on our task, and these cannot be deflected onto other things or other people.[35]

In conversing with the animals, Zarathustra exposes himself to the contagion of their worldly poverty: here, speaking with animals seems to effect a becoming-animal. By speaking with animals, one opens oneself to the vast negativity of a world under erasure; one renounces the presence of a world determined by language. Zarathustra's otherworldly intercourse with animals thus exceeds the parameters of language, blocking its ability to be represented in the human world. His dialogue takes place outside the exchanges that constitute the world community, in the interstices of communication. As Heidegger notes, it is in the suspended moment of Nietzsche's "midday" that the encounters occur: "These animals of his, eagle and serpent, . . . do not enter on the stage at some fortuitous point. Zarathustra first espies them at glowing midday, that part of the day which throughout the work *Thus Spoke Zarathustra* unleashes an essential image-generating force."[36] In suspended time and solitude, conversing here resembles its antithesis, seclusion and stasis. Conversation requires chronology, the movement of the sun. The solitude that Zarathustra achieves with animals is not to be confused with any familiar (or, for that matter, familial) comfort: it is, for Heidegger, a solitude emerging from the depths of alienation: "[The animals] seek to learn whether Zarathustra is still living, living as one who is prepared to go under. That should be enough to let us know that the eagle and serpent are not pets; we do not take them home with us and domesticate them. They are alien to all that is domestic and usual, all that is 'familiar' in the petty sense of the word."[37] Like Poe's orangutan, Zarathustra's animals do not belong at home, in homes—they are *unheimlich*. The "speech" of animals is uncanny because, even if it is only "jabbering," it manages to produce in Zarathustra the semblance of a world, of a full exteriority within which language circulates. Heidegger explains that "after such solitude the world *is* like a garden, even when it is invoked by mere empty talk, in the sheer play of words and phrases."[38] The discourse of animals thus provokes a deep sense of solitude, an abundance of emptiness. It is in this sense that those animals are uncanny: Zarathustra feels alone in their company. For Heidegger, Zarathustra's exchange with the animals portrays the "loneliest loneliness," an experience of solitude that reveals, for an instant (the shadowless moment of a suspended midday), the animal world.

Zarathustra's intercourse with the animals propels him into another world, another time: the transgressive communion aligns Zarathustra with an alternative world-history, a prehistory of world that explodes into his memory. In *On the Genealogy of Morals,* Nietzsche writes: "Indeed perhaps there was nothing more fearful and uncanny in the whole *prehistory of man* than his *mnemotechnics.*"[39] The fear and pain that accompany Zarathustra's entry into the abyss of an animal world arise from the depths of memory, or as Nietzsche phrases it, from the "prehistory of man." By engaging the animals, Zarathustra—and by inference, humanity—plummets from the edifice of world (language and memory) into the immemorial open of a time before world. And this time before world, this prehistory of man, returns to humanity as the figure of the animal. Animal being forces humanity to acknowledge the finitude of world: that is, animals tear humanity away from the imagined totality of world. In this way, the Nietzschean and Heideggerian animal meet at a point beyond language, world, and memory—at a point beyond mortality. The point beyond world is marked for Nietzsche by forgetting, for Heidegger by erasure; and for both Nietzsche and Heidegger, the beyond is recalled by the figure of the animal. For Nietzsche, however, the world beyond represents a "*robust health*," and the possibility of a new beginning, a "new promise," whereas for Heidegger it is a saddened and darkened affair.[40] The critical distinction between Nietzsche's *unheimlich* company and Heidegger's "crossed-through" world may indeed be one of affect. In an interview with Jean-Luc Nancy, Derrida notes the importance of affect to animal being. On the seeming melancholy of Heidegger's animals, Derrida responds to the following question:

> JEAN-LUC NANCY: . . . How could sadness be nonhuman? Or rather, how would sadness fail to testify to a relation to a world?
>
> JACQUES DERRIDA: . . . To come back to your remark, perhaps the animal is sad, perhaps it appears sad, because it indeed has a world, in the sense in which Heidegger speaks of a world as world of spirit, and because there is an openness of this world for it, but an openness without openness, a having (world) without having it. Whence the impression of sadness—for man or in relation to man, in the society of man. And of a sadness determined in its phenomenology, as if the animal remained a man enshrouded, suffering, deprived on account of having access neither to the world of man that he nonetheless senses, nor to truth, speech, death, or the Being of the being as such.[41]

The contrast in mood between the Nietzschean and Heideggerian animal, between ecstasy and depression respectively, brings the question of animal being to the limits of language—to its border with affect and the affective cry. This limit, which speaks to "the Being of the being as such," also marks the final line of a philosophical tradition that situates the distance of the animal in absolute terms. By tracking the animal across the philosophical spectrum, one discovers the systemic manner in which the figure of the animal comes to portray a serial logic: the animal is incapable of language; that lack prevents the animal from experiencing death; this in turn suspends the animal in a virtual, perpetual existence. The figure of the animal determines a radically antithetical counterpoint to human mortality, to the edifice of humanism.

3 | Evolutions: Natural Selection, Phenomenology, Psychoanalysis

We know it well, the world in which we live is
ungodly, immoral, "inhuman"; we have interpreted
it far too long in a false and mendacious way, in
accordance with the wishes of our reverence, which is
to say, according to our needs. *For man is a reverent*
animal. But he is also mistrustful; and that the world
is not *worth what we thought it was, that is about as*
certain as anything of which our mistrust has finally
got hold. The more mistrust, the more philosophy.

—FRIEDRICH NIETZSCHE,
"THE GAY SCIENCE" (EMPHASIS ADDED)

AS THE DISCUSSION of animals moves from philosophy toward the registers of psychoanalysis, aesthetics, and critical theory, it is necessary to address the impact of Charles Darwin (1809–82) on the configuration of animals in Western thought. During the late nineteenth century, Darwin's work profoundly altered the terms of philosophical, psychological, scientific, and sociological theory, causing a veritable reorganization of the epistemological order. And although earlier versions of evolutionary theory had already been in circulation prior to Darwin's publications, the appearance of *On the Origin of Species* in 1859 and *The Descent of Man* in 1871 initiated a polemic that would ultimately restructure the epistēmē.[1] For the present purposes, Darwin's report to the academy reinvigorated a discussion of zoological issues within the philosophical framework, challenging certain axioms of philosophical discourse and opening the way for further evolutions of animal thought.

More than a simple effect of the transition from the metaphysical to the biocentric idiom, Darwin's work actively forced the change by offering a rigorous theory of perpetual transition. As John Dewey wrote in 1909: "The influence of Darwin upon philosophy resides in his having conquered the phenomenon of life for the principle of transition, and thereby freed the new logic for application to mind and morals and life."[2] Darwin uprooted the fixtures of philosophy, what Dewey terms "the familiar furniture of the mind," and turned the dwelling of humanity inside out. Darwin's *unheimlich* legacy had a powerful influence on, among other theorists, Freud and his theses of the unconscious.

Before entering the terrain of the unconscious proper and discussing its relation to animal being, however, it is necessary to first gauge the impact of the "Darwinian revolution" upon the gestation of a nascent twentieth-century zoosemiotics. If the ontological exclusion of animals marked a distinct feature of the philosophical world, then the figure of the animal came to represent, for psychoanalytic thought, precisely the symbol for changing notions of subjectivity. Darwin's discovery of natural selection and the properties of biological adaptation had introduced new possibilities for the conception of a subject and its environment, or *Umwelt*. Not only did Darwin challenge the foundations of religious orthodoxy (among many controversial extrapolations, Darwin's findings pointed toward the historical inaccuracy of Biblical creation, the essential relationship between human beings and primates, and the dynamism of species), they also assailed many of the tenets of metaphysics, not least of which insisted upon a rigid distinction between humanity and animal.

By expanding the definition of community to include animals, Darwin's work precipitated the subsequent search for

modes of communication between animals and human beings, which in turn led to developments in genetic research—
a type of universal, biological language—as well as to the consideration of an unconscious realm of the mind in which
animal being could exist beneath the cultural stratum imposed
by language. Freud later credited Darwin with forging a passage toward the world of unconscious activity, claiming that
Darwin's theory of descent "tore down the barrier that had
been arrogantly set up between man and beast."[3] In fact, this
barrier between humanity's world and the animal kingdom
had been, as previously discussed, carefully constructed and
rigorously guarded throughout much of the Western philosophical tradition.

At the time of Darwin's intervention into the discourse of
animal and human subjectivity, Enlightenment principles had
designated reason as the dominant criterion for inhabiting the
world as sovereign. As the only reasonable creatures on earth,
human beings had, accordingly, assumed a position at the center of the world. Aided by these eighteenth-century ideals,
which heralded the triumph of reason and order over the chaos
of nature, the philosophical and scientific discourses had
sustained the anthropocentric tendencies of modern, post-
Cartesian thought. Darwin's intervention not only undermined
Enlightenment values, it also challenged the premise that was
embedded in the very definition of Enlightenment: namely, the
function of light—lucidity, illumination, and reason—as the
constitutive metaphor for humanity's knowledge. The conflict
between the metaphysics of human vision and animal smell will
return during this discussion of psychoanalysis. The move toward greater spiritual and intellectual enlightenment, taken for
granted throughout the course of Western metaphysics (from
theology to modern phenomenology), was replaced in Darwin's
revision by a more complicated set of genetic, unconscious, and
instinctive drives.

In her account of the "biocentric" movement, Margot Norris discusses the transformation of the "cultural" into the "creatural" as an aftereffect of Darwin's findings.

> Darwin replaced this cybernetic model of Nature as a machine with his theory of natural selection, which removed intelligence (and, by inference, a rational creator) altogether as the source of life and put in its place innumerable, dispersed, trivial organic forces operating unconsciously and irrationally, on an ad hoc basis subject to chance, over time. Darwin thereby liberated biology from its Enlightenment enthrallment to physics.[4]

More important than the distance that Darwin's work placed between scientific and religious doctrine (the rift between these competing discourses had, of course, begun long before Darwin's arrival), was the reversal of influence that it effected between the natural sciences and philosophy. Scientific investigation was no longer enslaved to Enlightenment values, and thus philosophical thought was forced to adjust to the infusion of new empirical data, in a manner not unlike the responses to Aristotle's revaluation of Greek metaphysics. As Bergson writes in *Creative Evolution:* "The ancients reduced the physical order to the vital order, that is to say, laws to genera, while the moderns try to resolve genera into laws."[5] Dewey places the burden of thinking through the implications of Darwin's research not upon the religious institution ("There is not . . . a single instance of any large idea about the world being independently generated by religion"), but upon the disciplines of "science and philosophy."[6]

The resulting discourses sought to reconsider the status not only of the human being but also of its two attendant attributes, corporeality and subjectivity. Of the impact that Darwin's work had upon the biocentric writing that followed, most notably that of Nietzsche, Norris makes the following claim:

The vitalistic, biocentric, zoomorphic energy . . . propels this Nietzschean *Anknüpfung*, this suture of the great cleft produced in our human being by the repression of the animal and the living body. But the biocentricity of this tradition—its valuation of the body and the body's effusion of power, its instinctual epistemology, its celebration of unmediated experience—renders its writings at war with themselves, hostile to art, impervious to representation, inimitable. As a result the short-lived tradition ends in a cul-de-sac, and one finds little evidence of it after the 1930s.[7]

The description that Norris offers of Nietzsche simultaneously succumbing to and resisting the Darwinian gaze—apparent in, according to Norris, Nietzsche's "autotelic biocentrism"—prefigures another hypnotic sway that immediately followed this coupling: Nietzsche eventually exerted the same type of influence over Freud.[8] Moreover, Freud established, from the outset of his oeuvre, his own indebtedness to Darwin. Besides positing the appearance of a writing that emphasized the autotelic body (among the other philosophers, thinkers, authors, and artists that Norris includes in her account of the biocentric tradition are Bergson, Freud, Kafka, Ernst, Lawrence, and Hemingway), Norris also points, in the above passage, to Freud's eventual focus on the "pleasure principle": the autotelic drive embedded within the human psyche.

Along with corporeality, the other concept touched by Darwin's theories was that of subjectivity. The ideological allegiance between Enlightenment doctrines and humanist subjectivity also suffered in the hands of Darwinism. Linking the Enlightenment—humanity's quest for dominion over, and thus liberation from, the forces of nature—to that of the humanist projects embraced by the modern philosophical tradition, Horkheimer and Adorno write of humanity's attempts to appropriate and humanize nature:

Enlightenment has always taken the basic principle of myth to be anthropomorphism, the projection onto nature of the subjective. In this view, the supernatural, spirits and demons, are mirror images of men who allow themselves to be frightened by natural phenomena. Consequently the many mythic figures can all be brought to a common denominator, and reduced to the human subject.[9]

In this passage, and throughout the text, Horkheimer and Adorno argue that according to processes of Enlightenment understanding, the elements of life that evade comprehension or rational analysis are transformed into mythical figures that are then appropriated into thought through anthropomorphic transfiguration. In this way, reason manages to recuperate, or "disenchant," even irrational and supernatural phenomena. ("The disenchantment of the world," the authors note, "is the extirpation of animism.")[10] Thus, everything that elides the category of "human" can still be reincorporated as "inhuman" into the body of humanity as a surfeit of humanity. For Horkheimer and Adorno, the dialectical process of reintroducing the monstrous into the folds of humanity through anthropomorphosis defines the principle of humanism and the Enlightenment. It was the ideological faculty that facilitated, among other disasters, the Third Reich and the atomic bombings of Hiroshima and Nagasaki: "The fully enlightened earth radiates disaster triumphant."[11]

By the early twentieth century, however, the philosophy of humanism had come under increasing attack from all sides of the political and intellectual spectrum. The humanist world, characterized by the ideal that had constituted and sustained the notion of "our" world through the exclusion of others, in this case the nonhuman being, had been unable to prevent a swift capitulation toward two world wars. The faith in progress, in a linear course to human perfection, had led instead to a hostile impasse in which the possibilities of communication, let *alone* community, were suspended. Alluding to the communicational aporia brought about by World War II and the ethical regimen that has ensued, Adorno muses: "Now that the world has made men speechless, not to be on speaking terms is to be in the right."[12]

The clash of history, humanity, and philosophy on the battlefields of World War II is perhaps most eloquently and cynically described by Kojève in a footnote to his discussion of nature's capacity to survive time and history, humanity's existence on earth.

> In point of fact, the end of human Time or History—that is, the definitive annihilation of Man properly so-called or of the free and historical Individual—means quite simply the cessation of Action in the full sense of the term. Practically, this means: the disappearance of wars and bloody revolutions. And also the disappearance of *Philosophy;* for since Man himself no longer changes essentially, there is no longer any reason to change the (true) principles which are at the basis of his understanding of the World and of himself.[13]

Humanity, and the metaphysics of humanism that had framed its existence, definitively ceased to exist, according to Kojève, under the annihilating gaze of World War II.[14] In the aftermath of the "end of history," humanity relinquished its struggle to exist as Humanity, that is, to strive for "recognition" against the forces of nature (e.g., by risking its animal life for the sake of a cultural identity, or by attempting to impose the technical world of Time and History onto the ontology of Nature). At the end of history, Kojève writes, humanity "returns to animality."

In Kojève's nuanced and allusive reading of Hegel, humanity, at the brink of history's finitude, must surpass itself, must overcome finite humanity, if it is to survive the devastation of history. These are, in fact, the exact terms that Dewey uses to describe the impact of Darwinism on philosophy. Arguing that philosophy needed first to exhaust the possibility of stable and transcendent standards of truth and identity, Dewey explains: "The human mind, deliberately as it were, exhausted the logic of the changeless, the final, and the transcendent, before it essayed adventure on the pathless wastes of generation and transformation."[15] Although different in tone from Kojève's despair, Dewey's essay nonetheless concludes with a similar assessment of the posthumanist condition of humanity. Dewey writes of humanity's overcoming of it:

> Old ideas give way slowly; for they are more than abstract logical forms and categories. They are habits, predispositions, deeply engrained attitudes of aversion and preference. Moreover, the conviction persists — though history shows it to be hallucination — that all the questions that the human mind has asked are questions that can be answered in terms of the alternatives that the questions themselves present. But in fact intellectual progress usually occurs through the sheer abandonment of questions together with both of the alternatives they assume — an abandonment that results from their decreasing vitality and a change of urgent interest. *We do not solve them: we get over them.* Old questions are solved by disappearing, evaporating, while new questions corresponding to the changed attitude of the endeavor and preference take their place. Doubtless the greatest dissolvent in contemporary thought of old questions, the greatest precipitant of new methods, new intentions, new problems, is the one effected by the scientific revolution that found its climax in the "Origin of Species."[16]

Dewey clears the way not only for "new methods, new intentions, new problems" but for a serious analysis of the massive cultural repression of old unsolvable questions. In abandoning these questions, Dewey beckons the arrival of the psychoanalytic science, whose first important discovery would be the existence of a mechanism of systematic repression in the human psyche. And although one cannot abandon the discipline of philosophy without even beginning to think through the consequences of its fragmentation, it is also necessary to turn to the new discourses on animal being that emerged from the metamorphoses of the philosophical *eidos,* or "species" (Dewey's translation), to understand the effects of a reorganized philosophical practice.

The notion of abandoning old ideas, advocated by Dewey, would play a crucial role in Freud's discovery of the unconscious. The passage of philosophy marked not so much the end of an era—and thus the inadequacy of the pre- and postmodern binarism in this context—as the expiration of *our* world. It was no longer a question of history, but rather of historicity; a question of the constitution of what must succeed the end of *our* history and *our* day in the sun, a sun that no longer stood transfixed at midday. As the midday sun (Nietzsche's figure for the "zenith of mankind"[17]) moved across the horizon and cast its shadow over the era of humanity, what Adorno and Horkheimer term its era of "enchantment," one finds Nietzsche, himself a fierce but ultimately enchanted opponent of Darwinism, undergoing a metamorphosis of sorts.[18] Convinced of the "misunderstanding" to which his work was destined, Nietzsche rejected humanism and human community, turning instead to the properties of the animal: "It is my fate that I have to be the first *decent* human being; that I know myself to stand in opposition to the mendaciousness of millennia. —I was first to experience lies as lies—smelling them out. —My genius is in my nostrils."[19] Nietzsche, upon whom Heidegger would bestow the title of "last philosopher," appears to fulfill Kojève's expectation by refusing the privileged sense of human beings—sight—for that most frequently associated with the animal: smell. In this sense, Nietzsche returns to animality by transforming himself into a smelling animal. Nietzsche's metamorphosis at the end of history—at the end of philosophy and at the end of humanity—completes a move from the death of god (Nietzsche's terminal for the end of metaphysics) into and beyond the realm of Freud's creatural expanse—what he calls the "pleasure principle."

Henri Bergson (1859–1941)

IN MOVING TOWARD the destination of this chapter—Freud's unconscious and its relation to the figure of the animal—it is necessary first to traverse the work of Henri Bergson, whose notion of the "cinematographic" function prefigures the topic of animality and technology that returns at the conclusion of this investigation. Bergson's focus upon "duration," the perpetual movement and becoming of things, ideas, and entities in time, as an essential structure of being ("the essence of life is in the movement by which life is transmitted") will also serve as a potent catalyst between Darwinian evolution and the unconscious dynamic.[20]

Bergson initiates *Creative Evolution* (1907) with this hypothesis concerning the capacity of being to "endure" the laws of physical animation: "The truth is that we change without ceasing, and that the state itself is nothing but change."[21] Far from an idealist principle (one that pertains only to stabilized things, ideas, or beings at rest), however, Bergson makes clear that the ontological dimension of change pervades both subjectivity and consciousness: "I change, then, without ceasing."[22] And of the spheres of consciousness that bear upon the question of being, Bergson makes this claim: "We are seeking only the precise meaning that our consciousness gives to the word 'exist,' and we find that, for a conscious being, to exist is to change, to change is to mature, to mature is to go on creating oneself endlessly."[23] In fact, for Bergson, "Life in general is mobility itself."[24] From this theoretical assertion, Bergson argues that both classical and modern philosophy and the natural sciences have relied too heavily on the analysis of immobilized states to derive the theories of being that humanity inhabits. These "snapshots," as Bergson calls them, necessarily interrupt the movement that is essential to their constitution. For Bergson, the object in motion is inaccessible to a methodology that concentrates on "privileged moments," or representations of the moving, becoming, and vital entity, that have been extracted artificially from the movement as a whole: *"Representation is stopped up [bouchée] by action."*[25] Thus Bergson proposes an examination of the interval between states, the transition from state to state, and the movement that determines the character of each state as a way to address the broader question of being.

As the object for this investigation Bergson chooses the model of the animal, a being that hangs in the balance between "instinct" and "intelligence." The ratio of instinct to intelligence determines, for Bergson, the degree of an animal's consciousness. *"The consciousness of a living being may be defined as an arithmetical difference between potential and real activity. It measures the interval between representation and action."*[26] Accordingly, consciousness for Bergson involves the capacity to integrate the philosophical or conceptual stases (snapshots) with the animal's instinctual, sensorial, or unconscious participation in the world of fluctuating entities. The mechanism particular to animal beings, one that allows for the constant exchange between instinctual and intelligent modes of behavior, is centralized in the nervous system: "a nervous system being pre-eminently a mechanism which serves as intermediary between sensations and volitions."[27] The greater the degree to which this nervous system is able to minimize the difference between sensations and volitions, or unconscious and conscious responses to stimuli, the more sophisticated the consciousness.

For example, if a given animal is unable to reduce the distance between the poles of a felt hunger and the willed, successful search for food (the ability to intelligently interpret environmental information), then its consciousness is reduced to the zero degree and becomes identical to the instinct itself. If, however, another animal is able to respond to sensations of hunger by immediately locating a source of nourishment and by so doing alleviate the nervous disturbance, then the registers of sensation and volition are working closely together and that animal exhibits a high degree of consciousness. Although those examples represent extreme cases of intelligence and instinct, Bergson sees all living beings as residing somewhere along this spectrum of instinct and intelligence, always possessing a blend of both and attended by the varying degrees of consciousness that result from the transaction between instinct and intelligence.[28] Bergson posits consciousness as "the *deficit* of instinct, the distance between the act and the idea."[29]

From this seemingly biologistic standpoint, Bergson gradually shifts the correlation of instinctual and intelligent acts toward the question of knowledge in general and the definition of consciousness in particular. "While instinct and intelligence both involve knowledge, this knowledge is rather *acted* and unconscious in the case of instinct, *thought* and conscious in the case of intelligence."[30] Bergson argues that in traditional philosophical inquiries, what is "thought," and is thus conscious, has been privileged over what is "acted" and unconscious. This prejudice has persisted at least since Plato, and even Aristotle's apparent challenges to the Platonic ideal never integrated the discrepancy between these two modes of knowledge. According to Bergson's recounting of the dichotomy between idea and matter, the problem has reached an impasse in the positivism of a philosophy that, attempting to absorb the advances made in the natural sciences, has credited the object with properties of totality while denying the object in transition, in the process of becoming, any status whatsoever. What is at rest thus garners the designations of presence; the mobile, transitory form receives no such recognition. Determinations of presence and absence, among the most resilient oppositions in metaphysics, thus come to haunt the polemic between conscious and unconscious states — thought and acted forms of knowledge — with the former term in each pairing qualified by presence and the latter terms relegated to negations and the categorizations of absence. Concerning the question of knowledge, Bergson argues that presence must be further defined as the presence of "order," whereas absence refers to the absence of the same, or "disorder." "The question, we then said, is to know why there is order, and not disorder, in things. But the question has meaning only if we suppose that disorder, understood as an absence of order, is possible, or imaginable, or conceivable."[31] In other words, one must be able to produce an image of disorder, or the absence of order, apart from the mere negation of order. This distinction is crucial for the present discussion of animals, since it invokes the problem of the animal's capacity to represent "as such."

The question of the presence of order on the one hand and its absence on the other presses ultimately not only upon the understanding of knowledge, the ways in which one apprehends, but upon consciousness itself — on the capacity to experience the phenomenal world. Turning toward the problem of disorder, Bergson offers two possible forms of unconsciousness that bear a striking resemblance to Heidegger's stages of world-forming powers among beings. Bergson describes these two states of unconsciousness in relation to absence, or what he calls "zero":

> But here we must point out a difference, not often noticed, between two kinds of unconsciousness, viz., that in which consciousness is absent, and that in which consciousness is nullified. Both are equal to zero, but in one case the zero expresses the fact that there is nothing, in the other that we have two equal quantities of opposite

sign which compensate and neutralize each other. The unconsciousness of a falling stone is of the former kind: the stone has no feeling of its fall. Is it the same with the unconsciousness of instinct, in the extreme cases in which instinct is unconscious? When we mechanically perform an habitual action, when the somnambulist automatically acts his dream, unconsciousness may be absolute; but this is merely due to the fact that the representation of the act is held in check by the performance of the act itself, which resembles the idea so perfectly, and fits so exactly, that consciousness is unable to find room between them.[32]

Like the stages of world asserted by Heidegger, the activity of the stone falling provides an example of absent consciousness; "the stone is worldless." The stone charts the realm of "zero," which remains beyond the possibilities of representation. Nullified consciousness, however, very much like Heidegger's vision of a "crossed-through" world, does not determine the radical absence of consciousness but rather its erasure by something other—by the act of language. Because, Bergson states, this subtle difference between two modes of consciousness is "not often noticed," philosophical inquiries have resulted in a crude positivism that only recognizes presence and absence, order and disorder, and consciousness and unconsciousness.

Emmanuel Levinas also notes the similarity between Bergson's nothingness and Heidegger's crossed-through world and connects those two articulations to the question of *Dasein,* which in Heidegger's terminology appears as the "es gibt," and in Levinas's translation as the "il y a." Against a positivist reading of the *there is,* Levinas writes: "When, in the last chapter of *Creative Evolution,* Bergson shows that the concept of nothingness is equivalent to the idea of being crossed out, he seems to catch sight of a situation analogous to that which led us to the notion of the *there is.*"[33] "Thus the problem of knowledge," Bergson explains, "is complicated, and possibly made insoluble, by the idea that order fills a void and that its actual presence is superposed on its virtual absence."[34] Accordingly, what must be posited, measured, and evaluated is the internal movement between "actual presence" and "virtual absence"; which is to say that since no state ever exists in an absolutely pure form (all states, Bergson argues, are constantly changing, are constituted by the shifts between the ideals of presence and absence), change itself must be considered ontologically, along with the ideal states that represent their totality and the material states that signify their singularity.

The problem reaches its apex in Bergson's argument over the movement between absolutes, which is, in fact, an "inner" movement, a movement intrinsic to the things themselves rather than an external movement between two established differentials. "All movement is articulated inwardly."[35] Since it is virtually impossible to distinguish between presence and absence (between "absent" and "nullified" consciousness) in the case of knowledge, Bergson proposes that one must first determine the sum total of all posited ideas and the absolute negative, zero, and then differentiate this totality by the movements of becoming, or the durations that define key transitions.[36] Bergson offers this solution:

> It is therefore something negative, or zero at most, that must be added to Ideas to obtain change. In that consists the Platonic "non-being," the Aristotelian "matter"—a metaphysical zero which, joined to the Idea, like the arithmetical zero to unity, multiplies it in space and time. By it the motionless and simple Idea is refracted into a movement spread out indefinitely. In right, there ought to be nothing but immutable Ideas, immutably fitted into each other. In fact, matter comes to add to them its void, and thereby lets loose the universal becoming. It is an elusive nothing, that creeps between the Ideas and creates endless agitation, eternal disquiet, like a suspicion

insinuated between two loving hearts. Degrade the immutable Ideas: you obtain, by that alone, the perpetual flux of things. The Ideas or Forms are the whole of intelligible reality, that is to say, of the truth, in that they represent, all together, the theoretical equilibrium of Being.[37]

Nothing, the metaphysics of nothing, animates the static idea, giving it an existence in space and time and in the duration of becoming. Nothing, according to Bergson, gives the idea life. *"The affirmation of a reality implies the simultaneous affirmation of all the degrees of reality intermediate between it and nothing."*[38] Bergson's utilization of this logic, which establishes that each particular reality possesses the sum of its possibilities and nothing divided by time (as opposed to the Platonic and Aristotelian versions of this thesis, which locate the totality of the real in an ideal temporicity), brings his analysis close to that of the Hegelian dialectic. The difference between the two, however, lies in Hegel's recourse to the subject, or the "happy consciousness," as an agent for the procurement of this truth, which he terms "absolute knowing." Unlike Hegel, who places the dialectical apparatus within the subject, Bergson externalizes the mechanism of becoming, deriving it from the sum total of being and nothing. In his introduction to *Creative Evolution,* Bergson already argues that consciousness cannot be reduced to human intellect; he claims that alternative forms of consciousness can be derived from a multiplicity of forms and beings throughout the physical and psychological universe. The totality of these forms of consciousness and nothingness are intersected by duration, which enables "the continual elaboration of the absolutely new" from these totalities, and represents, for Bergson, "a vision of life complete."[39] Linking evolutionary theory to the exteriority of being, Bergson writes:

But the line of evolution that ends in man is not the only one. On other paths, divergent from it, other forms of consciousness have been developed, which have not been able to free themselves from external constraints or to regain control over themselves, as the human intellect has done, but which none the less, also express something that is immanent and essential in the evolutionary movement. Suppose these other forms of consciousness brought together and amalgamated with intellect: would not the result be a consciousness as wide as life? And such a consciousness, turning around suddenly against the push of life which it feels behind, would have a vision of life complete—would it not?—even though the vision were fleeting.[40]

With this gesture, Bergson departs from Hegel's philosophy and moves forcefully into the frame of Darwin's thought. For Darwin formulates the hypothesis that the sum total of organic life subsides within each particular organism and is differentiated by that organism at the specific stage of its evolutionary history. "Ontogeny recapitulates phylogeny." The figure for this change is postulated by Darwin in his theory of natural selection—a complex interaction between organisms and their environment in perpetual and mutual flux. Ultimately, genetic theory provides a semiotic system capable of regulating the historicity and temporicity of the sum total of an organism's being in each particular body. What is crucial for Bergson's brand of evolution emerges in the articulation of the third term, duration, which intervenes in the dialectic between subject (consciousness) and object (the world).

The issue for Bergson, then, is how to figure the move between absolutes: the dynamic between instinct and intelligence (consciousness), action and thought (knowledge), disorder and order (the physical world), and absence and presence (phenomena). Bergson needs a figure for this third term, a source of the movement. In support of such a transitional figure, Bergson writes that "there is *more* in a movement than in the successive positions attributed to the moving object, *more* in a becoming than in the forms passed through in turn, *more* in the evolution of form than the forms assumed one after another."[41] The apparatus that Bergson chooses to exemplify the move, the indefinable surplus of movement and becoming, is the cinematograph. Bergson's cinematograph mediates fixed images, operating like the nervous system.

> It is true that if we had to do with photographs alone, however much we might look at them, we should never see them animated: with immobility set beside immobility, even endlessly, we could never make movement. In order that the pictures may be animated, there must be movement somewhere. The movement does indeed exist here; it is in the apparatus. . . . The process then consists in extracting from all the movements peculiar to all the figures an impersonal movement abstract and simple, *movement in general,* so to speak: we put this into the apparatus, and we reconstitute the individuality of each particular movement by combining this nameless movement with the personal attitudes. Such is the contrivance of the cinematograph. And such is also that of our knowledge.[42]

The figure is remarkable because it suggests, in the context of evolutionary and adaptive logic, a convergence of the animating properties of technology with the cognitive functions of the mind. As a hybrid analogue for knowledge, the cinematograph renders the mind as a technological apparatus, the machine as a form of animal.

The figure of the cinematograph is important not only for the consolidation of Bergson's philosophy but also as a means by which to deconstruct the series of metaphysical oppositions that Bergson presents in his analysis of evolution and philosophy. Retaining the concept of change from Darwin's theory of evolution—one that elevates the process of transition, the movement as a whole to an ontological status—Bergson applies this notion to the activities of consciousness and the perception of phenomena. According to Bergson, there is no phenomenology without this notion of change, which he specifies as duration: "There is no feeling, no idea, no volition which is not undergoing change every moment: if a mental state ceased to vary, its duration would cease to flow."[43] The figure of the cinematograph provides not only a locus for the movement of change but also an image of the change itself.

Change, according to Bergson, can be represented neither by the dynamic object nor by the idea of change—it needs an autonomous form. Language cannot fulfill this role because "forms are all that it is capable of expressing. It is reduced to taking as understood or is limited to *suggesting* a mobility which, just because it is always unexpressed, is thought to remain in all cases the same."[44] Likewise with scientific signs: "These signs undoubtedly differ from those of language by their greater precision and their higher efficacy; they are none the less tied down to the general condition of the sign, which is to denote a fixed aspect of the reality under an arrested form."[45] Thus movement cannot, Bergson explains, be derived from static representations, or ideas, nor can the moving object articulate its own dynamic. Instead, the movement must be sought separately, externally, neither in the subject nor in the object, but in the apparatus that mediates the absolute states of subjectivity and objectivity as a source of their oscillating movement. Bergson's cinematograph shares many of the properties of Freud's own medium, the unconscious.

Bergson's attempts to reconcile a critique of metaphysics with what remains unthought in the natural sciences are also echoed in the work of Heidegger and point the trajectory of a postphilosophical phenomenology in the direction of psychoanalysis.

New Currents

*La propriété du corps animal qui le rend susceptible de l'influence
des corps célestes et de l'action réciproque de ceux qui l'environ-
nent, manifestée par son analogie avec l'aimant, m'a déterminé à
la nommer* Magnétisme animal.

—FRANZ ANTON MESMER, 1779

*Now although it would be very foolish to see in the phenomena
of animal magnetism an elevation of mind above even Reason
with its ability to comprehend, and to expect from this state a
higher knowledge of the eternal than that imparted by philosophy, and although the fact is that the magnetic state must be
declared pathological and a degradation of the mind below the
level even of ordinary consciousness in so far as in that state
mind surrenders its thinking as an activity creative of specific
distinctions, as an activity contradistinguished from Nature;
yet, on the other hand, in the visible liberation of mind in
those magnetic phenomena from the limitations of space and
time and from all finite associations, there is something akin to
philosophy, something which, as brute fact, defies the skepti-
cism of the abstractive intellect and so necessitates the advance
from ordinary psychology to the comprehension afforded by
speculative philosophy for which alone animal magnetism is
not an incomprehensible miracle.*

—G. W. F. HEGEL, "'PHILOSOPHY OF SPIRIT,' INTRODUCTION"

BERGSON'S CHALLENGE TO metaphysics opens the possibility for
a new exploration of the animal world that does not call for the
complete abandonment of the philosophical idiom—only its
modification. In the work of Bergson and Freud, the philosophical question of animal being takes on new meaning. For
the first time since Montaigne's arguments in support of animal consciousness and reason (perhaps with the exception of

Nietzsche's projections of animal community), the possibility of the existence of an entirely other animal world is raised.[46] Granted the marginal space of an evolving world in Bergson's work, the figure of the animal can be seen entering the new environments opened up by psychological and phenomenological reflections on being. If the momentum that marks this change of attitude toward animal being can be traced to its origin in Darwin, then its culmination can be found in the work of Freud.

Sigmund Freud (1856–1939)

UNLIKE THE PHILOSOPHERS before him who sought to sublate the animal into the worlds of humanity and consciousness, Freud attempted to secure a place for the animal as other, which is to say as a property of the unconscious or nonrational dimension of being. Freud managed to create an animal world not by investigating the properties that determine animal being (although he did maintain a strong interest in the biological, neurological, and zoological sciences throughout his life) but by producing a radical theory of world. Freud's theory of world—exemplified by the unconscious—allows for the existence of multiple and other worlds removed from that of consciousness.

Freud's discoveries followed, in part, from his readings (and misreadings) of Lamarckian and Darwinian evolutionary theory. Freud's journey toward the origin of psychoanalysis began in the biological laboratories of post-Darwinian Vienna and with one of Freud's own conceptual axioms that "biological research destroyed man's supposedly privileged place in creation and proved his descent from the animal kingdom and his ineradicable animal nature."[47] Neither exiling animality to the domain of alterity (a realm of unreachable absence) nor domesticating it into a subdivision of the human order, Freud devised the system of the unconscious to accommodate the possibility of new worlds. A type of supplemental apparatus, the unconscious mediates between what Bergson refers to as excess "animal energies" and human consciousness. The unconscious stores the *eidos,* or idea of animal being. Freud's discovery of the unconscious helped surmount the ontological impasse at which psychology as well as philosophy had arrived.

"If Freud's discovery had to be summed up in a single word," claim psychoanalysts Jean Laplanche and J.-B. Pontalis, "that word would without doubt have to be 'unconscious.'"[48] The unconscious opened a previously closed passage not only to human consciousness but also to a multiplicity of unexplored and unrecognized forms of consciousness. It meant, however, a radical departure from the traditional confines of reason. Freud's unconscious, like Darwin's natural selection and Bergson's cinematograph, marks a locale outside the structure of conventional subjectivity—outside, that is, the topology of the human being. Nonetheless, the unconscious consolidates, for Freud, the possibility of individual identity and being. In his 1915 essay "The Unconscious," Freud explains that only by departing from the topography of consciousness can one hope to understand what otherwise remains scrambled and illegible in consciousness: "Conscious acts remain disconnected and unintelligible if we insist upon claiming that every mental act that occurs in us must also necessarily be experienced by us through consciousness."[49] Freud's unconscious functions as an interpsychic exchange that makes possible a new form of communicability between the worlds of humanity and animals. The first stage of that passage for Freud appears in his involvement with hypnosis.

Freud's new topography and communication have their roots in Athanasius Kircher's and Franz Anton Mesmer's experiments with "animal magnetism."[50] Hypnosis, or suggestion, makes its first appearance in Freud's work with Josef Breuer, *Studies on Hysteria.*[51] From the analysis of hysteria and hypnoid states, Freud carefully refined the idea of animal magnetism, transforming it into the concept of transference. Despite his ultimate move away from animal magnetism, however, Freud himself acknowledges a debt to the parapsychical technique: "Incidentally, even before the time of psycho-analysis, hypnotic experiments, and especially post-hypnotic suggestion, had tangibly demonstrated the existence and mode of operation of the mental unconscious."[52]

Freud and Darwin

IN *Darwin's Influence on Freud: A Tale of Two Sciences,* a rigorous history charting Freud's intellectual development under the influence of Darwinism, Lucille B. Ritvo situates Freud firmly in the *epistēmē* of Darwin: "The life of the creator of psychoanalysis coincides almost exactly with the onset of the 'Darwinian revolution.'"[53] Throughout her account, Ritvo chronicles Freud's careful translations of Darwin's theories of drives, recapitulation, and perhaps most importantly, the narrative of the primal horde.[54] Freud's assimilation of Darwinism leads to a revealing configuration of the unconscious and its relation to animal being.

From the outset, Freud established the topographical and dynamic functions of the unconscious. Freud's descriptions of the unconscious already resemble that of the animal. "The Freudian unconscious," write Laplanche and Pontalis, "is primarily —and indissolubly—a topographical and dynamic notion."[55] "Its 'contents' are representatives of the 'instincts,'" and they are "strongly cathected by instinctual energy."[56] Freud himself makes two crucial statements concerning the topographical and dynamic construct of the unconscious. The first statement is found in "The Unconscious": "Our psychical topography has *for the present* nothing to do with anatomy; it has reference not to anatomical localities, but to regions in the mental apparatus, wherever they may be situated in the body."[57] This distinction is important, for Freud has, in essence, displaced the site of consciousness and unconsciousness from the topology of the subject, that is, from the centralized body, and dispersed these same functions across the nervous system "wherever they may be situated in the body." Darwin also makes similar claims of the mind: "Experience shows that the problem of the mind cannot be solved by attacking the citadel itself—the mind is a function of the body."[58] The mental apparatus, then, as Freud calls it, has nothing to do with anatomy, but charts instead an autonomous region of psychical activity. Freud's second key statement also comes from the metapsychological essay. "The processes of the system *Ucs.* are *timeless;* i.e. they are not ordered temporally, are not alerted by the passage of time; they have no reference to time at all. Reference to time is bound up, once again, with the work of the system *Cs.*"[59] Again, one finds Darwin having made similar advances toward the Freudian paradigm. "Character of dreams no surprise, at the violation of all [rules] relations of time [identity], place, & personal connections —ideas are strung together in a manner quite different from when awake."[60] Returning for a moment to philosophical definitions, one recalls Kojève's Hegelian assessment of "Time": "Time *is* the History of Man in the World. And indeed, without Man, there would be no Time in the World."[61] From this philosophical *doxa,* one can see that Freud's projection of the unconscious marks an attempt to outline an entire world distinct from that of the human being. Dislocated from the body and timeless, yet intrinsically bound to the psychical functions of human beings, Freud's unconscious opens the possibility of a bridge between the animal and human worlds, which are vigorously kept apart in philosophical discourses.

The externality and extratemporal dynamic of Freud's unconscious are both features of natural selection that exist in Darwin's theory of evolution. Unlike Jean-Baptiste de Monet de Lamarck, the other name most frequently associated with evolution, Darwin insists that natural selection cannot be reduced to the individual organism's "will" to survive. Or rather,

Darwin rejects Lamarck's assertion that "acquired characteristics" can be passed from one individual organism to another through an "interior orthogenetic force, or law of progressive development toward perfection."[62] In this sense, Darwin is responsible for *deconstructing* Lamarckian evolution, for refusing to allow the agency of evolution to reside in either the individual subject or an omnipotent being. For Darwin, evolution occurs as an endless series of struggles between competing organisms for limited resources: and just as each species remains in flux, so too the world and environment around each species remain in motion, readapting to meet the changing needs of their inhabitants. The Freudian unconscious, taken in this light, is synonymous with a Darwinian environment: it is characterized by a material exteriority that still functions as a genuine exteriority, that is, removed from the chronologies of human time. One effect of Freud's parallel world, the unconscious, results in a decentering of the subject from the world of human existence. In fact, Freudian psychoanalysis insists upon the estrangement of the subject from consciousness as the sole determination of subjectivity. Lacan describes the psychoanalytic subjectivity as a diminishment in world: "The subject is the introduction of a loss in reality."[63] The loss in reality, in the "as such," brings human beings closer to the *poorer* world of animals.

Mimicking the narrative of evolution, Freud recounts the estrangement of human beings from subjectivity:

> Consciousness makes each of us aware only of his own states of mind; that other people, too, possess a consciousness is an inference which we draw by analogy from their observable utterances and actions, in order to make this behaviour of theirs intelligible to us. (It would no doubt be psychologically more correct to put it in this way: that without special reflection we attribute to everyone else our own constitution and therefore our con-

sciousness as well, and that this identification is a *sine qua non* of our understanding.) This inference (or this identification) was formerly extended by the ego to other human beings, to animals, to plants, inanimate objects and to the world at large, and proved serviceable so long as their similarity to the individual ego was overwhelmingly great; but it became more untrustworthy in proportion as the difference between the ego and these "others" widened. To-day, our critical judgment is already in doubt on the question of consciousness in animals; we refuse to admit it in plants and we regard the assumption of its existence in inanimate matter as mysticism. But even where the original inclination to identification has withstood criticism — that is, when the "others" are our fellow-men — the assumption of a consciousness in them rests upon an inference and cannot share the immediate certainty which we have of our own consciousness.

Psycho-analysis demands nothing more than that we should apply this process of inference to ourselves also — a proceeding to which, it is true, we are not constitutionally inclined.[64]

Freud duplicates the logic by which Darwin arrives at his evolutionary history of humanity. Consciousness, in Freud's version, begins in total harmony and identification with the world around it; as differentiation begins to occur, consciousness, in an effort to sustain understanding, clings to the rapidly diversifying state of things by acknowledging the loss of phenomenal similitude. In turn, consciousness turns to the idea of a metaphysical unity that transcends individual differences (religion, for example) for solace. Unable to maintain this function, consciousness retreats within the confines of its community of fellow consciousnesses, or "fellow men." Once restricted to this group, however, consciousness is forced, for the sake of differentiating itself from the others, to reflect upon its own capacity to know itself; this leads in turn to the discovery of a further difference in the self, or, as Freud calls it, the unconscious. Thus the history of consciousness, like the history of organisms, proceeds always toward further differentiation. In both cases, the evolutionary dynamic ends in the establishment of an exteriority, of a topography beyond the jurisdiction of the organism or consciousness. The exteriorities marked by genetics and the unconscious are two exemplary legacies of evolutionary theory.[65]

Both Bergson's phenomenology and Freud's psychoanalysis bear the stamp of Darwinism and evolution: both discourses, furthermore, produce supplementary apparatuses with which to process the new knowledge. Bergson's cinematograph and Freud's unconscious both store the overflow of subjectivity that can no longer be contained in one, unified topology. Unlike Hegel's "anti-theses," which are sublated by the subject, these apparatuses can never be integrated into a dominant system. The apparatuses that emerge from evolutionary theory provide distinct topographies that are not regulated by human time, what Kojève calls "technical" time.[66] The system *Ucs.*, genetics, the cinematograph, then, all represent, in some form, the possibility of a nonhuman world, unregulated by human consciousness and subjectivity.

4 | The Wildside: Theory and Animality

The hypnotist asserts that he is in possession of a mysterious power that robs the subject of his own will; or, which is the same thing, the subject believes it of him. This mysterious power (which is even now often described popularly as "animal magnetism") must be the same power that is looked upon by primitive people as the source of taboo. . . . The hypnotist, then, is supposed to be in possession of this power; and how does he manifest it? By telling the subject to look him in the eyes; his most typical method of hypnotizing is by his look.

—SIGMUND FREUD, "GROUP PSYCHOLOGY AND
THE ANALYSIS OF THE EGO"

THE COMMUNICATIVE POWERS of animal magnetism, which Josef Breuer and Freud emphasize in their analysis of hypnosis, hysteria, and the "splitting of the mind," *Studies on Hysteria* (1893–95), can be said to lie at the origin of psychoanalysis. In this work, published as a complete volume in 1895, Breuer and Freud introduce a new category of consciousness—neurosis—to the discourse on subjectivity.[1] The authors assert in a "Preliminary Communication" (a phrase already haunted by the manifestations of a hysterical symptomatology, since for hysterics, all communication is, in some way, always preliminary) that "unconscious ideas" can produce physiological disturbances in the daily operations of the body.[2] Unconscious ideas are those ideational elements that enter into the psyche without passing through any reflective mechanisms: they surpass the subject's conscious capacities (usually signaling and signaled by an unassimilable affective disruption) and fall beyond the mind's recuperative reach. Unabsorbed by the system *Cs.,* these unconscious forces inscribe various disturbances upon the surface of the body from a place outside consciousness. The authors initially designate this occurrence a "splitting of the consciousness," *"which . . . under the form of 'double conscience' is present to a rudimentary degree in every hysteria, and that a tendency to such a dissociation, and with it the emergence of abnormal states (which we shall bring together under the term 'hypnoid') is the basic phenomenon of this neurosis."* [3] Two psychic topologies emerge in the hysterical constitution: one conscious and accessible, the other beyond the grasp of memory, fundamentally remote. Breuer distinguishes the hypnoid condition from its classical counterpart, the "double conscience," in his theoretical capitulation. With hysterics, he writes, "their psychical ideational activity is divided into a conscious and unconscious part, and their ideas are divided into some that are admissible and some that are inadmissible to consciousness. We cannot, therefore, speak of a splitting of consciousness, though we can speak of a *splitting of the mind.*" [4] This subtle shift from consciousness to mind strikes at the core of a traditional subjectivity, recalling the case of paraneoplastic encephalopathy described in the introduction. The difference between "split consciousness" and "split mind" is not one of simple degree, but of essence: it allows the psychoanalysts to found an entirely new psychic topology.

From a philosophical vantage point, this basic psychoanalytic axiom (which posits the existence of an unconscious "subject") challenges the concept of a unified subject. A split consciousness simply means that two or more parts have developed from a single mind: the mind remains a single entity but comprises various fragmentary spaces. The notion of a split mind, however, introduces a secondary or supplemental consciousness such as the unconscious, or any other alternative mode of consciousness.[5] In other words, the idea of a split consciousness does not necessarily imply a split in the apparatus of subjectivity (duality is a common feature of a functional consciousness); the split mind, by definition, opens the way for a doubled agency of subjectivity—two autonomous centers of consciousness (one conscious and the other *un*conscious) located in the same body. The implications are significant. Split consciousness merely reveals the fragmentation of unity that may or may not be ultimately realized, whereas the split mind establishes the presence of an entirely other thinking that, in this case, remains dissociated from the cognitive, reflective, semantic, and ideational registers of consciousness. Thus the system *Ucs.,* whose existence manifests itself on the hysteric's body, cannot be identified by normal measures, such as language. Disengaged from the discursive indexes of consciousness, the unconscious quickly assumes, in *Studies on Hysteria,* the capacity to accept and nurture ideational complexes that—structurally as well as thematically—cannot otherwise find their way into the world of consciousness.

The discovery of the unconscious in hysterical disorders marks the appearance of an other world of subjectivity—a topology in which ideas, desires, and drives can circulate in the world without being made manifest in language. For the present purposes, the unconscious opens a space within the psychophilosophical constitution for the entry of a formerly inadmissible ideational plexus grouped under the figure of the animal. The discussion of "unconscious ideas" in Breuer and Freud's writing greatly resembles the animal world, and this resemblance between the operations of the unconscious and the properties attributed to the animal only grows stronger in the course of the text. In fact, one can read Breuer and Freud's excavation of the unconscious as a direct reversal of the animal's crossed-through world that Heidegger presents. In hysteria, animal world erupts onto the surface of human consciousness as a kind of primal scene. Hysteria is inscribed, according to Breuer and Freud by a form of chronic remembering: *"Hysterics suffer mainly from reminiscences."*[6]

Another affinity to the animal in Breuer and Freud's delineation of the unconscious idea emerges in their theory that unconscious ideas, like animals, are endowed with a perpetual vitality. Animals, as seen in the preceding chapters, are generally denied singularity and thus, according to the rhetoric of mortality, are incapable of death.[7] Consequently, as their name indicates, animals figure a type of collective vitality. Unimpeded by finitude, animal being passes from one organism to another, much like Leibniz's monads, without interrupting the flow of life. In a similar way, unconscious ideas, because of their isolation and dissociation from the conscious community of ideas, tend to remain in an unaging and undiminishing state of activity. Although conscious ideas, Freud explains, undergo endless interruptions and form incompatible units, unconscious ideas "exist side by side without being influenced by one another, and are exempt from mutual contradiction." In the system *Ucs.* there is "no negation, no doubt, no degrees of certainty."[8] And because they do not "associate," these unconscious ideas, when of a pathological nature, are never entirely drained of their energies. Thus the affective force that unconscious ideas potentialize remains constant and even when partially drained can be renewed, according to the authors, on a seemingly limitless basis. *"The ideas which have become pathological have persisted with such freshness and affective strength because they have been denied the normal wearing-away processes by means of abreaction and reproduction in states of uninhibited association."*[9] Unconscious ideas, like animals, remain alive through the processes of perpetual rejuvenation: the unconscious allows ideas to remain charged forever. These forces—unconscious ideas and animals—affect, in a manner yet to be determined, occurrences in the phenomenal world without, however, being a part of it. They themselves exist in the faint traces of an unexplored realm unrepresentable to what Derrida calls the "as such." One can hear the reverberations of a de facto animal immortality in the withholding of "the normal wearing-away processes" from pathogenic unconscious thoughts. Unconscious ideas are otherworldly.[10] Not only are they unable to enter into the present, unconscious ideas actually problematize the very possibility of such a present. Drifting in the unstable atmosphere of the detemporalized, or "timeless" world, Freud's magnetized unconscious not only disrupts the empirical subject (the neurotic body) but also the theoretical one.

Existing apart from the chronomechanical dynamic of technical time, unconscious ideas obstruct any attempt to construct a unified subject. Or rather, the parasubjective field that they create does not appear in any historical mode. And since the philosophical subject achieves its measure of authenticity in the reflection of its historicality (Hegel)—its mortality, what Heidegger defines as "Being-in-the-world"—the psychoanalytic, or neurotic, subject secures its existence in the span of an alternative historicity. Breuer and Freud name this supplementary register the "hypnoid state." (In fact, these states suggest a type of vegetal being: "[They] provide the soil in which the affect plants the pathogenic memory with its consequent somatic phenomena.")[11] The hypnoid condition intervenes, according to the authors, on the occasion of an abnormalized consciousness: "during the prevalence of severely paralysing affects such as fright, or during positively abnormal psychical states, such as the semi-hypnotic twilight state of day-dreaming, autohypnoses, and so on."[12] At this moment, the reflective mechanisms that interiorize perceptions are disengaged, and an array of unprocessed information passes directly into the unconscious. Once entrenched, this material can no longer be retrieved consciously. Although these unconscious ideas organize into intensive units they remain, throughout the course of their extended lives, disenfranchised and incapable of abreaction.[13] This is because "the ideas which emerge in them [hypnoid states] are very intense but are cut off from associative communication."[14] Languishing thus in the shadows of consciousness, the unconscious idea constructs a secondary force, which bypasses the cognitive route and directly afflicts the body. According to Breuer and Freud:

> Hysterical attacks, furthermore, appear in a specially interesting light if we bear in mind a theory that we have mentioned above, namely, that in hysteria groups of ideas originating in hypnoid states are present and that these are cut off from associative connection with the other ideas, but can be associated among themselves, and thus form the more or less highly organized rudiment of a second consciousness, a *condition seconde*. If this is so, a chronic hysterical symptom will correspond to the intrusion of this second state into the somatic innervation which is as a rule under the control of normal consciousness.[15]

In other words, when attacking, not only do unconscious ideas take over the nervous system but they implement an entirely other topography: unconscious ideas do not merely displace (and replace) consciousness, they add a "second consciousness" onto the nervous system. Not an altered state, then, the hypnoid attack implants an alternate state into the psychic topology.

The therapeutic strategy that Breuer and Freud propose involves re-creating the hypnoid condition during which the trauma occurred. Because the severance of the unconscious idea from the traffic of association remains absolute, the analysts argue that "as a rule it is necessary to hypnotize the patient and to arouse his memories under hypnosis of the time at which the symptom made its first appearance; when this has been done, it becomes possible to demonstrate the connection in the clearest and most convincing fashion."[16] The connection that is to dislodge the unconscious idea from the hysterical symptom cannot be produced internally, but must first be reintroduced by language:

> *It brings to an end the operative force of the idea which was not abreacted in the first instance,* by allowing its strangulated affect to find a way out through speech; *and it subjects it to associative correction by introducing it into normal consciousness (under light hypnosis) or by removing it through the physician's suggestion, as it is done in somnambulism accompanied by amnesia.*[17]

Breuer and Freud advocate the use of hypnosis to release the strangulated idea. By endorsing the use of hypnosis, suggestion, and somnambulism, Breuer and Freud link the psychoanalytic cure to its primitive roots in mesmerism and animal magnetism.

It is interesting to note that Breuer and Freud invert the sequence and causal logic that move from hysteria to hypnosis and grant the hypnoid condition an a priori status: "We should like to balance the familiar thesis that hypnosis is an artificial hysteria by another—the basis and *sine qua non* of hysteria is the existence of hypnoid states."[18] Rather than an artificial simulation of hysteria, hypnosis is an existential condition that hysteria recreates. There is already something hysterical in this account: by insisting upon the priority of the hypnoid and not the hysterical state, Breuer and Freud suggest the existence of a chronology between two imaginary states.[19] How can one decide between the priority of hypnoid and hysterical states, between the priority of two prelinguistic temporicities? It appears that a hysterical reaction has infiltrated Breuer and Freud's argument. The psychoanalysts seem to be stuck in the aporia of a preliminary communication that will ultimately cause them to break apart from one another. Choosing between the priority of hysterical and hypnoid time is not just a choice between two times, but a choice between two times that precede the existence of language, or time itself. One might call such a time before language *preliminal,* before the threshold of conscious sensory perception. Both hysteria and hypnoid states appear to take place within such a preliminal topography. In this light, preliminality can be understood as the communicative mode of an originary, as it were, hypnoid being.

Preliminal Communication: Josef Breuer (1842–1925)

The nonlinguistic channel of hypnosis and magnetism receives another articulation, another preliminal figuration, in Breuer's summary communication. Likening the establishment of hypnoid states to the siphoning off of electrical current during system breakdowns or short circuits, Breuer affixes the psychical and nervous networks onto the metaphorical switchboards of telephone lines and animated electrical apparatuses. Breuer stammers the analogy in the manner of a hysteric:

> *We ought not to think* of a cerebral path of conduction as resembling a telephone wire which is only excited electrically at the moment at which it has to function (that is, in the present context, when it has to transmit a signal). *We ought to liken it* to a telephone line through which there is a constant flow of galvanic current and which can no longer be excited if that current ceases. *Or better,* let us imagine a widely-ramified electrical system for lighting and the transmission of motor power; what is expected of this system is that the simple establishment of contact shall be able to set any lamp or machine in operation. To make this possible, so that everything shall be ready to work, there must be a certain tension present throughout the entire network of lines of conduction, and the dynamo engine must expend a given quantity of energy for this purpose. In just the same way there is a

certain amount of excitation present in the conductive paths of the brain when it is at rest but awake and prepared to work.[20]

Breuer's apparent hesitation before committing himself to the electrical figure suggests that the risk is high. For Breuer's figurative "galvanic current" that runs through the psychonervous apparatus introduces another semiological system into the unconscious. Breuer's electrical system overrides the functions of language and the normal channels of communication by remaining continuously "on." A few sentences earlier Breuer had already stumbled upon precisely that thought in the discussion regarding the dislocations of "perceptive" and "apperceptive" faculties. In what can be seen as a lapse, Breuer compares the deactivated status of most perceptions—those which have not yet been transferred to the field of apperceptions—to a spiritual communion or communication. In a parenthetical aside, Breuer remarks: "For instance, we find ourselves talking to a dead person without remembering that he is dead." This curious revelation, delivered parenthetically in a daydreamlike calm, suggests that the hypnoid states described by Breuer and Freud have crossed the thresholds of neurosis and have entered into and affected the larger economy of phantasmatic conversation. Breuer appears to have located a primordial function of communication that predates the appearance of language in the human organism and also exceeds the capacity of normative language to communicate. In a dissociated state, a hypnoid state (which according to Breuer and Freud constitutes an a priori condition of human being that hysteria only simulates), one can speak with a dead person "without remembering that he is dead." In Breuer's accidental discovery, the dead are brought back. By forgetting the dead, forgetting that they have died, the dead remain, like animals and unconscious ideas, present in another world—accessible, perhaps, to communication.[21]

The original question returns: can a medium be found that would make hypnoid communications possible? Throughout Breuer's figuration of the hysterical and hypnoid matrix, a certain unnameable, paralinguistic force seems to destabilize his discourse. Following the electrical current, Breuer stumbles upon a hypnoid language that allows him to communicate with the dead (whom he has forgotten are dead). The two factors—loss of memory and supernatural communication—are connected. It seems that this forgetting, perhaps pathological in Breuer's case, is directly connected to the appearance of new worlds, of the dead, for example. The preliminal or prelinguistic hypnoid condition affords the possibility of another language that opens onto this other world.

In the first stage of Breuer's analysis, electricity, as a figure for the nervous system, challenges the resilience of human language. Inefficient, prone to imprecision, and excruciatingly slow, the processes of language seem much weaker beside the high-density exchanges of the electrical semiotic. (Regarding the unwillingness of philosophers to surrender the singularity of language, that is, to reduce language to one element of communication among many, Friedrich Kittler has noted that Hegel, for one, rejected "Mesmer's attempts 'to think without words' only as 'unreason.'") [22] Breuer and Freud's appropriation of animal magnetism into the body of psychoanalysis under the guise of hypnotic therapy and hypnoid conditioning provides a crucial link between the development of psychoanalysis both as a discourse and praxis and the sublinguistic electrical stratum that Breuer locates in the human psychical and nervous systems. The linkage is important because it posits at the foundation of psychoanalysis an irrational process that remains in place throughout the attempts to legitimize psychoanalysis as a science. Accordingly, unlike the accepted sciences that observe the properties of material objects (the body, the earth, the universe) or mathematical systems, psychoanalysis would remain a science of the immaterial, of the unconscious. So, even while psychoanalysis sought to wrest animal magnetism from its association with magic, it was also clear that hypnosis would never enjoy the full privilege of scientific status. Animal magnetism under any name would continue to retain the traces of its nonrational nature. The immaterial force would forever be consigned to "the underworld of psycho-analysis," to the underworld of unconscious ideas.[23]

In his faltering attempts to implement the electrical figure, Breuer tries, shortly after his evocation of the electrical system, to retreat from the impact of his metaphor. The footnote begins: "I may perhaps venture here to indicate briefly the notion on which the above statements are based."[24] And still the matter persists. Like the constant activity of the intracerebral tonic excitation that he is here discussing, Breuer seems unready or unwilling to shut off his metaphorical and perhaps even synecdochal current. Breuer insists upon the electrical figure and indeed from the moment after its appearance, the electrical terminology seems to rewire, so to speak, and entirely pervade his theoretical apparatus. The border between the primary reference (in this case the psychical construct) and the metonymic supplement (the electrical dispatch) becomes virtually indistinguishable. With a shared phraseology and idiomatic register, the systems are collapsed into simulacra of one another. The result of this figuration is that the two systems become increasingly interchangeable and begin to lose their figurative dimension. Thus the order of reference, in which one system stands in for another, is dismantled, and the two systems emerge as originary dimensions in Breuer's psychotopology. For example, in another parenthesis Breuer interjects the electrical supplement at a moment when the discussion appears to be traversing precisely that electrical register, thus obscuring the status of the electrical idiom as a metaphor or supplement of the psyche. Breuer asserts his electrical matrix at a telling moment—at the moment that he introduces the primal scene of hypnoid conditioning, the hysterical conversion. Breuer, himself reaching a hysterical pitch, reiterates his figure at the same time that he denies its essentiality:

> I shall scarcely be suspected of identifying nervous excitation with electricity, if I return once more to the comparison with an electrical system. If the tension in such a system is excessively high, there is a danger of a break occurring at weak points in the insulation. Electrical phenomena then appear at abnormal points; or, if two wires lie close beside each other, there is a short circuit. Since a permanent change has been produced at these points, the disturbance thus brought about may constantly recur if the tension is sufficiently increased. An abnormal "facilitation" has taken place.[25]

The nervous and electric systems are modulated into a perfectly reciprocal state in which the precedence of one over the other can no longer be ascertained. It is a crucial moment when the figurative operation of a text exceeds its secondary function and begins to assume a primary status within the text. Breuer's electrical idiom appears to be undergoing this type of rhetorical expansion. What was begun as a tentative figure intended to describe the operation of the unconscious and the forces that excite it has grown throughout Breuer's presentation until it appears to replace the unconscious as the primary reference.

At this point, it is no longer clear what Breuer intends to accomplish: his argumentation itself appears to have undergone an abnormal facilitation. Some sort of metapsychological or metaphorical breaker has kicked into the work and caused a hysterical conversion. Breuer's delirium, if this is in fact the right term, only appears to increase. He continues to deny that he has installed an extraneous electrical stratum into the depths of the hysterical psyche at the same time that he persists in evoking it. Breuer appears to be, quite literally, at war with the specter of his own rhetoric and its production, the electrical system. Why has this simple figurative device caused so much havoc in Breuer's attempts to delineate a hysterical unconscious? What are the stakes in locating a figure that appears to precede and exceed the system it is meant to elucidate? It is important to remember that the unconscious appears first as a figure of the unconscious: the unconscious appears, as Derrida has shown in "Freud and the Scene of Writing," only in its representation. Derrida explains the logic of originary supplementation: "Since the transition to consciousness is not a derivative or repetitive writing, a transcription duplicating an unconscious writing, it occurs in an original manner and, in its very secondariness, is originary and irreducible."[26] Breuer, it seems, has begun to realize that the unconscious takes place in the first instance elsewhere, meaning that the representation of its existence (in Breuer's case the electrical system) in fact marks its originary site. This would imply that the unconscious determines an exterior place that is only reintroduced into the subject, the conscious subject, afterward. Thus, what is preliminal in communication—what is external to consciousness— returns to supplement but also to lay the foundation for the undercurrents that sustain the subject. Breuer appears to have stumbled upon the realization that the subject is already exceeded even as it is in the process of being constituted.

The unconscious, which forms, according to psychoanalysis, the subject's core, is in fact external to the subject and can only return to claim the subject as a supplement. There can thus be no self-sufficiency, autonomy, or closure in the world of consciousness without its completion by something foreign to it. Breuer has, in essence, discovered the radical alterity of the unconscious by realizing that its figuration, its supplement, determines the place of its incarnation. The supplement, trope, or figure of the unconscious is in fact the unconscious. The origin of the unconscious is not in the subject but outside it. In the first instance, this excess is marked by the electrical system and its magnetic, prelinguistic efficacy.

After committing to paper the thought, "what was originally an affective idea now no longer provokes the affect but only the abnormal reflex," Breuer again descends into the footnote to retract his "abnormal" compulsion:

> I am anxious not to drive the analogy with an electrical system to death. In view of the totally dissimilar conditions it can scarcely illustrate the processes in the nervous system, and can certainly not explain them. *But I may once more recall the case in which,* owing to excessively high tension, the insulation of the wires in a lighting system breaks down and a "short circuit" occurs at some point in it. If electrical phenomena (such as overheating or sparking) occur at this point, the lamp to which the wire leads fails to light. In just the same way, the affect fails to appear if the excitation flows away in an abnormal reflex and is converted into a somatic phenomenon.[27]

For Breuer, the magnetic lure of the electrical field appears to simulate, if not supplant, the attractive force of the death drive ("I am anxious not to drive the analogy . . . to death"). The death drive, as Freud later insists, expresses the desire to exist in a state beyond human life and consciousness: "Instinctual life as a whole serves to bring about death."[28] As he succumbs to the force of the drive's efficiency and speed, Breuer seems to act out the system breakdown he allegorizes.

Functioning much like the high-tension circuit that he summons, Breuer's inclination toward the electromagnetic figure develops in rapid contrast to Freud's psycho-organic metaphors (alien tissues, etc.) like "two wires [that] lie close beside each other." The ensuing short circuit manifests itself in Freud's violent conclusion where, with only a mild diplomacy, the *father* of psychoanalysis refutes Breuer's diagnosis and treatment of the hysterical state. (After raising serious doubts as to the validity of Breuer's analysis, Freud writes: "It would be unfair if I were to try to lay too much of the responsibility for this development upon my honored friend Dr. Josef Breuer. For this reason the considerations which follow stand principally under my own name.")[29] Freud would further distance himself from the world of hypnosis, whereas Breuer would remain, like unconscious ideas, tirelessly roaming in the surplus excitement of electrical figuration.

Despite the dialectical triumph of Freud's posthypnotic conclusions (the submergence of the hypnoid state), the departure from scientific measures into the figurative realm of unconscious forces and the affirmation of nonlinguistic currencies had been irrevocably instituted. (Breuer: "The persistence in the normal state of the symptoms that have arisen during the hypnoid one corresponds entirely to our experiences with posthypnotic suggestion. But this already implies that complexes of ideas that are inadmissible to consciousness co-exist with the trains of ideas that pursue a conscious course, that the splitting of the mind has taken place.")[30] Although Freud had eclipsed Breuer's short-circuiting systematology, the flicker of hypnosis would remain entrenched in the shaded depths of psychoanalytic writing.

Before moving away from Breuer and Freud's preliminary gesture toward the reorganization of subjectivity and its thresholds of perception, a few further passages from Breuer's writings are worth mentioning. Even while attempting to install his electrical figure into the topology of the unconscious, Breuer has recourse to another metaphorical system. In an attempt to illustrate the tensile force of charged excitability, Breuer, again parenthetically, offers this simile: "compare the aimless running round of a caged animal."[31] What is interesting in his statement is not the figure of the animal per se; nor is it the referential relapse to a biologism (in fact, the essence of the animal, as seen in the case of animal magnetism, is frequently equated with the movement of electricity); rather, what is most revealing in Breuer's insight is his evocation of the animal as captive. Whereas *animated* imagery—animal magnetism, animation, animism, and animal phobias and fabulations—sustains the underlying dynamic of the *Studies on Hysteria,* as well as much of Freud's oeuvre, here the animal is represented not as a figure of wildness but of captivity. The animal's restlessness emerges as an effect of its incarceration, and the distressed excitability it exhibits reflects its environment: the parenthetic field of psychical intensity it occupies determines the animal's habitat and world. Thus the traditional view of the animal's nature, its wildness, is here transformed to suit the animal's condition as captive. The nature of the animal is, in Breuer's figure, its restrictedness, its pent-up energy. By comparing the animal to the tensile charges that roam the unconscious, by placing the animal into the psychical realm, Breuer positions the animal in the world as captive.

Distinguishing between the stimulatory states of "incitement" *(Anregung)* and "excitement" *(Aufregung),* Breuer asserts that "while incitement only arouses the urge to employ the increased excitation functionally, excitement seeks to discharge itself in more or less violent ways which are almost or even actually pathological."[32] Incitement (Breuer mentions "interesting conversation and a cup of tea or coffee" as an example) stimulates the organism toward releasing energy while excitement (such as that initiated by narcotics) forces the body to expend energy. Incitement is thus the conscious regulation of stimuli through the nervous system; excitement is the state that appears when the stimuli has surpassed these mechanisms and caused an overflow of energy. At this point, the animal again enters Breuer's protopsychoanalytic landscape. Questioning the role of hunger within the spectrum that spans the energetic poles of incitement and excitement, Breuer concludes that although the symptoms of hunger exhibit many qualities of excitation (violent behavior, for one), its ultimate purposefulness remains intact (the survival of the organism) and thus ultimately falls short of that pole of stimulation. Except for, however, the case of the caged animal in which the excitement that precedes "feeding-time" has no causal link to the search for food. Breuer explains this agitation: "It is true that we see animals in a zoo running backwards and forwards excitedly before feeding-time; but this may no doubt be regarded as a residue of the performed motor activity of looking for food, which has now become useless owing to their being in captivity, and not as a means of freeing the nervous system of excitement."[33] Not only is the caged animal exhibiting a new behavioral system based on its environment, but it actually suffers from the hysterical clamor of a remembered "motor activity." The memory of its freedom, induced by the rituals of feeding, comes to determine the process of this animal's hysterical response: the remembering animal awakens the memory of its traumatic incarceration.

Does the animal remember an actual state of freedom, or does the remembered freedom—in the case of animals born in captivity—actually represent an innate longing for freedom that only returns in the form of a memory? "Hysterics," one recalls, "suffer mainly from reminiscences." This animal suffers, according to Breuer, not from the need to free "the nervous system of excitement" but from the memory of itself in "another life or state." If Nietzsche's animal forgets, Breuer's animal represses, then suffers from reminiscences. By introducing the animal into the unconscious topology, Breuer transforms the animal from an empirical creature to a conceptual figure: the animal has migrated from the traditional exteriority of reason (nonconsciousness) to a new, fortified, and psychoanalytic exteriority, the unconscious. In the process, the animal has become, along the contours of Breuer's own unfolding, a psychomagnetic engine—none other than the mind itself. The exteriority that the animal determines secures the foundation of the psychic structure and is, indeed, its principal figure. This final development achieves its maximal articulation when Breuer asserts that the arousal of the sexual instinct presents the most explosive challenge to the psychical construct. Effecting a sensory overflow, this form of excitability demolishes the organism's capacity to maintain consciousness:

> The sexual instinct is undoubtedly the most powerful source of persisting increases of excitation (and consequently of neuroses). Such increases are distributed very unevenly over the nervous system. When they reach a considerable degree of intensity the train of ideas becomes disturbed and the relative value of the ideas is changed; and in orgasm thought is almost completely extinguished.[34]

During this surge of excitation the faculties of ideation are paralyzed, the overcharged creature bursts forth from the cages of its thought, and the organism kicks into the accelerated drives of self-destruction. Breuer here stages a rebellion against the conscious forces from which the animal emerges. At the moment of arousal, "an animal which is normally timid and cautious becomes blind and deaf to danger. . . . Peaceable animals become dangerous until their excitation has been discharged in the motor activities of the sexual act."[35] At the breaking point of excitability, the animal drive assumes control over the conscious organism and supervises the discharge of its excitement, the surge of its unconscious instincts, or death drive. In Breuer's diagrammatical configuration, the animal represents the surplus psychical energy that is released in excess of conscious intentions. By surpassing the regulatory mechanisms of consciousness, the animal as surplus energy likewise exceeds the linguistic system. Electric currents and the alleged "magnetic fluids" of animals designate a transmissive system that operates beyond language; they are utilized by Breuer to prefigure a psychical structure that overruns the limits of linguistic representation. (Here, one must remember the emphasis placed upon the relationship between animals and language, or rather the absence of such a relationship, which separates the two spheres in the philosophical readings previously addressed.) The animal, like Breuer's electrical system, portrays the excess psychical apparatus that, as an originary figure (a supplemental figure that founds the existence of the unconscious), precludes the possibility of any further figuration. Pointing out the inadequacy of attempts to spatialize the interaction between the conscious and unconscious zones of cerebral coordination, Breuer notes:

> All our thinking tends to be accompanied and aided by spatial ideas, and we talk in spatial metaphors. Thus when we speak of ideas which are found in the region of clear consciousness and of unconscious ones which never enter the full light of self-consciousness, we almost inevitably form pictures of a tree with its trunk in daylight and its roots in darkness, or of a building with its dark underground cellars. If, however, we constantly bear in mind that all such spatial relations are metaphorical and do not allow ourselves to be misled into supposing that these relations are literally present in the brain, we may nevertheless speak of a consciousness and a subconsciousness. But only on this condition.[36]

The psychical realm remains indescribable in a language that, as a set of material signs, tends to spatialize its references.

Freud resumes the question of representing the unconscious in *Civilization and Its Discontents,* where he compares two modes of data storage, the historical and the psychical. Arguing that the historical mode of preservation functions according to a spatial logic (juxtaposition) in which each unit of information occupies a singular site, Freud contrasts the psychical system in which sensory materials are superimposed over one another and passed along in a dense configuration into the psychic order. "The fact remains that only in the mind is such a preservation of all the earlier stages alongside of the final form possible, and that we are not in a position to represent this phenomenon in pictorial terms."[37] For both Breuer and Freud, the unimaginable representation of the psychical system must follow a dimensional rather than spatial configuration—a dynamic rather than pictorial circuit. Freud and Breuer's revision is crucial, for it not only offers a critique of history (of the spatial conceptions of historiography) but also facilitates a theory of becoming that rests upon the forms of movement and change rather than upon stable ideas. As seen earlier during the discussion of Bergson's evolutionary philosophy, the study of movement itself—the investigation of transitions between fixed states—results in the discovery of an essential exteriority, the site of an otherness in which the morphology of beings takes place. And thus one finds in Breuer's projections—the electrical matrix and the expressive animal—the similar figuration of a dynamic rather than a static unconscious. One can hear the echoes of the word *animal* in the description of an animated unconscious—a resonance that grows clearer when the question turns to the invention of the cinema and the principle of its artificial electrical movement, animation.

The electrical and animal figures that Breuer contributes to the fledgling science underscore the impact of animal magnetism, hypnosis, and other nonlinguistic circuits on the early stages of psychoanalytic investigation: hypnosis and the analysis of the hypnoid state soon passed, however, into the recesses of the psychoanalytic doctrine. In the nineteenth lecture of his *Introductory Lectures to Psychoanalysis,* published between 1916 and 1917, Freud makes this definitive claim: "I have been able to say that psychoanalysis proper *[die eigentliche Psychoanalyse]* began when I dispensed with the help of hypnosis."[38] While Freud would reconstruct the dwelling of subjectivity and the logocentric structures that constitute analysis and interpretation, Breuer's alternatives to linguistic communication—facilitated by electromagnetic and animal magnetic currents—would fade into the obscure regions of psychoanalysis alongside its original deposits. And yet, for the present purposes, a critical shift had been accomplished in the nascent logic of psychoanalysis. Psychoanalysis had undone the exclusion of animals from the field of subjectivity.

No longer exiled from the site of subjectivity, the animal had become, through Breuer's tropes, aligned with electric circuitry and signification. In the small shift in logic, animals, as conductors in a relay of information that superseded the exclusive regime of language, were assigned to the outer limits of consciousness—to the supersemiotic field of the unconscious. And although animals have always been accorded the faculties of transmitting affect, it is in the psychic generators of Breuer's states that animals were endowed not only with an ideational capacity but also with a means of communication. The nervous system and the unconscious together form the basic elements of the animal being. It is through Breuer, whose own disappearance from the frontiers of psychoanalysis was imminent, that the animal was brought to the liminal threshold.

Smell

IF THE BARRIER of language continued to restrict contact between the spheres of consciousness and unconsciousness, between the human and animal worlds, another mode of communication would come to play an important role in bridging the existential divide and solidifying the psychoanalytic idiom. The sense of smell, frequently associated with animals and animality, serves the psychoanalytic corpus both as a feature and as a figure. Thinking about smell possesses a long history in Western philosophy, converging at times with the discourse on animality. In *Timaeus and Critias,* Plato states that "[all] smells are half-formed things, and none of our regular figures corresponds to any particular smell."[39] Plato concludes that smells, like the two poles of affect that animals communicate, "have no names and do not consist of a plurality of definite types; the only clear distinction we can make is between the pleasant and unpleasant."[40] Against this reduction, Vicki Hearne asserts that in the case of some animals as well as human beings, aroma functions as "a metonymy for knowledge."[41] Hearne adds that scents cannot be translated into language: "We can draw pictures of scent, but we don't have a language for doing it the other way about, don't have so much as a counter for a representation of something visual by means of (actual) scent."[42] The unrepresentable nature of scent in language appears in Hearne's presentation of the dog's capacity to track, a capacity that determines the epistemological basis of the dog's existence. The movement from dog to human being, from scent to language, necessitates an impossible translation from the semiology of animals to that of human beings. "'Scent' for us," explains Hearne, "can be only a theoretical, technical expression that we use because our grammar requires that we have a noun to go in the sentences we are prompted to utter about tracking. We don't have a 'sense' of scent."[43]

Alain Corbin explains the traditional resistance to olfaction as a means of obtaining knowledge:

Smelling and sniffing are associated with animal behavior. If olfaction were his most important sense, man's linguistic incapacity to describe olfactory sensations would turn him into a creature tied to his environment. Because they are ephemeral, olfactory sensations can never provide a persistent stimulus of thought. Thus the development of the sense of smell seems to be inversely related to the development of intelligence.[44]

The inability to record and sustain the impressions of scent, their ephemerality, forms the grounds for their dismissal. Scents do not provide material and thus repeatable signifiers, and therefore cannot form a semiotic system. In his famous footnote to *Civilization and Its Discontents,* Freud also charts the emergence of humanity from the olfactory world of animals by following the movement of humanity away from the sense of smell and toward that of sight. The shift in emphasis from smell to sight is marked, according to Freud, by a change in human posture from a quadruped stance to a biped one: it also effects the sudden exposure of the genitals. The visibility of the genitals and the subsequent need to hide them, in turn, has been understood from Genesis to Kant as the inceptive moment of visual representation, indeed of language.[45] In this manner the move from smell to sight coincides with the appearance of a material, that is, visual semiology. Returning to the faculty of smell, Freud writes: "The diminution of the olfactory stimuli seems itself to be a consequence of man's raising himself from the ground, of his assumption of an upright gait; this made his genitals, which were previously concealed, visible and in need of protection, and so provoked feelings of shame in him."[46] Horkheimer and Adorno support the claim that smelling stirs up the recollection of distant and shameful forms of existence.

> The multifarious nuances of the sense of smell embody the archetypal longing for the lower forms of existence, for direct unification with circumambient nature, with the earth and mud. Of all the senses, that of smell—which is attracted without objectifying—bears clearest witness to the urge to lose oneself in and become the "other." As perception and the perceived—both are united—smell is more expressive than the other senses. When we see we remain what we are; but when we smell we are taken over by otherness. Hence the sense of smell is considered a disgrace in civilization, the sign of lower social strata, lesser races and base animals.[47]

In Horkheimer and Adorno's description of the sense, smell becomes an emblem of the other, the passage to a place of loss and a longing for that loss. When one smells, one is "taken over by otherness," taken over by the distance of otherness, taken over by the scent of animality that clings to that otherness. At the same time, smells are "more expressive than the other senses." The paradox between the association of smell with "the sign of lower social strata, lesser races and base animals" and its expressive and annihilating capacities underscores the complex structure of animality, language, and being. The atopic force of smell described by Horkheimer and Adorno illuminates the inadequacies of visual metaphors to name new topologies such as those of the animal or unconscious. Horkheimer and Adorno's other topology can be read as the same *Umwelt* inhabited by animals and signified by smells. For animals, the foundations of perception and cognition (and perhaps even affect) remain entrenched in an atmosphere determined by odors. Of the dog's relation to the sensual realm, for example, Hearne asserts: "He *sees* what we see—his eyes aren't defective—but what he *believes* are the scents of the garden behind us."[48]

If, however, olfaction appears at odds with the Platonic prejudices of intellectual activity, its relations to the subcategory of memory are even more complex. Between the mnemic regions of philosophical and psychoanalytic interpretation, animals occupy a significant though disputed status. Corbin describes the initial clash between the functions of smelling and remembering: "Olfactory sensations are ephemeral, and thus defy comparisons through memory; any attempt to train the sense of smell always results in disappointment."[49] Freud has also insisted that of all sensations, scents alone cannot be remembered. To this paradox—the incommensurate proximity of odor and remembrance—Corbin ascribes a history:

On the other hand, doctors since ancient times have untiringly stressed the importance of the nose as the sensory organ closest to the brain, the "origin of sensation." . . . Thus, in contrast to the claims made in the first paradox, the extraordinary subtlety of the sense of smell appears to grow with the development of intelligence. . . . In the nineteenth century it was elevated to being the privileged instrument of recollection, that which reveals the coexistence of the self and the universe, and, finally, the precondition of intimacy.[50]

Freud tracks the *scent* of the unconscious toward its discovery. Of humanity's change in posture and the new sensuality that attends to it, Freud rehearses his famous narrative as he pens the following double-parenthetical note to his mentor and celebrated nasologist, Wilhelm Fliess, on 14 November 1897:

(Privately I concede priority in the idea to no one; in my case the notion was linked to the changed part played by the sensations of smell: upright walking, nose raised from the ground, at the same time a number of formerly interesting sensations attached to the earth becoming repulsive—by a process still unknown to me.) (He turns up his nose = he regards himself as something particularly noble.)[51]

Freud explains to Fliess that humanity's former posture has been imprinted on its memory as a trace of residual animality. The continued significance of the olfactory mechanism in animals distinguishes these "lowly" creatures from their walking, talking descendants: "In animals these sexual zones continue in force in both respects [as sensual and libidinal stimulant]; if this persists in human beings too, perversion results."[52] Concluding his hypothesis, Freud asserts that the forgotten erogenous systems, or "abandoned sexual zones," continue to remain embedded in the (collective or historical) psyche of each individual, and in fact secrete over time an unpleasurable sensation. "Deferred action of this kind occurs also in connection with a memory of excitations of the abandoned sexual zones. The outcome, however, is not a release of libido but of an unpleasure, an internal sensation analogous to disgust in the case of an object."[53] As he moves along the trail, closer to the source of the scent, Freud suddenly discovers its—the repressed id's—vulgar proximity. Dropping all vestiges of polite discourse, Freud exclaims: "To put it crudely, the memory actually stinks just as in the present the object stinks; and in the same manner as we turn away our sense organ (the head and nose) in disgust, the preconscious and the sense of consciousness turn away from the memory. This is *repression*."[54] And so, at the precise moment that Freud reaches for a theory of repression and the survival of memory traces, he finds himself plunged into the miasmic atmosphere of repression—put crudely, repression stinks. As if to complete the cycle that sends animals through the detours of memory, fragrance, and the hypnoid continuum, Freud conveys this hypothesis, again to Fliess, on perversion and zoomorphic degeneration:

> Perversions regularly lead to zoophilia and have an animal character. They are explained not by the functioning of erogenous zones that later have been abandoned, but by the effect of the erogenous *sensations* that later lose their force. In this connection one recalls that the principle sense in animals (for sexuality as well) is that of smell, which has been reduced in human beings. As long as smell (or taste) is dominant, urine, feces, and the whole surface of the body, also blood, have a sexually exciting effect. *The heightened sense of smell in hysteria presumably is connected with this.*[55]

For Freud, perversion—the forced implementation of re-pressed matter into the expressive acts of daily life—indicates an eruption not only of the sensations of aban-doned erogenous zones but also of the memories they har-bor. In other words, the primary effect of smell exists not in its perception but in the remembering it effects—in its sta-tus as a memory.

One might here recall Heidegger's depiction of the animal world as one under erasure. Like the repression that Freud dis-covers in the stench of the unconscious, Heidegger's crossed-through words also reveal through the animal not the world "as such" but rather the traces of a world under erasure. Smells then, like animals, but unlike conventional signs, do not open the world from which they have come. Or rather, scents and animals do open the world they inhabit but open that world as closed, shrouded, as a world that has faded, without ever hav-ing been present, into the recesses of memory and the uncon-scious. In thus arguing for the affinity between smells, smell-ing, and animals and their cohabitation in the unconscious, Freud revives the philosophical notion that animals (denied the capacity of *logos*) cannot and do not die: like Dewey's old ideas, animals are simply abandoned. Figured as an undying "anti-*logos*" in philosophy and as transhistorical mnemic traces in psychoanalysis, animals emerge as creatures characterized by their ability to last, to remain, without, however, entering the finite world.

Becoming-animal

WHILE CONVENTIONAL PHILOSOPHY maps animal being outside human worlds, the discovery of the unconscious opens a route for animals to reenter the world, or what Gilles Deleuze and Félix Guattari rename the "rhizome."[56] Deleuze and Guattari characterize it thus: "The rhizome connects any point to any other point, and its traits are not necessarily linked to traits of the same nature; it brings into play very different regimes of signs, and even nonsign states. . . . It is composed not of units but of dimensions, or rather directions in motion."[57] The rhizome facilitates the entry of the animal into the phenomenal world not as a fixed entity but as a dynamic, a "direction in motion," a system that interacts with other systems. In the logic of the rhizome, Deleuze and Guattari discover a creative solution to the blocked communication between human and animal worlds. Each line of being or "intensity," they argue, connects with and traverses other such lines; the intersection of lines forms plateaus, which in turn combine to form rhizomes or worlds; the assemblages, however, are never permanent and are eventually dismantled. In this way, the world stays in permanent flux. In a more sober version of a similar schema, Thomas A. Sebeok writes: "All animates are bombarded by signs emanating from their environment, which includes a *milieu intérieur,* as well as, of course, other animates sharing their environment, some conspecific, some not."[58] Deleuze and Guattari call such movement between worlds, "becoming-animal."

In Deleuze and Guattari's reinvention of the world as becoming-animal, the subject of a human system is also exposed to the forces that other systems and plateaus impose upon it.[59] Humanity's being is opened to animal being, "which is continually dismantling the organism, causing asignifying particles or pure intensities to pass or circulate, and attributing to itself subjects that it leaves with nothing more than a name as a trace of an intensity."[60] In another idiom, Sebeok refers to the lines or systems that form heterogeneous communities as "symbionts": "organisms of different species living together, in ceaseless informative commerce."[61] The work of Deleuze and Guattari seeks to map, against every convention of mapping, a terrain open to animal being. In a theory they develop around the body of Kafka's work, Deleuze and Guattari describe the rhizomatic mode as "becoming-animal," that is, "absolute deterritorialization."[62]

> To become animal is to participate in movement . . . to cross a threshold, to reach a continuum of intensities that are valuable only in themselves, to find a world of pure intensities where all forms come undone, as do all significations, signifiers, and signifieds, to the benefit of an unformed matter of deterritorialized flux, of nonsignifying signs. . . . There is no longer anything but movements, vibrations, thresholds in a deserted matter: animals, mice, dogs, apes, cockroaches [in Kafka's stories] are distinguished only by this or that threshold, this or that vibration, by the particular underground tunnel in the rhizome or the burrow.[63]

From this provisional definition of becoming-animal, Deleuze and Guattari attempt to reterritorialize the discourse of natural and unnatural being.

In a critique of natural history, Deleuze and Guattari attack the method they identify as "series and structure." "Natural history can only think in terms of relationships (between A and B), not in terms of productions (from A to x)."[64] "Relationship" is the method by which conventional evolutions, genealogies, and filiations between organisms, genera, and species are introduced into knowledge as related terms. Relationships block potential lines of communication between members of unrelated groups. The blockage results, in part, from the need to rely upon the principle of resemblance or natural affinity to facilitate movement from one state to the next, one body to the next, one moment to the next. Like the function of signifiers in Saussurean linguistics, each term must be matched against another term according to a differential but predetermined series. Based on the existence of resemblance, the pairs are figured as either series or structures. In this way, the relation between every set of terms is determined dialectically.

In the case of series, I say *a* resembles *b, b* resembles *c,* etc.; all of these terms conform in varying degrees to a single eminent term, perfection, or quality as the principle behind the series. . . . In the case of structure, I say *a* is to *b* as *c* is to *d;* and each of these relationships realizes after its fashion the perfection under consideration. . . . In the first case, I have resemblances that differ from one another in a single series, and between series. In the second case, I have differences that resemble each other within a single structure, and between structures.[65]

Against such dialectical organizations of the world, Deleuze and Guattari propose the alternative force of the rhizome. Rhizomes comprise beings that may have no resemblance or affinity to one another: rhizomes are essentially and radically heterogeneous in nature. Any field of intensity within a rhizome can, at any moment, realign itself with another such field to form further rhizomes. The resulting formations are never, according to the authors, the effect of lineation but rather of "alliances." Rejecting the series and structure approach of conventional natural history, Deleuze and Guattari argue that temporary alliances are formed when intensities intersect.

Thus packs, or multiplicities, continually transform themselves into each other, cross over into each other. . . . A multiplicity is defined not by its elements, nor by a center of unification or comprehension. It is defined by the number of dimensions it has; it is not divisible, it cannot lose or gain a dimension *without changing its nature.* Since its variations and dimensions are immanent to it, *it amounts to the same thing to say that each multiplicity is already composed of heterogeneous terms in symbiosis, and that a multiplicity is continually transforming itself into a string of other multiplicities, according to its thresholds and doors.*[66]

In this manner, individual beings continually dissolve and metamorphose into new rhizomes. Appropriating the logic of becoming from Darwinian and Bergsonian evolution, Deleuze and Guattari emphasize becoming as the most advanced state of existence. This is not to say, however, that Deleuze and Guattari establish an opposition between being and becoming; they see these two categories of existence also in rhizomatic terms: being is intersected continually by the dynamic of becoming, and becoming passes through numerous states of being—the two processes are inseparable.

Deleuze and Guattari insist on the idea of multiplicity as an essential feature of their theory of becoming. To this end, animals are the perfect embodiment of multiplicity, since they, unlike human beings, can never be reduced to individual beings. Following Georges Bataille's description of the animal as being in the world like "water in water,"[67] Deleuze and Guattari posit: "Every animal is fundamentally a band, a pack. . . . it has pack modes rather than characteristics."[68] Or again: "becoming-animal always involves a pack, a band, a population, a peopling, in short, a multiplicity."[69] Animals are often rendered in groups, or "hordes" to use Darwin's and Freud's term. More than an empirical condition, however, this groupness or multiplicity defines the being of animals. Becoming-animal thus involves a relation to multiplicity, which Deleuze and Guattari explain is at the center of all becomings: "Multiplicity is defined not by the elements that compose it in extension, not by the characteristics that compose it in comprehension, but by the lines and dimensions it encompasses in 'intension.'"[70] In this sense all becomings are animal becomings: "Becoming can and should be qualified as becoming-animal even in the absence of a term that would be the animal become. The becoming-animal of the human being is real, even if the animal the human being becomes is not."[71] Deleuze and Guattari arrive at an ontological dynamic that begins with becoming or, more precisely, with becoming-animal.

Although philosophical ontology is determined by language and the site of subjectivity that it enframes, the animal symbiont configures, in the terms established by Deleuze and Guattari and Sebeok, a communicational tissue through which information passes, moving toward the constitution of energetic ontologies. These impermanent loci are constantly being extinguished, disappearing, only to re-form, like Leibniz's monads, into new corporealities and informational alliances. Each particular rhizome, once dissolved, never reappears in quite the same formation. What perishes with each organism is not, however, an essence but an informational assemblage, a transitory order of data that is unique but not essential. Thus Sebeok concludes that "every time a population of animals is exterminated, the draining of the gene pool is concurrently and irreversibly accompanied by the elimination of a unique communicative code."[72] Fragments of the eliminated code are, however, transported to other bodies and reorganized into further intensities. In this manner the animal world is never truly extinguished. This process of perpetual intensification links the monadic visions of Leibniz's world with the biological properties of genetics and the vicissitudes of unconscious forces.

In the present attempt to navigate the "rhizosphere," the discussion has moved from evolution to psychoanalysis, from electricity to aromatology. Not only do animals enter the world, they figure a communicational medium, a technology of being. And although the discussion has only hinted at the universe of animal discourse that issues from the disenchantment of metaphysics, one can perhaps sense the dynamic of animal being. Throughout the discussion, however, no mention of literature has been made as such. For the literary corpus encloses a special world of animality: it retains a place within the body of its *logos* for what Deleuze calls elsewhere the "anti-*logos*."[73] Unlike other epistemological bodies such as philosophy, for example, literature is defined by its heterogeneity, its contamination, its impurity as a genre. Literature possesses many of the features with which Derrida describes the *pharmakon*. In a passage from "Plato's Pharmacy" that could equally describe the animal, Derrida writes:

> This *pharmakon,* this "medicine," this philter, which acts as both remedy and poison, already introduces itself into the body of discourse with all its ambivalence. This charm, this spellbinding virtue, this power of fascination, can be—alternately or simultaneously—beneficent or maleficent. The *pharmakon* would be a *substance*—with all that that word can connote in terms of matter with occult virtues, cryptic depths refusing to submit their ambivalence to analysis, already paving the way for alchemy —if we didn't eventually have to come to recognize it as antisubstance itself: that which resists any philosopheme, indefinitely exceeding its bounds as nonidentity, nonessence, nonsubstance; granting philosophy by that very fact the inexhaustible adversity of what funds it and the infinite absence of what founds it.[74]

Although Derrida's reference here points to a chemical property, one might posit the same capacity to exceed *logos* in the figure of the animal. The animal exceeds language both literally and figuratively as a site of contagion: "Animals," write Deleuze and Guattari, "form, develop, and are transformed by contagion."[75] The nonidentity and nonessence of the animal are indeed "inexhaustible," as Derrida says of the *pharmakon,* since animals are not capable of death, and even as each individual organism perishes it is immediately replaced by another from among the multiplicity that constitutes it. Accordingly, animals exhaust philosophy, exhaust *logos,* draining the body of its ability to resist the swarming deterritorializations that animals threaten. Only in the literary text does the animal remain in the body as a foreign element without, at the same time, corrupting that body irreversibly. Literature can be seen, in the tradition of Freud's *unheimlich* economy and Derrida's *pharmakon,* as an example of "antiliterature," a vaccine against itself and the animality it harbors.

5 | The Literary Animal: Carroll, Kafka, Akutagawa

Languages, like organic beings, can be classed into groups under groups; and they can be classed either naturally according to descent, or artificially by other characters. Dominant languages and dialects spread widely and lead to the gradual extinction of other tongues. A language, like a species, when once extinct, never . . . reappears. The same language never has two birth places. Distinct languages may be crossed or blended together. We see variability in every tongue, and new words are continually cropping up; but as there is a limit to the powers of the memory, single words, like whole languages gradually become extinct. As Max Müller has well remarked: —"A struggle for life is constantly going on amongst the words and grammatical forms in each language."

—CHARLES DARWIN, "THE DESCENT OF MAN
AND SELECTION IN RELATION TO SEX"

DARWIN'S SUPPOSITION THAT languages are a type of dynamic organism and thus behave no differently from any other class of organic entities—that they struggle, evolve, and ultimately succumb to extinction—modifies the conventional view of language as humanity's first acquisition. Languages are not just effects of humanity's existence, Darwin argues, but they possess lives of their own. Darwin's remarkable gesture appears to transport language from the register of artifice to that of nature. Languages, according to Darwin, like animals and plants, are consigned to the sequences of a morphological existence: life, struggle, selection, change, and death. Darwin's vitalization of language highlights another important point: by addressing the question of language from a scientific perspective, Darwin exhibits how concepts of science, philology, and technology were commingling at this historical juncture. One can take note of the profound influence that studies in genetics, adaptation, filiation, and the evolutionary dynamic have had on literary, filmic, and psychoanalytic theory in particular, and communication or semiotic theory in general.

Three authors, Lewis Carroll, Franz Kafka, and Akutagawa Ryunosuke, have contributed to the acceleration of literature toward a certain limit. In their work, the literary language of the novel is transformed, as is the role of the literary subject, in a process that, following Deleuze and Guattari, can be described as the becoming-animal of literature. The following analyses are not intended to provide extensive readings of each author's complex corpus but rather to illustrate how these authors thematized the return of animal being and world in literature and questioned the capacity of language to contain animality. All three help establish the framework within which a cultural shift from logocentric modes of representation evolved into genetic or transferential media such as cinema.

Lewis Carroll (1832–98)

Artaud says that Being, which is nonsense, has teeth.
—GILLES DELEUZE, "THE LOGIC OF SENSE"

LEWIS CARROLL'S THEMATIZATION of animals and discourse, sense and nonsense, and childhood and animality in *Alice's Adventures in Wonderland* (1865) and *Through the Looking-*

Glass (1871) displays on the surface a familiar modernist trope: an awareness of the premises—reason, logic, language—that constitute the writing of fiction. As narratives, however, the novels engage a broader set of assumptions about the existence of the human species. Carroll published the original *Alice* on the heels of Darwin's *Origin of Species* (1859); the publication of his later work, *Looking-Glass,* coincided with the appearance of Darwin's *Descent of Man* (1871). Carroll's two works show the rapid impact that evolutionary thought had on the literary culture of that period. Also apparent in Carroll's writings are the reconceptions of animal and human morphology that Darwin's conclusions made possible. Carroll's novels, however, signal the author's resistance to evolution at the same time that they try to think through some of its implications. Of the connections between Darwinism and *Alice,* William Empson writes: "The first Neanderthal skull was found in 1856. *The Origin of Species* (1859) came out six years before *Wonderland,* three before its conception, and was very much in the air, a pervading bad smell. It is hard to say how far Dodgson [Carroll] under cover of nonsense was using ideas of which his set disapproved."[1] According to Empson, Carroll was undoubtedly aware of Darwin's theories. What is not clear is the extent to which Carroll approved of those concepts. Although Empson ultimately sees Carroll's ambiguous approach to evolutionary thought as a form of political shrewdness, there is no doubt that the circulation of Darwinism led Carroll, who was also an accomplished mathematician, to consider the new physical and psychic worlds that opened up before him.[2] As a result, Carroll's literary assemblage of animals, space, language, and childhood brings together the elements of the human world but in an entirely other configuration.[3] In particular, the fluid relation between physicality and figures of speech places Alice in a world no longer grounded by a referentially stable language. In Wonderland, bodies are allegorized and idioms are literalized in a seemingly unrestricted exchange. In the rabbit hole, for example, a physically and emotionally erratic Alice slips into a pool of her own tears: "'I wish I hadn't cried so much!' said Alice, as she swam about, trying to find her way out. 'I shall be punished for it now, I suppose, by being drowned in my own tears.'"4 The miniature Alice faces the danger of drowning in the tears that she shed as a larger being: the figure of drowning in one's own tears here moves from the rhetorical to the literal level. Alice's tears are not only a figure for self-pity, they actually threaten to drown her—Alice is in danger of being drowned in her own bodily refuse. Here as elsewhere, Carroll's words turn back upon the body where their meanings, like Alice's bodily dynamic, are never firm.

In another episode, one learns that the Mock Turtle's education consists of subjects that parody the curricula of human children. The punned course of studies described by the Mock Turtle (who gets his name from a food and not an actual animal) refers to bodily and affective rather than intellectual pursuits: basic "Reeling and Writhing"; "the different branches of Arithmetic—Ambition, Distraction, Uglification and Derision"; the arts of "Drawling, Stretching, and Fainting in Coils"; and the classics, "Laughing and Grief."5 The reversal of intellectual and bodily references frames a more specific exchange between the two poles of orality, speaking and eating. One leads to sense, the other to the stomach. When Alice first enters Wonderland, she encounters a bottle marked "DRINK ME" and a cake inscribed with the words "EAT ME." In this scene, Carroll links language with food, reading with consumption and emphasizes their essential proximity.

In the "Pig and Pepper" chapter, which opens in a kitchen, one witnesses the gradual transformation of an infant into a pig: the metamorphosis of a human being into an edible animal. The transformation is first brought to Alice's attention by the infant/pig's grunting: "The baby grunted again, and Alice looked very anxiously into its face to see what was the matter with it. There could be no doubt that it had a *very* turn-up nose, much more like a snout than a real nose: also its eyes were getting extremely small for a baby: altogether Alice did not like the look of the thing at all."[6] The infant/pig's voice or grunt remains constant while its body changes form, suggesting the continuity of voice in both human and animal beings. By linking the infant and the pig with their grunts, Carroll draws attention to orality in general and the mouth in particular. Besides being used for making noise, mouths are also used for eating. In the kitchen, Carroll emphasizes the various functions of the mouth. When Alice enters the room, the Duchess is "nursing" the baby, who is "howling," the Cheshire cat is "grinning from ear to ear," and the cook is "leaning over the fire, stirring a large cauldron which seemed to be full of soup."[7] By placing those activities—nursing, howling, grinning, and cooking—in one room, Carroll indicates their proximity in Wonderland. Oral functions remain unstable throughout Carroll's texts. The transformation of the baby into a pig thus makes the creature vulnerable. Alice worries that the pig will be killed, if not eaten. As she runs from the kitchen with the creature in her arms, Alice thinks: "If I don't take this child away with me . . . they're sure to kill it in a day or two."[8] That the child, which was being nursed in the first instance, might eventually be killed, and perhaps eaten, suggests that for Carroll, mouths are dangerous places. One cannot relax in the presence of mouths, since they are constantly being used for different purposes. Carroll's focus on the mouth is further emphasized at the chapter's end, when the talking Cheshire cat "vanishe[s] quite slowly, beginning with the end of the tail, and ending with the grin, which remained some time after the rest of it had gone."[9]

From the kitchen of the "Pig and Pepper" chapter, the reader moves to a different place of orality in "A Mad Tea-Party." This chapter brings together the themes of eating (or drinking) and speaking, and shows how they can be readily interchanged. When Alice states at the tea-party, for example, that saying what one means is the same thing as meaning what one says, she is reprimanded by the Hatter: "'Not the same thing a bit!' said the Hatter. 'Why you might just as well say that "I see what I eat" is the same thing as "I eat what I see."'"[10] The scene at the table shifts between eating and speaking, until Alice seems unable to distinguish between the two. In the end, Alice leaves the table unsatisfied, claiming: "It's the stupidest tea-party I ever was at in all my life."[11]

Without adult supervision, without the mediating mechanism of the adult human being, the distinctions between eating and speaking are plunged into chaos. Language loses its bearing. One effect of a deregulated language becomes apparent in the question of who or what speaks. Animals and plants speak in Carroll's texts, whereas human personages (who are in fact animations of playing cards and chess pieces, or figures of figures, and appear less endowed with reason than their bestial and vegetal counterparts) seem closer to automata. Another effect of language without stability erupts in the fluctuating scale that pervades Wonderland. The inability of Alice to maintain a size relative to her surroundings dramatizes the dynamic that allows animals to overshadow human beings in a radically free economy of language. It is a condition that hints at cinematic representation.[12]

Among the searching readers of Carroll's work is Antonin Artaud, who has recorded his violent reaction against the "smell of happy leisures and of intellectual success" that he sensed in the reverend's texts.[13] In his most vitriolic assault on Carroll, Artaud accuses him of foraging in the world of others, without himself suffering in that other world. In a letter from Rodez to Henri Parisot, dated 22 September 1945, Artaud assails Carroll's "Jabberwocky" as the work of "a sort of a hybrid mongrel who pulverized his consciousness in order to produce writing":

> "Jabberwocky" is the work of an opportunist who wanted to feed intellectually on someone else's pain, although he himself was satiated from a well-served meal. . . . When one digs out the caca of existence and of language, the poem must smell bad, and "Jabberwocky" is a poem which its author has been careful to protect from the uterine existence of suffering in which every great poet has been immersed and from which when he is delivered he smells bad. There are in "Jabberwocky" passages of fecality, but it is the fecality of an English snob who forces the obscene in himself into curls and corkscrews as if with hot tongs, a kind of dilettante of the obscene who is very careful not to be obscene himself. . . . "Jabberwocky" is the work of a coward who was not willing to suffer his work before writing it, and this can be seen. It is the work of a man who ate well.[14]

In his denunciation of Carroll's poem, Artaud propels the oral duality of speaking and eating into a further stage, writing and excreting. For Artaud that extension serves not only as a critique of Carroll but also as a transformation of Carroll's text into what Deleuze terms a "language without articulation."[15] In *The Logic of Sense,* Deleuze argues that while Carroll challenges the notion of a unified body of language, Artaud takes that challenge a step further and calls for the total annihilation of language. Carroll plays with the surfaces of language while Artaud attacks its depths; Carroll always restores language to its proper place while Artaud ruins language in an attempt to make it meaningless. Despite their similarities, the difference between Carroll and Artaud is, according to Deleuze, the difference between sense and nonsense. By assailing Carroll, Artaud seeks to shatter the careful surfaces of Carroll's writing and move the language of literature closer to its limit. Deleuze explains the contrast between Carroll's "logic of sense" and Artaud's "schizophrenic body":

> In this collapse of the surface, the entire world loses its meaning. It maintains perhaps a certain power of denotation, but this is experienced as empty. It maintains perhaps a certain power of manifestation, but this is experienced as indifferent. And it maintains a certain signification experienced as "false." Nevertheless, the word loses its sense, that is, its power to draw together or to express an incorporeal effect distinct from the passions of the body, and an ideational event distinct from its present realization. Every event is realized, be it in a hallucinatory form. Every word is physical, and immediately affects the body.[16]

In contrast to Carroll, who like Alice returns, in the end, to his senses, Artaud calls for a militant invasion of Wonderland: a permanent incursion that precludes return. For Artaud, Carroll does not proceed far enough away from or beneath the surface: Carroll's mimetic trips into Wonderland merely reaffirm the body of *logos* against the schizoid inhabitants of Wonderland. In the end, Carroll's desperate grasp on sense prevents him from truly crossing over into the other world. Deleuze describes the scene on the other side of sense:

> Although sense results from the actions and passions of the body, it is a result which differs in nature, since it is neither action nor passion. It is a result which shelters sonorous language from any confusion with the physical body. On

the contrary, in this primary order of schizophrenia, the only duality left is between the actions and the passions of the body. Language is both at once, being entirely reabsorbed into the gaping depth. There is no longer anything to prevent propositions from falling back onto bodies and from mingling their sonorous elements with the body's olfactory, gustatory, or digestive affects. Not only is there no longer any sense, but there is no longer any grammar or syntax either—nor, at the limit, are there any articulated syllabic, literal, or phonetic elements.[17]

Schizophrenics, Deleuze claims, treat the body not as a reference, not as *logos,* but as a part of their language. Artaud does not, for example, distinguish between body and language. For Artaud, body and language are not clashing terms of an opposition but belong instead to the same system: the schizophrenic's body is composed of language, its language made of flesh. Words hurt Artaud, wound his body. At the same time, when there are no words, when there is only silence—or worse, when there is only sense—Artaud feels disembodied, nonexistent. One can consider Lyotard's argument that the challenge for modernity consists of "mak[ing] thought without a body possible" in the context of Artaud's pain. Can one conceive a thinking being that has no body?[18] In a way, Artaud has answered that the conception of the body itself must change, that the body must engender a language that participates in the functions of the body. Artaud's language without articulation can be seen as a language of the animal: it moves freely throughout the body because it is a part of that body. Artaud's language is, paradoxically, a language without *logos*—a language without language. And without language one can no longer speak of literature: Artaud's language, his "animated hieroglyphs," moves the discussion from Carroll's word games to another medium, another genre, another dimension of voluminous bodily dispersal—cinema.[19]

Franz Kafka (1883–1924)

"—then you don't like all insects?*" the Gnat went on, as quietly as if nothing had happened.*

"I like them when they can talk," Alice said. "None of them ever talk, where I come from."

—LEWIS CARROLL, "THROUGH THE
LOOKING-GLASS"

STILL MOVING TOWARD the cinema under the shadow of Artaud, Franz Kafka's domain of animal stories and parables helps illustrate the role of literature in reconfiguring the animal. One can observe the resumption of Carroll's trajectory in Kafka, especially with regard to the question of animal morphology and metamorphosis. In Kafka's narratives the transformative process cannot be reversed, and the lines that separate the human and animal worlds cannot be so easily traversed. Deleuze and Guattari's focus on "becoming-animal" in Kafka is especially useful. *The Metamorphosis* addresses the topic of becoming-animal—or more precisely, becoming-insect—in response to the oppressive confines of familial, social, and religious conventions. Deleuze and Guattari write of the becoming-animal as a way out of the oedipal configuration (the *epistēmē* that for them comprises the familial, social, and religious conventions of a capitalist society)—an "absolute deterritorialization" that allows the subject to escape from the discourse that constitutes and binds it. Becoming-animal does not, however, promise total freedom: it is, Deleuze and Guattari insist, only a line of escape and retreat—animal being carries its own finitude.

One effect of becoming-animal concerns the relocation of the body with regard to acts of articulation. In *The Metamorphosis,* Gregor Samsa's new body forces him to develop new methods of expression. Shortly after his transformation, Gregor begins to lose control over his voice:

Gregor had a shock as he heard his own voice answering hers, unmistakably his own voice, it was true, but with a persistent horrible twittering squeak behind it like an undertone, that left the words in their clear shape only for the first moment and then rose up reverberating round them to destroy their sense, so that one could not be sure one had heard them rightly.[20]

From this initial deterioration of his vocal capacity, Gregor progressively loses the ability to communicate with words. His final descent into unintelligibility is registered by the chief clerk, who responds to Gregor's futile attempts to explain his absence at work by exclaiming: "Did you understand a word of it? . . . That was no human voice."[21] Not only words, however, but the familiar sounds emitted by human bodies are also withdrawn from Gregor's world until he doubts even his ability to engage in a recognizable cough: "To make his voice as clear as possible for the decisive conversation that was now imminent he coughed a little, as quietly as he could, of course, since this noise too might not sound like a human cough for all he was able to judge."[22] Ultimately, as Gregor slips away from the world of human language—"No entreaty of Gregor's availed, indeed no entreaty was even understood"—his body begins to adjust to its new shape, functions, and surroundings.[23] And although Gregor never fully loses the ability to understand human language, he does gradually lose interest in it at the same time that he grows more accustomed to his own audio emissions: "But Gregor was now much calmer. The words he uttered were no longer understandable, apparently, although they seemed clear enough to him, even clearer than before, perhaps because his ear had grown accustomed to the sound of them."[24]

Communication, however, is only one area in which Gregor makes adjustments to his new existence as an insect. Gregor finds that he must also explore the new appetites that follow naturally from this state. Perhaps as a sign of his de-oedipalization or dehumanization, Gregor finds himself immediately revolted by his once favorite substance, milk: "Although milk had been his favorite drink and that was certainly why his sister had set it there for him, indeed it was almost with repulsion that he turned away from the basin and crawled back to the middle of the room."[25] Not only does Gregor finds the mammalian liquid disgusting, he is attracted to human refuse, garbage.

> There were old, half-decayed vegetables, bones from last night's supper covered with a white sauce that had thickened; some raisins and almonds; a piece of cheese that Gregor would have called uneatable two days ago. . . . "Am I less sensitive now?" he thought, and sucked greedily at the cheese, which above all attracted him at once and strongly. One after another and with tears of satisfaction in his eyes he quickly devoured the cheese, the vegetables and the sauce; the fresh food, on the other hand, had no charms for him, he could not even stand the smell of it and actually dragged away to some little distance the things he could eat.[26]

The changes in Gregor's body lead him to reconsider the world he inhabits, the new world that opens about his body: "He had formed the habit of crawling crisscross over the walls and ceiling. He especially enjoyed hanging suspended from the ceiling."[27] Although Gregor's body has been turned into that of an insect, his consciousness still remains that of a human being. Gregor hangs between two worlds—between the insect and human worlds. For Gregor to complete the metamorphosis, he must willingly leave behind the human world of consciousness and language.[28] Kafka suggests that once one's existence is no longer regulated by language, by the convergence of language and body, the entire world is thrown into an animated state of disarray. Ceilings, for example, no longer seem upside-down but rather right-side-up, and Gregor's mind must make the adjustments that follow from the reality of his insect body. Since language is the means by which human beings are said to determine their existence, and since Gregor lacks that capacity to be human, he must instead allow his insect body to lead him to a new identity. Like Alice's fluctuating size in Wonderland, Gregor's lack of a functional language forces him to reconstruct every relation between his body and the environment anew. In reconnecting each bodily motion with the space that surrounds him, new modes of expression become necessary. Like Artaud's call for a new language without articulation, Kafka's literary creatures develop new forms of signing that play an increasingly important role in the metalinguistic worlds he depicts.

In addition to Gregor Samsa's screeching and scratching, Kafka offers another case of animal signing in "Josephine the Singer, or the Mouse Folk." Josephine's singing, described by Kafka as a kind of "piping," reflects the nonhuman reality of her bodily structure. Kafka's narrator, presumably also a mouse, states of Josephine's singing:

> So is it singing at all? Is it not perhaps just a piping? And piping is something that we all know about, it is the real artistic accomplishment of our people, or rather no mere accomplishment but a characteristic expression of our life. We all pipe, but of course no one dreams of making out that our piping is an art, we pipe without thinking of it, indeed without noticing it, and there are many among us who are quite unaware that piping is one of our characteristics.[29]

In the description of Josephine's singing, her so-called art moves from a special skill or talent to a general characteristic of the mouse folk's existence until it passes entirely out of consciousness: "There are many among us who are quite unaware that piping is one of our characteristics." Kafka describes through the vehicle of Josephine's piping, which is "nothing out of the ordinary," a type of sonorous metamorphosis from human notions of art (music) to the animal's "characteristic expression": crying, or in this case, piping. The audible spectrum between language and music, words and noise, determines for Kafka the space and process of the metamorphosis. In Josephine's world, music cannot be fully differentiated from natural sounds. Somewhere between human and animal being, Kafka searches for another aurality. It is this in-between of transformation that occupies Kafka's animal stories—the moment at which identity floats in transit.

Invariably, the expression that erupts from Kafka's transitory beings involves music. Returning to *The Metamorphosis,* one remembers Gregor's response to his sister's violin playing. Kafka narrates Gregor's thoughts as he is mesmerized by the music: "Was he an animal, that music had such an effect upon him? He felt as if the way were opening before him to the unknown nourishment he craved."[30] (Not unlike the various potions that Alice ingests, Gregor's experience of sensation also appears to pass first through the register of orality. By likening his musical seduction to an "unknown nourishment," Gregor displays the confusion with which he experiences the world in his new animal being. Although it is no longer used for speaking, the mouth remains a crucial orifice for the transformed body.)[31] An indeterminate semiotic medium, music resonates between the registers of a sophisticated artistic form and a simple display of sentiment and emotion.

"Howling" precedes the discourse of the jackals in another of Kafka's animal tales, "Jackals and Arabs." It is the jackals' howling that first alerts the narrator to their presence before they begin to speak to him hypnotically, "eye to eye."[32] In this instance, the howling mediates between the language of the human being and the animal. Deleuze and Guattari note that "music always seems caught up in an indivisible becoming-child or becoming-animal, a sonorous block that opposes the visual memory."[33] Music, or the artifice of animal sound, appears in Kafka's texts as an ambiguous representation—somewhere between technique and noise—that marks the shift from words to sounds, intellect to affect, and human to animal being. As a literary motif, animal noises indicate a place of communication beyond the limits of language.

Another such index to the nonhuman world appears in "A Report to an Academy." In this reply to the Darwinian call of the wild, Kafka's talking ape describes an irreversible path toward humanization: "My memory of the past has closed the door against me more and more. . . . even if my strength and my will power sufficed to get me back to it, I should have to scrape the very skin from my body to crawl through."[34] An apparent reversal of the move toward animality, Kafka's former ape appears to fall into line with the evolutionary convention by "becoming-human." Yet that humanization of the beast does not result in an unqualified endorsement of anthropomorphism. The ape's transformation accompanies a noticeable becoming-animal of its human captors and proceeds around the oral/aural loci.

The first mention of sound in connection with the captured ape occurs when it states: "I am supposed to have made uncommonly little noise, as I was later informed, from which the conclusion was drawn that I would either soon die or if I managed to survive the first critical period would be very amenable to training."[35] By suppressing the expressions of its animal noise, the ape risks its animal life. By taking the risk, however, it increases its chances of becoming human, of being trained to be human. While the ape struggles to overcome its nature, its captors display their nature proudly, a nature that differs little from that which the ape is expected to shed. "Their laughter had always a gruff bark in it that sounded dangerous but meant nothing. They always had something in their mouths to spit out and did not care where they spat."[36] In this characterization of the sailors, it is they who appear to have lost the capacity for language, replacing it instead with meaningless laughter and a compulsion to expectorate. Their mouths are not used for language but rather for the expression of affect (laughing), ingestion (smoking and drinking), and excreting (spitting). Thus even in reversing the apparent dynamic toward becoming-animal, Kafka refuses to allow another, more conventional dynamic to supplant it. Deleuze and Guattari explain this process: "There is no longer man or animal, since each deterritorializes the other, in a conjunction of flux, in a continuum of reversible intensities."[37] Accordingly, although Kafka's metamorphoses are themselves irreversible, they are infectious—they initiate a chain of radical transformations.

In the end, the ape crosses the threshold that separates the human and animal worlds through a process that in psychoanalysis is referred to as "introjection." Overcoming the smell that revolted it, the ape learns to swallow the sailors' schnapps, which had become the symbol of its final obstacle to reaching the human world. Pressing toward the ontological limit, the ape learns to imitate in sequence its captors' orality: spitting, smoking, and finally drinking. The ape's final success in mastering its repulsion and breaking into the human community is marked by the eruption of human language from its mouth. Kafka's ape narrates its achievement:

> I took hold of a schnapps bottle that had been carelessly left standing before my cage, uncorked it in the best style, while the company began to watch me with mounting attention, set it to my lips without hesitation, with no grimace, like a professional drinker, with rolling eyes and full throat, actually and truly drank it empty; then threw the bottle away, not this time in despair but as an artistic performer; forgot indeed to rub my belly; but instead of

that, because I could not help it, because my senses were
reeling, called a brief and unmistakable "Hallo!" breaking
into human speech, and with this outburst broke into the
human community, and felt its echo: "Listen, he's talking!" like a caress over the whole of my sweat-drenched
body.[38]

In a scene that recalls the ingestions of Alice, Kafka's ape
swallows the totemic liquid and regurgitates the human greet-
ing, "hallo." The oral economy slides into an aural one, blur-
ring the distinctions between the various functions of animal
orifices.[39]

The motif of becoming by ingestion resembles the process
of introjection that Freud discusses in relation to mourning.
Laplanche and Pontalis describe introjection as an act in which
"the subject transposes objects and their inherent qualities
from the 'outside' to the 'inside' of himself."[40] Further, it is
"characterised by its link to oral incorporation."[41] Tracing the
term's origin to Ferenczi, Laplanche and Pontalis cite its oppositional relation to the concept of projection and the proximity of it to incorporation. According to the logic that Freud
sets forth in "Mourning and Melancholia" (1917), introjection is the psychic means by which the ego regains a lost
object. Through introjection the subject learns to forgo the
loss of a cathected object.[42] But not only objects. In *Civilization and Its Discontents* (1929–30), Freud applies that
same logic of introjection to the whole of civilization. According to Freud, each individual must relinquish personal
desires so that a community can arise. In answer to his own
question, "What happens in him to render his desire for aggression innocuous?" Freud says: "Something very remarkable, which we should never have guessed and which is nevertheless quite obvious. His aggressiveness is introjected,
internalized; it is, in point of fact, sent back to where it came
from — that is, it is directed towards his own ego."[43] Like the

ape, the individual swallows its aggression whole in a gesture akin to mourning—renunciation. Or rather, the ape, in a gesture similar to the human being's, swallows the unpleasant substance in a symbolic act that sublimates its former self into its new ego—an ego constituted on the occasion of this gesture. In both versions, a communion or transubstantiation takes place during introjection.

In contrast to introjection, incorporation involves a significantly more phantasmatic economy—one that proceeds without ever establishing the position of the subject. Incorporation results in what Nicolas Abraham and Maria Torok describe as the "crypt": a secret place of articulation no longer accessible to the subject that carries it.[44] In Kafkaesque fashion, Abraham and Torok pursue the narrative of Sergei Pankeiev's transformation into the Wolf Man and the cryptonymy that envelops his being. Kafka's narratives of metamorphosis are important in the present context not only because they thematize the figure of the animal and its world but also because they involve the question of language and metamorphosis. What happens to language when the transformed subject is no longer a speaking entity? In their assessment of that problem, Deleuze and Guattari argue that the becoming-animal that occupies Kafka's stories results in the substitution of a multivocal being for the speaking subject. As seen earlier, for Deleuze and Guattari, animal being is essentially multiple. Animal being is defined by that multiplicity. Consequently, the animal never assumes the position of a discursive subject. Animal being is a "machinic assemblage, the parts of which are independent of each other but which functions nonetheless."[45] In Kafka's animals and the metamorphoses that mark their entry into the world, the speaking mouth of the human subject is replaced by a multitude of orifices that provide an infinite number of introjective functions. Kafka's animals determine a massive introjection apparatus.

Akutagawa Ryunosuke (1892–1927)

But what I fear is the mysterious Greece, hidden in the shadows of their Wests like an eternally wakeful, immortal phoenix. Did I say fear? No, it is probably not fear. But I cannot help feeling, even while I strangely resist it, a kind of animal magnetism inexorably drawing me in.

—AKUTAGAWA RYUNOSUKE, CITED IN
"ORIGINS OF MODERN JAPANESE LITERATURE"

THE FINAL EXCURSION in this brief literary investigation ventures into Japanese literature and Akutagawa Ryunosuke's satirical and mythical writings. Concepts of introjection, projection, and ultimately incorporation play an important part in the writings of Akutagawa, who grappled with the issue of Japan's past and its relation to the modern West. For Akutagawa, writing in the early twentieth century, the task of absorbing Japan's literary past and appropriating the Western notion of the subject came to be increasingly polarized projects. By the end of his life, Akutagawa had largely abandoned his "historical" writings (rewritings of classical Japanese narratives such as his 1915 "Rashomon," which was taken from the eleventh-century *Konjaku monogatari*) and had adopted the *shishosetsu,* or "I-novel" form (autobiographical writings developed from European naturalist novels). Akutagawa's life can be seen as an endless string of personal, cultural, artistic, and religious introjections, which led to a final introjection, suicide. On 24 July 1927, Akutagawa, clutching a Bible, swallowed a lethal dose of kaliumcyanid.

Akutagawa's above comment, which notes his ambivalent relation to the West—his simultaneous attraction to and repulsion from it—was written shortly before his suicide. It comes from Akutagawa's reflection on modern literature (especially that of the West), titled "Bungeitekina, amari ni bungeitekina" (Literary, all too literary). Akutagawa's transcription of

Nietzsche's famous title *Human, All Too Human* supplants the notion of the human with that of the literary, suggesting a series of dichotomies between human and literary being, West and East, old and new, and in the context of one of his last works *Kappa* (1927), between human and nonhuman being. Written in part as a response to Swift's *Gulliver's Travels,* Akutagawa's *Kappa* tracks the story of a man's descent into the underworld of the mythical Kappas, amphibious creatures that reside, according to Japanese folklore, beneath swamps and marshes. Like the *Alice* novels (which it also resembles)[46] and *Gulliver's Travels,* Akutagawa uses the imaginary creatures for satirical purposes but also as a medicinal relief for his increasing "revulsion from the whole of human life."[47] In this respect, *Kappa* also resembles *Gulliver's Travels* in tone, especially those moments when Swift interjects his contempt for the human species. Gulliver, for example, remarks of "those filthy Yahoos," the humanoid creatures that he initially fails to perceive as such: "Although there were few greater lovers of mankind, at that time, than myself, yet I must confess I never saw any sensitive being so detestable on all accounts."[48] Adopting a similar stance, Akutagawa delivers a thinly-veiled thrust at the human race in general and the Japanese in particular, during a sequence in which an unborn Kappa refuses to enter into the world. Asked whether or not it wants to be born, the Kappa fetus replies: "I do not wish to be born. In the first place, it makes me shudder to think of all the things that I shall inherit from my father—the insanity alone is bad enough. And an additional factor is that I maintain that a Kappa's existence is evil."[49] The erratic scale that forces Gulliver at times to incorporate and at others to be incorporated by the creatures and cultures that he encounters returns in Akutagawa's prenatal Kappa. The Kappa's desire to remain in fetal form can be read as a form of nostalgia, on Akutagawa's part, for a time untouched by the difficulties that attend to one's entry into the world. However, the desire to remain in the womb can also be seen as a reverse introjection, as the desire to be introjected. The desire to remain inside the other — in this case, the mother — counters the normal route of introjecting others on the way to constructing a self, effecting instead a deconstruction of the self.[50]

The reception of *Gulliver's Travels* has determined a recurrent moment in the constitution of Japanese modernity, for it addresses the themes of civility, society, bestiality, and madness as they are measured in the eyes of Western culture.[51] For the Japanese, who were themselves the objects of considerable curiosity when Commodore Perry arrived upon Japanese shores in 1856, *Gulliver's Travels* persists as a singular reminder of their own strangeness from the perspective of the other. And that other's perspective, whether actual or imagined, has served as a locus of identification for some Japanese writers. In particular, Gulliver's encounter with the horselike Houyhnhnms and humanoid Yahoos explores the possibility that not only languages and customs but also species and entire life forms may separate countries and their cultures from one another.[52]

Having maintained a virtual closed-door policy until 1868, Japan's modernization resulted in two related but different events: Japan's entry into the outside world and the entry of the outside world into Japan. *Gulliver's Travels* reminds Japan of its own isolation, of its own history of introjection and projection. In his short story "Kamigami no bisho" (Smiles of the Gods, 1922), Akutagawa summons a Japanese "spirit" who warns a seventeenth-century Jesuit missionary of Japan's ability to introject every aspect of the other:

> It is possible that Deus himself could turn into a native of our country. China and India were transformed. Now the West, too, must change. We inhabit the woods. We are in

the shallow streams. We are in the breeze that wafts over the rose. We are in the evening light that lingers on the temple wall. We are everywhere, always. You must be very careful, very careful.[53]

Akutagawa's animistic account of the Japanese spirit exhibits both the author's paranoia (directed in this instance at the spectral Japanese spirit that surrounds and threatens to engulf him) and his conception of the nation-body as a fluidal, *disorganized* (in Artaud's sense) stomach function that gains its identity through the consumption of others. The satirical *Kappa* exposes Japanese culture from the vantage point of an internalized other, from the perspective of an introjected self that has ceased to exist in the empirical world. Thus for Akutagawa, *Kappa* was not only a response to *Gulliver's Travels,* it was a response to the call of the whole of a phantasmatic Western culture and literature (especially modern Western literature) that he once termed the "call of the wild."[54] It is a call whose source, by Akutagawa's time, could no longer be located as either outside or inside Japan. Karatani Kojin writes of Akutagawa's dialogue with the other: "What Akutagawa called 'Deus' was the Western novel, which was 'remade' into the *shishosetsu.*"[55]

Akutagawa spent much of his literary career reworking and reinterpreting classical Japanese texts, but also saturated his writings with allusions to Western literature from Poe to Nietzsche, displaying a special affinity for the fantastic. (In Kappaland, for example, the anarchist Tok describes himself as "a superman," to which Akutagawa's narrator adds: "Actually, the word that he used translates literally as super-Kappa.")[56] In the course of his writing, which culminated in madness and suicide at the age of thirty-five, Akutagawa began the literary construction of a distinct world located between the Western and Eastern hemispheres, reality and hallucination, subjectivity and multiplicity, and the human and animal worlds. Depicting a transient world, Akutagawa's writing occupies a realm most commonly identified with madness. (It is important to remember that madness is inextricably linked to the site of animality through the *notion* of irrationality.)[57] Yet Akutagawa's madness, like that of Poe, Nerval, and Nietzsche, cannot be summoned as a mere clinical fact to explain the strangeness of his work; rather, one must read Akutagawa's madness as it assumes form in his writing. In the case of Akutagawa, the theme of madness appears in the guise of the supernatural: haunting, madness, and monstrosity are dominant features of Akutagawa's fictive landscape and characters.[58]

A mental asylum frames *Kappa,* which begins with an author's prefacing remark ("This is the story of Patient No. 23 in one of our mental homes . . .")[59] and concludes in the same home, with the narrator since diagnosed with dementia praecox. The narrator's symptoms include hallucinations and delusions, and he believes that he has discovered a mythical race of creatures called Kappas. Akutagawa describes the Kappas as follows:

> The average height of a Kappa is just over three feet, and . . . its average weight varies between twenty and thirty pounds. . . . The distinctive feature is the oval-shaped saucer to be found on the top of its head. . . . it is the colouring of the Kappa's skin that is its most remarkable feature. The Kappa's skin does not retain a uniform colour as is the case with us humans; it always changes so as to blend with that of the environment.[60]

A humanoid amphibian with chameleon-like skin, "webbed hands and feet," and a "pouch in his belly, rather like a kangaroo's," the Kappa's identity hangs in a delicate balance between land and water, man and beast, natural and supernatural.[61] Yet it is also caught up in a matrix of differences. The Kappa's perennial enemy is the otter, and for a Kappa, being "called a frog in this country is tantamount to being called a swine."[62] Their language, Kappanese, consists primarily of exclamations that have "no real meaning."[63] Ultimately, although the Kappas are and aren't projections of the Japanese, are and aren't projections of Akutagawa himself, it is, paradoxically, the motif of introjection that introduces animality and madness into Akutagawa's narrative.

The story commences when the narrator falls into "a pitch black abyss" that opens onto the world of the Kappas.[64] The Kappas themselves maintain a peculiar relation to internalization and consumption, practicing a form of ritual cannibalism whereby they devour the flesh of unemployed workers. "'We slaughter any worker who loses his job,' a Kappa explains, 'and we use his flesh as meat.'"[65] In this manner, the state maintains a perfect economic ratio between the unemployment rate and the price of meat. The cannibalistic economy is also represented in the prebirth custom already mentioned. Before a Kappa is born, it is asked whether indeed it wishes to leave the womb and enter the world.

> Just as we would, the Kappa calls in a doctor or a midwife to assist at the delivery. But when it comes to the moment just before the child is born, the father—almost as if he is telephoning—puts his mouth to the mother's vagina and asks in a loud voice:
> "Is it your desire to be born into this world, or not? Think seriously about it before you reply."[66]

The child thus exists as a preborn entity, a being whose ego is constituted not by introjecting others but rather by being introjected. That condition is important with regard to Akutagawa's treatment of the issue of genetics. As the response of the unborn Kappa to its father indicates, the question of heredity (here, the father's madness) remains a serious concern for the Kappas. The narrator learns that the Kappas practice a form of selective breeding intended to eliminate "unsound and unhealthy" infants. Against the usual logic of selection, however, the Kappas seek to couple the sound with the un-sound, the healthy with the unhealthy, in an attempt to absorb or sublate the undesired hereditary traces. In this sense, the in-herited trait remains internalized, like the unborn Kappa, wait-ing to make its entry into the world or the horizon of the psy-che. It is with exceptional urgency that Akutagawa considers this question, since he watched his mother succumb to schizo-phrenia. "My mother was a madwoman. . . . When my sister and I pestered her to, she would draw pictures for us on sheets of paper. . . . But the people she drew all had foxes' faces."[67]

The becoming-animal depicted by Akutagawa's schizo-phrenic mother can be discerned in the Kappas, who behave like people but possess the faces and bodies of animals. It is as if Akutagawa explodes his mother's madness—a madness he had inherited through a genetic introjection—across the land-scape that constitutes Kappaland. Akutagawa, who had resisted autobiographical writings throughout the early part of his career only to succumb to the "I" (along with madness) in his later writings, can be seen to undergo what might best be termed a becoming-mother—a return to the site of the mad-ness that spawns him, that incorporates him, even while intro-jecting it into the figure of the mother and the animal. Akutagawa's madness takes the form of a becoming-mother, a becoming-animal that allows him to escape from the self he finds increasingly unbearable.

The link between the becoming that Akutagawa exhibits in *Kappa,* the becomings that Deleuze and Guattari enumerate in Kafka, and those that Deleuze finds in Carroll and Artaud all concern the collapse of a stable human subjectivity. In each case, the impending collapse of the subject, the corruption of the ideal of a stable subject, precipitates in some form the ap-pearance of animal or otherwise nonhuman creatures. In each instance, the breakdown of language accompanies or imple-ments a bodily crisis that is only resolved by transforming oneself into another form, by adapting to the new environment that now surrounds one. Alice argues with animals and flowers, Gregor crawls on ceilings, Akutagawa's narrator learns to converse in exclamations. Each instance adheres to Artaud's vision of a "body without organs." A body no longer defined by the singularity of its structure but rather by its fluidity, Artaud's organless body functions like a "body-sieve," absorbing its surroundings from which it is no longer distinguished. Deleuze explains that "the consequence of this is that the entire body is no longer anything but depth—it carries along and snaps up everything into this gaping depth which represents a fundamental involution."[68] In Artaud's projected corpus, organs and words become indistinguishable, as do interiorities and exteriorities. "Everything," writes Deleuze, "is a mixture of bodies, and inside the body, interlocking and penetration."[69] Instead of structure, then, one is left with a multiplicity of openings and orifices that continuously absorb, introject, incorporate, excorporate, dissolve, transform, and resurface the world ad nauseam. That vision of language as a perforated and solvent body can also be read in terms of animal being, which lacks density, finitude, and definite borders. Artaud's, Kafka's, Akutagawa's, and to a lesser degree Carroll's writings signal the advent of the novel made animal.

In his final polemic with Japanese novelist Tanizaki Junichiro (who derided Akutagawa for lacking the "physical stamina" to write full-length novels), Akutagawa calls for a "novel without plot."[70] Responding to Tanizaki's preference for "powerful breathing, muscular arms, robust loins" in the body of a novel, Akutagawa opts for a less cohesive figure of writing.[71] Akutagawa likens the ideal novel to a painting by Cézanne, which "depend[s] more on color than on *dessin* for its vitality."[72] The notion of a writing that comprises splashes of color, porous word residues, an infinitesimal monadic flow—"an organism without parts which operates entirely by insufflation, respiration, evaporation, and fluid transmission"—leads to the threshold of literary language and its possible extinction.[73] As Darwin's earlier assertion suggests, languages, like organisms, are prone to extinction and can only survive that finitude by multiplying, by expanding from singular organic entities into full animal species. Literary language and modern literature perhaps most aggressively explored the possibilities in language of sustaining animal being. As a linguistic apparatus, modern literature can be understood as having opened a unique topology of the animal. The work of Carroll, Kafka, and Akutagawa, among others during the nineteenth and early twentieth centuries, pushed the relationship between a revitalized notion of language and animality to a possible limit: the word made animal, *zoon,* may also have exhausted language. At the place of such a limit, the animal *has* language, although its mode of having must be radically rethought. The literary animal is a hybrid being, a *zoologos,* that forces human language to adapt in order to survive.

The changes to language that the figure of the animal effects also open another realm for animals to occupy. The technological media, exemplified by photography and cinema, provide a destination for the animal trajectory. It is a space made possible by the extinction of a certain form of language. The technological media can be seen as the afterlife of that language— animals survive language in the cryogenic topographies of technological reproduction. In the twentieth century, language becomes, after literature, a form of technology.

6 | Animetaphors: Photography, Cryptonymy, Film

A PHOTOGRAPH

Six captive horses, their white
Forms overlapping

Interstices, a series
Of spaces where love, blackened

By chemistry to pure
Shade will answer white with black,

Black with white. You will betray
This photograph day and night

But still the horses from your
Wall will emerge, captive, bright.

—VICKI HEARNE, "NERVOUS HORSES"

BECAUSE THE DIFFERENTIAL system of language can refer to things or ideas that lie outside its referential chain, the semiology of language is haunted by a profound negativity. The system of language, which operates according to a dialectical logic, can posit (qua antithesis), concepts that elude its grasp. Things can be named, like Heidegger's animal graphic, as negations of language. In the present context, the figure of the animal has come to occupy just such a negative space—one that language can point to without naming, subsume without securing. The capacity of language to point beyond its limits allows it to exceed a communicative function. In the literary works of Carroll,

Kafka, and Akutagawa, language, extended beyond its usual limits, reaches across the categorical divide and brushes the site of its antithesis, the ontology of animals. These works represent instances of contact made possible by language, even as they assail the stability of that language. They operate in the negativity of the animal field. In the previously discussed literary projects, the dynamic of language undergoes a demetaphorization: words are thrust, like Artaud's corporeal language, into living animal bodies.

The question of language, which is inextricably linked to human and animal being, is necessarily implicated in the encounter with animality and the figure of the animal. If the animal is said to lack language, to represent the site of radical alterity, then words cannot circumscribe the being of animals as animals. The contact between language and the animal marks a limit of figurability, a limit of the very function of language. The proximity to the threshold of language is a trait common to animals and to another medium, photography. The two semiotic systems are mediated by the logic of the unconscious and the forces of a fantastic visuality. Freud himself makes a curious reference to animals in his theses on the dreamwork.

In concluding chapter 3 of *The Interpretation of Dreams,* Freud offers a final illustration of his thesis, "A Dream Is the Fulfilment of a Wish." After a series of empirical observations, citations, speculations, and interpretations, Freud confesses abruptly: "I do not myself know what animals dream of."[1] He follows the rare moment of restraint, however, by citing a proverb in the form of a riddle: "What do geese dream of? Of Maize."[2] The dreams of animals, like those of human beings, express desires. Freud closes the paragraph by affirming the force of the parabolic insight: "The whole theory that dreams are wish-fulfilments is contained in these two phrases."[3] Even animals, it would seem, at least those in proverbs, participate in the logic of dreams. It is thus in the form of an animal proverb that Freud configures the secret of dreams.

Freud's recourse to proverb underscores the complex nature of figuring the unconscious in general, and dreams in particular. The distance that animal metaphors evoke creates a further layer of complexity. Yet the Freudian logic, as Derrida has shown at length, often requires such radical detours. Freud frequently turns to metaphors, citations, and footnotes to extend the proper body of his thought into areas that resist conventional paths of representation. However, the specific allusion that Freud makes in defense of his theory of dreams—the dreams of animals—resonates with a crucial aspect of that theory, namely regression. If, as Freud believes, the origins of dream wishes are revealed in regression, then the recourse to animality here suggests a point of contact between the deepest recesses of memory and the animal world.[4] Freud's fascination with and appropriation of certain tenets of Darwinian thought, discussed earlier, erupt here as a version of the recapitulation theory, "ontogeny recapitulates phylogeny." Every organism repeats the stages of its evolution, reenacting, as it were, the history of the species in the process of its individuation. For Freud, "dreaming is on the whole an example of regression to the dreamer's earliest condition, a revival of his childhood. . . . Behind this childhood of the individual we are promised a picture of a phylogenetic childhood—a picture of the human race, of which the individual is in fact an abbreviated recapitulation."[5] The wishful dreams of animals can be understood in this light as a primal scene of the dreamwork; every dreamer carries the trace of animality.

The space between the unconscious and the animal's dream is traversed, in Freud's account, by the metaphor. The transferential function of the metaphor allows the archaic material of the unconscious, derived from the prehistory of the species, to move into the registers of language. It is the other language, the shared cryptography of dreams, which grants a passage between the human and animal worlds. On another occasion, Freud insists on the necessity of speaking in a "dry and direct" fashion in general, of referring to "bodily organs and processes by their technical names" in particular. Appearing to reject the use of figurative language, Freud declares in French: "J'appelle un chat un chat."[6] When Freud calls upon the cat to speak directly, it responds as other, in another idiom. In both instances the animal figure responds to Freud's call in the form of an originary translation: it says what it means to say in another semiotic.

At two critical junctures—one that elaborates the dreamwork, the other that emphasizes direct language—Freud resorts to animal metaphors. And in each case the animal becomes intertwined with the trope, serving as its vehicle and substance. Although the recourse to animality may be a feature of Freud's own neuroses—Freud had already insisted to Fliess in a letter dated 11 January 1897 that "perversions regularly lead to zoophilia and have an animal character"—the intervention of the animal figure raises questions about the origin of the metaphor, its place in the world of language.[7] One might posit provisionally that the animal functions not only as an exemplary metaphor but, within the scope of rhetorical language, as an originary metaphor. One finds a fantastic transversality at work between the animal and the metaphor—the animal is already a metaphor, the metaphor an animal. Together they transport to language, breathe into language, the vitality of another life, another expression: animal and metaphor, a metaphor made flesh, a living metaphor that is by definition not a metaphor, antimetaphor—"animetaphor." The animetaphor may also be seen as the unconscious of language, of *logos*. As cited earlier, Derrida has written, apropos of the pre-Socratic sophists and rhetors: "*Logos* is a *zoon*. An animal that is born, grows, belongs to *phusis*."[8]

The genealogy of language, like that of the dream, returns to a place outside *logos*. The animal brings to language something that is not a part of language and remains within language as a foreign presence. That is, because the animal is said to lack the capacity for language, its function in language can only appear as an other expression, as a metaphor that originates elsewhere, is transferred from elsewhere.

The other side of thought, the place where metaphysics shatters the surfaces of metaphor, appears in the animal's visage —a countenance that, for Giorgio Agamben, "always seems to be on the verge of uttering words."[9] On the verge of words, the animal emits instead a stream of cries, affects, spirits, and magnetic fluids. What flows from the animal touches language without entering it, dissolving memory, like the unconscious, into a timeless present. The animal is magnetic because it draws the world-building subject toward an impossible convergence with the limits of world, toward a metaphysics of metaphor. The magnetic animal erases the limits of the metaphor, effecting an economy of the figure that is metamorphic rather than metaphoric. ("Metamorphosis," insist Deleuze and Guattari, "is the contrary of metaphor.")[10] The magnetic animal forces a transformation of the figure. Thus for Deleuze and Guattari, one recalls, all "becomings" are animal becomings: "Becoming can and should be qualified as becoming-animal even in the absence of a term that would be the animal become. The becoming-animal of the human being is real, even if the animal the human being becomes is not."[11]

The magnetic property of the animetaphor does not simply sway language but actively transforms it, assailing *logos* with the catachrestic force of affect. Defined as the capacity to effect concrete changes in the material world through an immaterial or fantastic medium, magnetic power, like that of dreams, transforms the traditional rapport between action and reaction. With magnetism, reactions, in the sense of affective responses, can be said to cause actions. In the animal, the magnetic capacity appears both destructive and generative. Montaigne, for example, claims, "Tortoises and ostriches hatch their eggs just by looking at them, a sign that their sight has some ejaculative value."[12] Montaigne's psychosexual economy is not too far from the idea of mesmerism and its place in psychoanalysis. Through hypnosis, the animal trace infiltrates thought, instituting a pathic communicability that, as Mikkel Borch-Jacobsen argues, evolves into transference. From metaphor to metamorphosis, transference to transformation and back again, the animetaphor conducts a magnetic trade into and out of language. What is transferred magnetically, moreover, speaks to and from the originary animal topology, the animal den, *ethos*.

The questions of ethics, metaphor, and animal converge in another animal fable, this time recounted by Adorno. Titled "People Are Looking at You," Adorno's narrative tracks the slippage between mortality and morality, murder and violence, through the look of the animal. Locating the ethics of the animetaphor in the transferential power of the animal look, Adorno's aphorism reads:

Indignation over cruelty diminishes in proportion as the victims are less like normal readers, the more they are swarthy, "dirty," dago-like. This throws as much light on the crimes as on the spectators. Perhaps the social schematization of perception in anti-Semites is such that they do not see Jews as human beings at all. The constantly encountered assertion that savages, blacks, Japanese are like animals, monkeys for example, is the key to the pogrom. The possibility of the pogroms is decided in the moment when the gaze of a fatally-wounded animal falls on a human being. The defiance with which he repels this gaze—"after all, it's only an animal"—reappears irresistibly in cruelties done to human beings, the perpetrators having again and again to reassure themselves that it is "only an animal," because they could never fully believe this even of animals. In repressive society the concept of man is itself a parody of divine likeness. The mechanism of "pathic projection" determines that those in power perceive as human only their own reflected image, instead of reflecting back the human as precisely what is different. Murder is thus the repeated attempt, by yet greater madness, to distort the madness of such false perception into reason: what was not seen as human and yet is human, *is made a thing,* so that its stirrings can no longer refute the manic gaze.[13]

According to Adorno's transferential logic, violence originates in the encounter between human and nonhuman beings. The recourse to figure, "it's only an animal," transcribes violence metaphorically as murder. Since the capacity for murder is limited to the world of human beings, the ethics of violence must first be transferred then transformed, according to Adorno, from the outside. The ethics of murder is made possible by seeing the animal first as nonhuman, then inhuman. If one's victim can be seen as inhuman, the aggressor reasons, one is then justified in performing acts of violence, even murder upon that inhuman body, since those acts now fall beyond the jurisdiction of the anthropocentric law.[14] For Adorno, violence always involves such a delusional economy. Adorno has located a crucial moment in the rhetoric of violence: as a performative statement, "it's only an animal" transforms other beings into *things* "so that [their] stirrings can no longer refute the manic gaze." Adorno's insight reveals that the animal as such is never a mere animal, its gaze exceeds the "thingness" of a nonhuman being and penetrates the human sphere—which is to say, that the "it's only an animal" utterance fails, in the first instance, to perform the immunity from guilt that the metaphor promises to the perpetrator of violence. Thus the series of pathic projections that leads inevitably to the pogrom begins with the collapse of the metaphor, with the failure of the figure to prevent a fundamentally ethical exchange: an irrevocable contact between human and nonhuman beings. Pathic projections, for Adorno, do penetrate and affect the ethical and linguistic structures of world. The animal and its remote, even technological being—Descartes, one recalls, likens animals to "automata"—are never far enough away to establish an ethical field distinct from that inhabited by human beings.[15] Although the human and animal worlds may be separated by the world of language, the animal's pathic projection pierces the global divide, facilitating an encounter between the human and animal topoi.

The animal's pathic projection opens a passage between worlds, but also to the end of the world, to the end of metaphor. "Metaphor," writes Derrida, "always carries its death within itself."[16] The living metaphor, the animetaphor, projects its own finitude, always anticipating its own disappearance. Metaphors, in this sense, are a priori figures of mourning. For Nicolas Abraham and Maria Torok, who have also described a fabulous animal, metaphors end where they begin—in the mouth.[17] When the subject is confronted with an insurmountable loss, they argue, the loss of the possibility of loss, a certain countersemiotic force, intervenes. "We propose to call this figure *antimetaphor.*" They continue: "Let us make clear that it is not simply a matter of reverting to the literal meaning of words, but of using them in such a way—whether in speech or deed—that their very capacity for figurative representation is lost."[18] The phantasmatic process of incorporation, according to Abraham and Torok, disfigures the metaphor, transforming it from figure to flesh. By destroying figures and tropes, by initiating the "active destruction of representation," incorporation provides a secret, nonrepresentational path to the topographies of loss, absence, and death. In this light, Heidegger's melancholic animal can be understood as suffering from the impossibility of representing loss as such. Recalling Heidegger's insistence that only mortals can "experience death as death," that "animals cannot do this," Derrida explains, in *Aporias,* that although Heidegger juxtaposes the capacity to die properly, to experience death as death, with the ability to speak, he does not insist on their synthesis.[19] Language invokes the capacity for death, the exemplary moment of the end of metaphoricity, without naming it. The animal, then, cannot experience death as death, according to Heidegger, nor can it speak: it can only incorporate death unnamed. For Abraham and Torok, *"Incorporation entails the fantasmatic destruction of the act by means of which metaphors become possible: the act of putting the original oral void into words."*[20] If the animal enters the world then, it does so not through representation but through incorporation, not through the dynamic of language but through the economy of a cryptic fantasy.

When the metaphoricity of the metaphor collapses, the concept becomes a metonymic thing that can be eaten. The animetaphor is, in this sense, never absorbed, sublated, or introjected into world but rather incorporated as a limit, an absolutely singular and cryptonymic idiom. The animetaphoric figure is consumed literally rather than figuratively. Derrida has added to this term, "animetaphorality."[21] At the edges of the mouth where the metaphor has ceased, one senses, perhaps tastes, the end of the world as such. It is against this limit of language that Derrida locates the end of metaphor: "This *end* of metaphor is not interpreted as a death or dislocation, but as an interiorizing anamnesis, a recollection of meaning, a *relève* of living metaphoricity into a living state of properness."[22] The animal returns like a meal that cannot be digested, a dream that cannot be forgotten, an other that cannot be sublated. The animetaphor can be seen as a kind of *zoon,* inhabiting the edges of figurative language, marking the absence of subjectivity.

Photograph

THE ABSENCE OF subjectivity ascribed to animals also appears in the haunted look of the photograph. "Every photograph, writes Roland Barthes, signals "the return of the dead."[23] Barthes connects the vacant subjectivity of the photograph to the absence of metaphor—of discourse—in the photograph:

> In Photography, the presence of the thing (at a certain past moment) is never metaphoric; and in the case of animated beings, their life as well, except in the case of photographing corpses; and even so: if the photograph then becomes horrible, it is because it certifies, so to speak, that the corpse is alive as corpse: it is the living image of a dead thing.[24]

The photograph represents, as André Bazin writes in "The Ontology of the Photographic Image," the culmination of a desire that has sustained the plastic arts: the desire to preserve the dead. "If the plastic arts were put under psychoanalysis, the practice of embalming the dead might turn out to be a fundamental factor in their creation."[25] Unlike painting or literature, the key element of the photograph is the object itself. Whereas the representational systems of the plastic arts rely on materials (paint, paper, clay) to re-create the represented object, and writing uses words to describe it, photography captures the rays that reflect directly from the subject's body. Of the relationship between photography and the object it represents, Barthes asserts: "A specific photograph, in effect, is never distinguished from its referent (from what it represents) . . . as is the case of every other image, encumbered—from the start, and because of its status—by the way in which the object is simulated."[26] Because the body's effusions are transposed, the photograph's effects are tactile. Barthes names this uncanny effect the photograph's *"punctum,"* a prick, puncture, or wound:

The photograph is literally an emanation of the referent. From a real body, which was there, proceed radiations which ultimately touch me, who am here; the duration of the transmission is insignificant; the photograph of the missing being, as Sontag says, will touch me like the delayed rays of a star. A sort of umbilical cord links the body of the photographed thing to my gaze: light, though impalpable, is here a carnal medium, a skin I share with anyone who has been photographed.[27]

Barthes sees the spectator as an incorporated body whose orifices, like Artaud's, are penetrated by the photographic rays of the other in a carnal exchange—a becoming-photograph.[28]

The photograph provides a moment of encounter with radical absence. Every photograph "mortifies," writes Barthes, at the same time that it generates, effects a filiation.[29] The uncanny duplication, which simultaneously mortifies and generates, forces the photographed object into another temporal dimension. "To preserve," writes Bazin, "artificially, bodily appearance is to snatch it from the flow of time, to stow it away neatly, so to speak, in the hold of life."[30] The distinction between killing life and killing time, or life in time, is a crucial one, for it bears upon the question of animal vitality and temporality. The earlier discussion of animals and philosophy noted the philosophical axiom that animals, lacking the capacity for language, also lack the capacity for death: animals lack the ability to experience death as an integral feature of life. Because animal being is not thought of as singular, the death of each individual organism is survived by the entire species. All animals of a given species are, according to this logic, extensions of one other. Unlike human beings, whose existence is founded on the metaphysics of the individual (the singularity of the soul, for example), animal being cannot be reduced to individual identities. It is dispersed throughout the pack or horde, which preserves the individual organism's death within the framework of a group body or identity. Similarly, photography facilitates this form of survival. According to Barthes, the photograph preserves in the *now* the future death of the object. Photographed objects never die, although they are always represented as "going to die." "At the limit, there is no need to represent a body in order for me to experience this vertigo of time defeated."[31] One can read Barthes's description of photographic time in relation to the temporality of animals. Beings that are inscribed as photographic images, like animals, do not die, are incapable of death. A direct relation between the nature of the photograph and that of the animal resides in the look—a look without subjectivity—that both media project.

In his 1977 article "Why Look at Animals?" essayist John Berger describes the fascination that gazing at animals affords human beings: "The image of a wild animal becomes the starting-point of a daydream: a point from which the day-dreamer departs with his back turned."[32] A type of inverted trauma, the animal look effects, Berger argues, a kind of reflection, a non-communication with the animal being. Berger adds that human beings recognize something in the animal look, something that reminds them of themselves.

> The eyes of an animal when they consider man are attentive and wary. The same animal may well look at other species in the same way. He does not reserve a special look for man. But by no other species except man will the animal's look be recognised as familiar. Other animals are held by the look. Man becomes aware of himself returning the look.[33]

According to Berger, human beings find the animal's look familiar because they recognize themselves in this look; they find themselves caught in the act (of looking at themselves) by the animal look as if at a mirror. Between the looks, animal and human, there lies, claims Berger, "a narrow abyss of non-comprehension"—a fascinatory divide.[34] In lieu of comprehension, animals provide humanity with a glimpse of subjectivity at its limit. Animals fascinate human beings. Fascination sets into motion the apparatus of subjectivity at the same moment that it arrests its operation. Addressing the relation between subjectivity and fascination, Lacan argues that fascination is one way in which the subject experiences the "terminal time of the gaze."[35]

As an affective state, fascination suspends the subject in the gaze of the other. Of that gaze which determines the subject from the outside, that is, from a point outside subjectivity, Lacan writes: "In the scopic field, the gaze is outside, I am looked at, that is to say, I am a picture."[36] The gaze positions the subject within the lapse of a suspended moment, like a photograph: "I am," writes Lacan, *"photo-graphed."*[37] Fascination determines one instance of that power of the gaze: in front of the other, the fascinated subject stands transfixed by the sudden appearance of an unassimilable exteriority, the *fact* of alterity that halts the movement of the subject. Lacan explains the effect of fascination and names the point at which it occurs, the object that instigates it the *"fascinum"*:

> The evil eye is the *fascinum*, it is that which has the effect of arresting movement and, literally, of killing life. At the moment the subject stops, suspending his gesture, he is mortified. The anti-life, anti-movement function of this terminal point is the *fascinum*, and it is precisely one of the dimensions in which the power of the gaze is exercised directly.[38]

According to Lacan, the *fascinum* blocks the dialectic of seeing and introduces an entirely other topography. Fascinated being no longer dwells in subjectivity, wandering instead on the outside like an animal, unable to reenter the world of being. Such exteriority can be seen in the present context as a kind of

"ecstasy."[39] Fascination creates ecstatic consciousness, or unconsciousness, which does not reside in the individual but
rather is directed outward, toward the exterior community.
Jean-Luc Nancy writes that ecstasy, "strictly speaking, . . . denies the possibility, both ontological and gnosological of absolute immanence . . . and consequently the impossibility either
of an individuality, in the precise sense of the term, or of a pure
collective totality."[40] For Nancy, ecstasy is a transit between the
individual and the group, singularity and multiplicity, humanity and the animal. Fascination and ecstasy are here linked because together they describe the temporal and spatial dislocation of the subject from itself. Fascination and ecstasy define a
time and place between subjectivity and objectivity—a photograph. Barthes's account of being photographed, for example,
registers this ecstatic awareness: "I am neither subject nor object
but a subject who feels he is becoming an object: I then experience a micro-version of death (of parenthesis): I am truly
becoming a specter."[41] He is, quite literally, becoming a photograph, in Deleuzian terms, becoming-photograph: "Photography transformed subject into object, and even, one might say a
museum object."[42] Fascination and ecstasy found a topography
that can be read as the topography of the photograph, one that
is ultimately shared with the animal.

According to Barthes, photography suspends in transition
the shift from subjectivity to objectivity (biology to biography)
—the movement that usually characterizes representation.
As such, photographic images are deictic rather than discursive (the photograph "cannot *say* what it lets us see"), and the
transient, unresolved space that the photograph depicts is always carried as a reference.[43] "It is as if the Photograph always
carries its referent with itself, both affected by the same
amorous or funereal immobility, at the very heart of the moving world."[44] Photography freezes the transformation of beings at an impossible moment between consciousness and

identity. Neither *here* nor *there,* the photographed object is in fact nowhere, atopic. (Of such ontological ellipses, André Bazin writes: "All the arts are based on the presence of man, only photography derives an advantage from his absence.")[45] Looking at the photograph, one realizes that one is looking into a place without subjectivity and, moreover, that something like a nonsubject returns that look. Barthes writes: "One might say that the photograph separates attention from perception, and yields up only the former, even if it is impossible without the latter; this is the aberrant thing, *noesis* without *noeme,* an action of thought without thought, an aim without a target."[46] Photography projects both "the effect of truth and the effect of madness."[47] The image it shows is always both there and not there. The photographic look exhibits an attention without perception, a type of being without subjectivity. On this view animals are, in essence, like photographs. Animals are phenomenal beings that exist— that is their truth. Nonetheless, animals are said to exist without taking place in the world of being—and that is the madness. The contradiction between the animal's truth and its madness is brought together, like the photograph, in the animal's look. Barthes closes the penultimate section of *Camera Lucida* by relating the photographic affect to a scene of animality, to Nietzsche's collapse, during which the philosopher allegedly embraced a carriage horse. Linking the experience of his own pathos before certain provocative photographs to Nietzsche's notorious episode, Barthes writes:

In each of them [the photographs], inescapably, I passed beyond the unreality of the thing represented, I entered crazily into the spectacle, into the image, taking into my arms what is dead, what is going to die, as Nietzsche did when, as Podach tells us, on January 3, 1889, he threw himself in tears on the neck of a beaten horse: gone mad for Pity's sake.[48]

Photography elicits that madness, that hallucination of the other that allows the spectator, in a momentary *jouissance,* to enter into the spectacle, to commingle with the spectacle, to embrace, as it were, the spectral other or dying animal.

Barthes closes the final section of his last book by noting the political desire to "tame the Photograph."[49] He writes of the urgency with which society seeks "to temper the madness which keeps threatening to explode in the face of whoever looks at it."[50] For photography transforms not only the photographed object, the subject of the photograph, but also the spectator. In front of the photograph, the spectator is also dissolved into the field of fascination, what Barthes names in conclusion "the photographic *ecstasy* [*l'extase photographique*]."[51]

One finds, by the latter half of the nineteenth century, a set of terms—animal, photography, unconscious—coalescing to form a distinct topology. Each term defines or portrays a distinct locus of being that cannot be inhabited by the subject. It is, nonetheless, a place of being or becoming. Animals and photographs can be seen as resembling versions of the unconscious. One can interpret the animal as a version of the unconscious in nature and the photograph as a technological unconscious. In this regard Benjamin writes: "It is through photography that we first discover the existence of this optical unconscious, just as we discover the instinctual unconscious through psychoanalysis."[52] It would appear that the unconscious arose—both in photography and psychoanalysis—to capture what Derrida terms "a memory of the present," the division of the present from itself, from closure, from the totality of the click.[53]

In one of a series of interviews with David Sylvester, Francis Bacon makes the following assessment of photographs of animals in slaughterhouses:

I've always been moved by pictures about slaughterhouses and meat. . . . There've been extraordinary photographs which have been done of animals just being taken up before they were slaughtered; and the smell of death. We don't know, of course, but it appears by these photographs that they're so aware of what is going to happen to them, they do everything to attempt to escape.[54]

The precise nature of Bacon's sentiment ("moved," he says) remains ambiguous in this account—a delicate mixture of arousal, pity, indignation, fascination, and even love, perhaps. (Kojève has suggested that human beings love animals for the same reasons, and with the same capacity, that they love the dead.)[55] Regardless of the exact emotion, Bacon appears overwhelmed by a torrent of sensation. He imagines not only the intentions of the animals ("attempt[ing] to escape") but also their odor—the smell of animals—intermingling with the more ambient "smell of death." In his reaction, Bacon appears to shift from the vantage point of a witness to that of a participant. He has slipped into the diegesis of slaughter, somewhere between slaughterer and slaughtered—in a kind of "photographic ecstasy," to return to Barthes's phrase. Bacon appears to identify with the soon-to-be-slaughtered animals.

In the same exchange with Sylvester, Bacon continues his identification: "We are meat, we are potential carcasses. If I go into a butcher shop I always think it's surprising that I wasn't there instead of the animal."[56] Bacon's rediscovery, in front of the photograph, of a totemic and sacrificial economy is here revealing. The factuality of meat appears to be an issue not for the ecstatic fact that it reveals—that corporeality continues beyond the threshold of mortality; that even after we die, we remain as animal facts, artifacts, and after the fact—but rather, for the excessive force of its facticity. The force of this fact, here in the form of a photographic image, seems to "puncture," to use Barthes's idiom, a register that was not stimulated by the initial phenomenon. In this case, the olfactory organs appear to have been activated in the wake of a visual perception. Bacon, as it were, smells the photograph, both its brutality and its facticity. In smelling the photograph, the animals in the photograph, Bacon assigns the two media a referent, a body. Between the figure of the animal and the materiality of the photograph, Bacon posits a mutual body of movement, intention, odor. He inscribes a locus of identification, a will, a dynamic that in turn moves him as spectator. In the figure of impending death, evoked by its smell in the photograph, Bacon sees himself. Between the slaughterhouse and the butcher shop, the animal and the photograph, Bacon finds himself slipping into the temporality of identification—Bacon sees himself in the place of the animal subject, an imminent corpse: "We are potential carcasses."

Bacon's utterance exposes a problem concerning animals and identification—namely, the assumption that human beings cannot identify with animals. Since the animal possesses no discernible subjectivity, the human subject cannot rediscover itself in the place of this other. Although a human being can project anthropomorphic characteristics onto the animal or experience emotions (such as pathos or sympathy) in response to its being, an impenetrable screen—language—divides the loci of animal and human being. If Bacon has indeed effected an identification with this image, then where does one locate the source of Bacon's identification, in the animal or in the photograph? The question raised by Bacon's uncanny sentiment addresses the possibility that the combination of the animal subject and the photographic image alters in some essential fashion the structure of identification. Although both the animal and photograph impede the dialectical flow of subjectivity (the effects of fascination and ecstasy result in the termination of the subject), as an assemblage, as a *rhizome,* animals and photographs appear to found and animate an entirely other topology: one that allows for an economy of the gaze, identification, and becoming.

Identifications result from encounters with sensual excess: a subject identifies with an image when that image exceeds the visual register and penetrates the polymorphic body. By entering the mise-en-scène of the slaughterhouse, Bacon not only advances from the secondary to the primary level of identification, he crosses the frame that separates reality from photographic reproduction, nature from the artwork, animality from humanity, and life from death. Identification is a mode of becoming, of mimesis, a method by which the ego assumes the properties of an other.[57] Identifying with the animal is part of the process of becoming-animal. The photograph's carnal reach that Barthes has noted appears to have here touched Bacon. He is becoming-animal, becoming-photograph, and the two becomings are inseparable. As with Barthes's characterization, the photograph's *punctum,* its sensational excess, initiates the spectator's feelings of identification. Although a hallucination, the spectator feels, in front of certain photographs, a sense of identification with them. It is this perverse trespass that facilitates identification. The photograph effects the subtle shift of being into an entirely other world. Of the slight distances traversed in photographic replication — the otherworldly vestige of its remove — Bacon reflects: "I think it's the slight remove from fact, which returns me onto the fact more violently."[58] Photography brings the spectator violently back to the reality of the real that appears, in the first instance, elsewhere.

The remove from fact that restores an awareness of that fact's truth to the spectator is not a feature exclusive to photography. The slight remove from fact is also a property of the animal look. Even at a distance, the animal look, as Berger notes, elicits a type of recognition from the gazing subject. Krafft-Ebing offers this glimpse into the psychopathology of "zooerasty," or pathological bestiality: "In numerous cases, sadistically perverse men, afraid of criminal acts with human beings, or *who care only for the sight of the suffering of a sensitive being, make use of the sight of dying animals, or torture animals, to stimulate or excite their lust.*"[59] In Krafft-Ebing's account, animals supplant the immediacy of human encounters. Animals, or rather images of animals, mediate the violent act. The image of the suffering animal facilitates, in this case, a move beyond the conventions of so-called human behavior. Violating the image of the animal allows one to exceed the permissible limits of human violence. The animal look does not terminate the momentum of identification, but rather deflects it into another economy. Thus displaced, identification mutates in kind: it no longer adheres to or circuits through the subject, but opens onto another space of identification unimpeded by the responsibilities of reason, language, and consciousness. By projecting the vector of identification into the animal world, the subject avoids what Derrida refers to as "the call that originates responsibility."[60] This impossible identification with the animal can be likened to an ingestion of the animal, invoking the transferential logic of sacrifice.

By consuming the animal in identification, the subject undergoes a becoming-animal in an effort to escape the realm of responsibility. As evidenced in anthropological research, the act of eating is commonly conceived of as a method of incorporating and becoming the other. Funeral feasts as well as most other forms of ritual consumption are directly linked to the notion of becoming-other, of harnessing the powers of the other (especially in the case of animals) by consuming its flesh. And because the animal inhabits an apolitical world, identification with this sphere exempts humanity from participating in human ethics. The sacrificial eating that concludes the act of identification—an identification that transpires in the act of eating—transfers onto humanity what Adorno calls the dying animal's "manic gaze."[61] The human being becomes other, and thus returns violently to the fact of itself, by consuming the animal, by engaging in what Derrida terms "eating well *(bien manger)*."[62] Regarding animal consumption, Derrida questions the constitutions of humanity and humanism in relation to nature and the animal:

> The subject does not want just to master and possess nature actively, . . . In our cultures, he accepts sacrifice and eats flesh. I would ask you: in our countries, who would stand any chance of becoming a *chef d'Etat* (a head of State), and of thereby "acceding to the head," by publicly and therefore exemplarily declaring him- or herself to be a vegetarian? . . . The *chef* must be an eater of flesh (with a view, moreover, to being "symbolically" eaten himself). . . . In answering these questions, you will have not only a scheme of the dominant, of the common denominator of the dominant, which is still today in the order of the political, the State, right, or morality, you will have the dominant schema of subjectivity itself.[63]

One now recognizes in Bacon's ecstatic shudder over the sight of slaughtered animals—a vision that seems to jolt him violently back into the place of the real—the source of his excitement. A convergence between eating and seeing, the two modes of phenomenal consumption that involve animals and photographs, brings these two entities together in a sacrificial economy. At the same time, this economy institutes a specific temporality. In an x-ray view of the animal, Bacon sees the animal's essence, its future. Animals can only appear as matter—meat—because they possess no discernible identity. The photographs thus show the spectator the future of the animal. Such disclosures are, for Barthes, a salient feature of photography. In *Camera Lucida,* Barthes also stumbles upon this realization, this anterior future tense of the photograph.

> In 1865, young Lewis Payne tried to assassinate Secretary of State W. H. Seward. Alexander Gardner photographed him in his cell, where he was waiting to be hanged. The photograph is handsome, as is the boy: that is the *studium.*

But the *punctum* is: *he is going to die.* I read at the same time: *This will be* and *this has been;* I observe with horror an anterior future of which death is the stake. By giving me the absolute past of the pose (aorist), the photograph tells me death in the future. What *pricks* me is the discovery of this equivalence. In front of the photograph . . . I shudder, like Winnicott's psychotic patient, *over a catastrophe which has already occurred.* Whether or not the subject is already dead, every photograph is this catastrophe.[64]

Like the condemned man in Barthes's photograph, animals are both dead and alive, suspended in the photograph.

Regarding Bacon's professed identification with animal carcasses, one must consider the metaphorics of eating, the act or gesture that circumscribes most sacrificial ceremonies. Concerning the relationship between eating and all phenomenal activity, Derrida asserts: "For everything that happens at the edges of the orifices (of orality, but also of the ear, the eye—and all the 'senses' in general) the metonymy of 'eating well' *(bien manger)* would always be the rule."[65] Looking at the photograph, Bacon recognizes his own death in the future by internalizing the corpse as a narcissistic fact. All photographs, as Barthes says, are of future corpses.

What is shared by animals and photographs is a crypt, in Abraham and Torok's sense, in which the antitheses—animal and technology—are united without, however, producing a sublation. A secret synthesis that cannot signify, the photograph brings into focus the alliance between animal and technology. One realizes that animals and photographs often produce the same phantasmatic and liminal effect, disrupting the flow of figurative language. Animals are, in this sense, fleshly photographs.

Animals can be seen as predecessors of photography, the two joined by the ecstatic feature of their look. Animals expose an unnameable aspect of fascination. And if Bacon transfigures the dynamic of the animal into that of its flesh, then he is only accelerating what is already embodied in the image of the animal, its corpse. For Bazin, the idea of embalming distinguishes the *technē* of the photographic image. But how do animals facilitate this transit between corporeality and photography? Why are animals the ideal subjects of photographs? One remembers that animals have never properly belonged to any ontology. Derrida explains that in traditional philosophy, "there is no category of original existence for the animal."[66] This is because animals have been excluded from the essential categories that constitute being. Nonetheless, animals have sustained the existence of every category of being as essential supplements: without belonging to any ontological category animals have made those categories possible by situating their borders. It is only in the imaginary topology of the photograph that one is able, perhaps, to perceive or discern the animal world. It is in such an exposure that the animal enters, for the first time, the phenomenal world. The animal look can be seen as a continuation of the photographic look. One recognizes that similitude in Bacon's photograph as a kind of *punctum*.

Technology

When, as a child, I was told about the invention of the telegraph the question which most interested me was, wherever did the swallows gather for their autumn migration before there were telegraph wires?

—KARL VON FRISCH, "THE DANCING BEES: AN ACCOUNT OF THE LIFE AND SENSES OF THE HONEY BEE"

CINEMA, WHICH BUILDS hallucinatory space, can be seen as a cryptic topography in which animals and the reproductive media converge, forming a Deleuzian rhizome. As animals began to disappear from the phenomenal world, they became increasingly the subjects of nineteenth- and twentieth-century reproductive media.[67] In 1872, Eadweard Muybridge began the task of bringing movement to the still image, of arousing an animate vitality from the catatonic corpus of photography. In his work, animals began to move across the reproductive media. In sequence after sequence, the photographer's animals pushed against the cryogenic frames of a fixated medium until they seemed to surpass the limits and enter the interstices, creating the semblance of motion—persistence of vision.

Muybridge's collection, *Animals in Motion,* which was begun in 1872 and appeared in copyrighted book form in 1899, and its sequel, a zoomorphic treatment of human bodies, *The Human Figure in Motion* (copyrighted in 1901), display the fascination with which animals and animal movement captured the photographic imagination.[68] Muybridge, whose technical contributions also include the zoopraxiscope, a projected version of the zootrope, has been positioned along a track that leads to the discovery of cinema. What is remarkable in Muybridge's work, what immediately seizes the viewer's attention, is the relentless and obsessive manner in which the themes of animal and motion are brought into contact—as if the figure of the animal had always been destined to serve as a symbol of movement itself. The movement of Muybridge's animals, at first across the frames and then eventually the screens of a new industrial landscape, not only aided the advent of a new mode of representation—cinema —it also introduced a new way to transport information from one locale to another; from one forum to another; one body to another; one consciousness to another. By capturing and recording the animals' every gesture, pose, muscular disturbance, and anatomical shift with such urgency, Muybridge seemed to be racing against the imminent disappearance of animals from the new urban environment. Distinct from the stillness of photography, cinema added the possibility of electric animation.

Christian Metz explains the relationship of cinema to time. In film "everything is recorded (as a memory trace which is immediately so, without having been something else before)."[69] Film is a parasite of the real, of the now, which is precisely why it cannot be restricted to a theory of language. Films are graphic constitutions of the real in the past: they record and then exhibit the past—a past that has never been, in the first instance, present. In this sense, film projects a totally imaginary relation to time and the world. For Metz, "What is characteristic of the cinema is not the imaginary that it may happen to represent, but the imaginary that it *is* from the start, the imaginary that constitutes it as a signifier."[70] As such an a priori expression of the imaginary, film calls into question the primacy of language in the constitution of the human world. This is because film simulates, in a manner to be discussed shortly, the effects of transference—the rapid movement of affect from one entity to another.

This is not to suggest that film determines a facile dialectic with language, that the properties of image, sense, and projection can be readily set against those of language, reason, and presence. Film does not replace language, for it cannot exist without it. Film displaces language, exposes the abyss that threatens to engulf every semantic signification. Film parasitizes language, much as the animal does, drawing into its imaginary panorama that which remains undisclosed in discursivity. Cinema is a parasite.

The *Oxford English Dictionary* places the first known usage of the word *anthropomorphism* in the context of "an injunction against attributing human traits to animals" in the second half of the nineteenth century.[71] (Until this referential shift, the word was used to indicate mistaken attributions of human qualities to deities.) It is during the nineteenth century, with the rise of modernism in literature and art, that animals came to occupy the thoughts of a culture in transition. As they disappeared, animals became increasingly the subjects of a nostalgic curiosity. When horse-drawn carriages gave way to steam engines, plaster horses were mounted on tramcar fronts in an effort to simulate continuity with the older, animal-driven vehicles. Once considered a metonymy of nature, animals came to be seen as emblems of the new, industrial environment. Animals appeared to merge with the new technological bodies replacing them. The idioms and histories of numerous technological innovations from the steam engine to quantum mechanics bear the traces of an incorporated animality. James Watt and later Henry Ford,[72] Thomas Edison,[73] Alexander Graham Bell,[74] Walt Disney, and Erwin Schrödinger,[75] among other key figures in the industrial and aesthetic shifts of the late nineteenth and early twentieth centuries, found uses for animal spirits in developing their respective machines, creating in the process a series of fantastic hybrids. Cinema, communication, transportation, and electricity drew from the actual and fantasmatic resources of dead animals. Technology, and more precisely the technological instruments and media of that time, began to serve as virtual shelters for displaced animals. In this manner, technology and ultimately the cinema came to determine a vast mausoleum for animal being.

Crypt

A PARADOX SURROUNDS animal death. Since animals are denied the faculties of language, they remain incapable of reflection, which is bound by finitude, and carries with it an awareness of death. Undying, animals simply expire, transpire, shift their animus to other animal bodies. Of the complete absence of death among animals, Bataille asserts: "Not only do animals not have this consciousness [of death], they can't even recognize the difference between the fellow creature that is dead and the one that is alive."[76] Animals thus function as the incarnation of a tech-nological fantasy—perpetual motion machines. Thomas Sebeok writes of the animal: "Whatever else an animal may be, it is clear that each is a living system, or subsystem, a complex array of atoms organized and maintained according to certain principles, the most important among these being negative entropy."[77] From the viewpoint of both quantum mechanics and meta-physics, animals appear capable of moving at will between the states of life and afterlife. By facilitating such perpetual engines, animals brought technology to life—the animal spirits that en-tered into the technological body turned technology into a species. Machines might fail, suffer, experience the breakdowns of exhaustion and confusion, but animated machinery as a *technogeny* would survive the demise of individual apparatuses.

In *The Wolf Man's Magic Word*, Abraham and Torok argue that Freud was unable to cure his famous Wolf Man patient, Sergei Pankeiev, because the latter had formed a crypt, a radi-cally other locus of subjectivity that could not be opened by the instrument of language.[78] Because the encrypted subject was not bound by language in the ordinary sense of the term (Pankeiev, according to the authors, had created a secret and absolutely singular idiom), he was not restricted by its finitudes. The Wolf Man was not mortal: he was incapable, according to the authors, of dying.

In presenting their theses on cryptic subjectivity—one that incorporates the other in its entirety without processing or in-tegrating its alterity—Abraham and Torok further enable the logic of an *illicit union* (Deleuze and Guattari's term) between technology and the animal. In this context, modern technology can be seen as a massive mourning apparatus, summoned to in-corporate a disappearing animal presence that could not be properly mourned because, following the paradox to its logical conclusion, animals could not die. It was necessary to find a place in which animal being could be transferred, maintained

in its distance from the world. Abraham and Torok's maintenance system in which the encrypted other is "crossed *out*,"
writes Derrida, "kept alive so as to be left for dead," resembles
Heidegger's crossed-through animal world.[79] As Leibniz writes
of animal death: "There is therefore no *metempsychosis*, but
there is *metamorphosis*."[80] If the animal cannot die but is
nonetheless vanishing, then it must be transferred to another
locus, another continuum in which death plays no role.
Animals must be transformed into cryptological artifacts.

The technological crypt resembles its psychic counterpart to
the extent that both preserve the radically absent other in a state
that can be defined as neither life nor death. Put another way,
the structure of the crypt preserves the presence of an absent
other that has never been present. Like Metz's cinema, which
records everything as a memory trace before it has been anything else, the crypt presents the absent other before it has ever
been present. This cryptological other has no world of its own,
appearing for the first time as an absent other in the crypt. This
is close to the complicated structure of world assigned to the
animal. It is thus perhaps more than mere coincidence that
Abraham and Torok find in the case of the Wolf Man the elements of a crypt.

Another factor links the crypt with technology and cinema.
The crypt itself is an effect of psychic *technē*. The crypt,
Derrida writes, is an "artificial unconscious"—the "Self's artifact."[81] Like Jean-Louis Baudry's notion of film, which induces
an artificial psychosis, Derrida's crypt establishes an artificial
unconscious—an artificial subjectivity.[82] Derrida describes the
unnatural topology of the crypt: "Carved out of nature, sometimes making use of probability or facts, these grounds are not
natural. A crypt is never natural through and through. . . . The
crypt is thus not a natural place [*lieu*], but the striking history
of an artifice, an *architecture*, an artifact.[83] Crypts are, according
to Derrida, technological in nature. They effect a technology of

the subject. The brutality of the cryptic artifact transforms the self into other, even as it transforms the other into self or subject. In the crypt, in the synthetic unconscious, the absent other becomes subject. Technology becomes a subject when it gains an unconscious; that artificial unconscious is established by the incorporation of vanishing animals.

Like the Wolf Man's irreducibly singular "verbarium"—his world composed of cryptonyms—technology also produces a structure and site of communication that avoid conventional language. In its most basic manifestation, electricity determines the currency of technological communication. (Recall Breuer's fixation on the electrical metaphor to describe the excitations that administer to the hypnoid state.) In the case of Freud's Wolf Man, the crypt is cracked by a dream, the Wolf Man's dream of "six or seven" white wolves on a tree.[84] In their analysis of this dream, Abraham and Torok suggest that the Russian word for window, *okno,* hinges upon a similar word for "'eye,' that is *oko* or *otch,* the root for its inflected forms."[85] The polysemic slide that Abraham and Torok discover is compelling not only because it marks the transition from organ (eye) to apparatus (window), perhaps even to the cinematic apparatus (lens), but also because it displays the method by which cryptonyms enter into the bodies of other words. Abraham and Torok write of the secret word or words that determine the crypt:

The key word, no doubt unutterable for some reason, and unknown for the moment, would have to be polysemic, expressing multiple meanings through a single phonetic structure. One of these would remain shrouded, but the other, or several other meanings now equivalent, would be stated through distinct phonetic structures, that is, through synonyms. To make our conversations about this easier, we would call them *cryptonyms* (words that hide) because of their allusion to a foreign and arcane meaning.[86]

Those synonyms or cryptonyms construct an unconscious dimension within the words that carry their meanings. Secret words travel parasitically from one host body to another in a movement that closely resembles transference. (In fact, as Abraham and Torok note, Freud and Otto Rank fought over the Wolf Man's dream. Freud trusted its authenticity; Rank claimed that the dream was a product of the patient's transference with Freud.)[87] The logic and history of transference carry the trace of animal magnetism into the psychoanalytic field. Transference is the means by which nonverbal energy circulates within the world.

Sandor Ferenczi defines transference as "[The] means by which long forgotten psychical experiences are (in the unconscious phantasy) brought into connection with the current reaction exaggerated by the affect of unconscious ideational complexes."[88] Laplanche and Pontalis add: "a particular instance of displacement of affect from one idea to another."[89] In *The Interpretation of Dreams,* Freud establishes the "indestructibility" of unconscious wishes or affects as the groundwork for transference. The reserved force of unexpressed desire is harnessed to various persons or acts that enter into the unconscious field and is released, in this manner, into the world. And because, like animals, unconscious wishes are indestructible, undying, they are recycled constantly throughout the world. Freud writes: "I consider that these unconscious wishes are always on the alert, ready at any time to find their way to expression when an opportunity arises for allying themselves with an impulse from the conscious and for transferring their own great intensity on to the latter's lesser one."[90] In this way, then, the affect is transferred from an inarticulate vehicle to a word, sign, or body. These affects operate like parasites, they are transferred by contact even when two conscious directives fail to reach an accord. Transference may thus take place even where communication does not—a kind of telepathy, or unmediated contact between metalinguistic forces.

In a footnote to the above passage, Freud follows the current of the perpetual unconscious affect through its metamorphic cycle. Of the perennial wishes that fill the reservoir of transferential activity, Freud writes:

They share this character of indestructibility with all other mental acts which are truly unconscious, i.e. which belong to the system *Ucs.* only. These are paths which have been laid down once and for all, which never fall into disuse and which, whenever an unconscious excitation re-cathects them, are always ready to conduct the excitatory process to discharge. *If I may use a simile, they are only capable of annihilation in the same sense as the ghosts in the underworld of the Odyssey—ghosts which awoke to new life as soon as they tasted blood.*[91]

Unconscious wishes, like phantom animals, cannot be destroyed. They lie dormant until another source awakens them. Because animals are unable to achieve the finitude of death, they are also destined to remain "live," like electrical wires, along the transferential tracks. Unable to die, they move constantly from one body to another, one system to another.

Cinema

In this glum desert, suddenly a specific photograph reaches me; it animates me, and I animate it. So that is how I must name the attraction which makes it exist: an animation.

—ROLAND BARTHES, "CAMERA LUCIDA:
REFLECTIONS ON PHOTOGRAPHY"

"CINEMA BEGINS," WRITES Sergei Eisenstein, "where the collision between different cinematic measures of movement and vibration begins."[92] A kind of origin of cinema, Eisenstein's assertion, like the writings of Dziga Vertov, Germaine Dulac, Antonin Artaud, and others who sought to discuss the new medium in ritual forms, bears the trace of an organic metaphor, an attempt to describe technological animation in animist terms. Much of Eisenstein's extensive writings on cinema are figured by an organic idiom. Describing the physiological status of cinema, Eisenstein writes:

> This montage is not constructed on the *individual dominant* but takes the sum of *stimuli* of all the stimulants as the dominant.
>
> That distinctive montage *complex within the shot* that arises from the collisions and combinations of the individual stimulants inherent within it,
>
> of stimulants that vary according to their "external nature" but are bound together in an iron unity through their reflex physiological essence.
>
> Physiological, in so far as the "psychic" in perception is merely the physiological process of a *higher nervous activity.*
>
> In this way the physiological sum total of the resonance of the shot *as a whole,* as a complex unity of all its component stimulants, is taken to be the general sign of the shot.
>
> This is the particular "feeling" of the shot that the shot as a whole produces . . .
>
> The *sum totals* thus achieved can be put together in any conflicting combination, thereby opening up quite new possibilities for montage resolution.
>
> As we have seen, because of the actual genetics of these methods, they must be accompanied by an extraordinary *physiological* quality.[93]

According to Eisenstein, the edit or montage of the scene is sustained only to a degree by the dominant stimulus of the shot.

With each edit, a multiplicity of extraneous information is also carried across the discursive threshold. A series of minor or imperceptible edits accompanies every major edit. Vertov refers to these minute edits as intervals: "*Intervals* (the transitions from one movement to another) are the material, the elements of the art of movement."[94] The intervals are like unconscious thoughts or genetic codes, passing like secrets through the dominant semiotics of the shot. Whether seen as psychology or physiology, Vertov and Eisenstein argue for a biology of the cinema, for an understanding of cinema as organism.

Referring to montage as hieroglyphic "copulation," Eisenstein extends the notion of film editing as a system that resembles the confluence of genes in organic reproduction. As each montage sequence within a film text combines with further and more detailed units of montage, the culminating effect of "their interrelationships . . . move[s] towards more refined variants of montage that flow organically from one another."[95] The term *organic* in Eisenstein's usage moves beyond the idiomatic nuance of a seamless flow to denote, rather, the transmission of complex data from one shot to another—all of which may not cross the viewer's perceptual threshold. According to Eisenstein's fantasy, filmic shots, like genetic structures, comprise dominant and recessive traits: when they are crossed, certain features are exposed upon the surface of the filmic body while others perform a subliminal function, sustaining the linkage between shots. Cinema cannot exhibit all of its features: as with any genetic code, certain materials are made manifest while other information remains recessed. For Eisenstein, the filmwork gradually evolves into a body distinguished by an exterior and interior dimension, if not by a conscious and unconscious capacity. Eisenstein brings his articulation of the cinema virtually to that of a biological organism. The characteristics with which he describes the medium, "reflex physiological essence" and "higher nervous activity," apply to the filmwork itself rather than to its spectator. One senses in Eisenstein's cinema a biomorphic hallucination. Films exist here as complex organisms—they have become animal, or animetaphor.

Eisenstein's animetaphor here functions as a technology, as do all instances of animetaphoricity. Despite the concept of nature it references, the animetaphor is itself profoundly unnatural, prosthetic, pressing the limits of world against the void. In an entirely different sense from that put forth by Descartes, the animal as figure functions as a technological trope, a technological index. The animal projects from a place that is not a place, a world that is not a world. A supplemental world that is, like the unconscious, like memory, magnetic in the technological sense. Thus when Freud speaks of the animal's dream, it is not a simple figure or illustration. His inability to know as such what animals dream of articulates concretely the very mechanism of dreams. One experiences the dream as a world under erasure; dreams mark the becoming-animal of human beings. And because dreams originate in a place that is not a place and arrive only as an originary translation or technological reproduction, they appear only within the frames of a mediating apparatus. Of Freud's dream logic, Derrida notes: "Everything begins with reproduction."[96] Derrida's mention of reproduction here refers not to the duplication of something that already exists, however, but rather to the introduction of something else, something other through a technology of representation. Regarding Freud's struggle to inscribe a metaphor for the apparatus of memory, Derrida stresses the inevitable turn in Freud's rhetoric from biological (1895) to technological (1925) figures. The *Wunderblock,* a fantastic machine that is not without its animal traces, evolves in Derrida's narrative from the organic memory cell. "Metaphor as a rhetorical or didactic device is possible here only through the solid metaphor, the 'unnatural,' historical production of a *supplementary* machine, *added to* the psychical organization in order to supplement its finitude."[97] In a similar manner, the animal as metaphor, the animetaphor, supplements the dream, language, and world systems, providing an external source of energy that charges the machine. The animetaphor is in this sense both alien and indispensable, an electromagnetic spirit that haunts the unconscious.

Thought of as technology, as a *technē* that opens worlds, the animetaphor operates like a fabulous machine. Trace and memory, Nietzschean amnesia or Heideggerian erasure, the discourse on the animal reveals at its origins a technological *atopia*—a world that, as Derrida claims, always begins on the occasion of its reproduction. Another apparatus, cinema, which arrives with psychoanalysis in 1895, provides, perhaps, the proper metaphor for the impossible metaphor, the animetaphor. The function of *unheimlich* reproduction, the vicissitudes of affect, the dynamics of animation and projection, the semiotics of magnetism, and the fundamental properties of memory can be seen as the basis of cinema, but also of the animal. Cinema is like an animal; the *likeness* a form of encryption. From animal to animation, figure to force, poor ontology to pure energy, cinema may be the technological metaphor that configures mimetically, magnetically, the other world of the animal.

One final speculation: the cinema developed, indeed embodied, animal traits as a gesture of mourning for the disappearing wildlife. The figure for nature in language, animal, was transformed in cinema to the name for movement in technology, animation. And if animals were denied the capacity for language, animals as filmic organisms were themselves turned into languages, or at least, into semiotic facilities. The medium provided an alternative to the natural environment that had been destroyed and a supplement to the discursive space that had never opened an ontology of the animal. In a radical departure from the framework of nature, the technological media commemorated and incorporated that which it had surpassed: the speechless semiotic of the animal look. Animal magnetism had moved from the hypnotist's eye to the camera eye, preserved in the emblematic lure of cinema. As a genre, animation—from Oskar Fischinger's spermatic ballets to Walt Disney's uncanny horde—encrypted the figure of the animal as its totem. Thomas Edison has left an animal electrocution on film, remarkable for the brutality of its fact and its mise-en-scène of the death of an animal. The single shot of an animated film–elephant collapsing from the surge of electrical current brings together the strange dynamic of life and death, representation and animal, semiotic and electricity. It is emblematic of the uncanniness of the medium. In the filmwork, one experiences the convergence of a traditional opposition between nature and artifice, *phusis* and *technē,* animal and technology. Cinema, then, can be seen as the simultaneous culmination and beginning of an evolutionary cycle: the narrative of the disappearance of animals and that of the rise of the technical media intersect in the cinema. The advent of cinema is thus haunted by the animal figure, driven, as it were, by the wildlife after death of the animal.

Notes

Introduction

01. John Berger, "Why Look at Animals?" in *About Looking* (New York: Vintage, 1980), 26.

02. The term *undead* appears most notably in Bram Stoker's 1897 *Dracula.* Michael Fried has suggested that the vampire can be seen as a super-animal, a being that dissolves the boundaries between human and animal existence. Moreover, Stoker's Dracula also possesses the ability to turn himself into various animals as well as to communicate with them. Stoker's supernatural figure can be read as following from the changed status of a modern animal being. Fried describes a series of painter-animal exchanges in Courbet's work, from the "brushness" of a horse's tail to Courbet's signature in the blood of a wounded animal (Fried, *Courbet's Realism* [Chicago: University of Chicago Press, 1990]).

03. Berger, "Why Look at Animals?" 21. Berger notes these founding dates for the following European metropolitan zoos: "the London Zoo in 1828, the Jardin des Plantes in 1793, the Berlin Zoo in 1844" (21).

04. Jacques Derrida, *Memoires for Paul de Man,* trans. Cecile Lindsay, Jonathan Culler, and Eduardo Cadava (New York: Columbia University Press, 1986), 60.

05. Rachel Wilder, "Rare Brain Disorder Sheds Light on How We Think," *Johns Hopkins Gazette,* 14 September 1992, 1.

06. David Clark, "On Being 'The Last Kantian in Nazi Germany': Dwelling with Animals after Levinas," in *Animal Acts: Configuring the Human in Western History,* ed. Jennifer Ham and Matthew Senior (New York: Routledge, 1997), 168.

07. It is worth noting that another form of encephalopathy, Bovine Spongiform Encephalopathy, or "mad cow disease," has raised further questions about the relationship between animals and human beings. The question of the transmission of this disease from animals to human beings focuses on the properties of the brain.

08. Wilder, "Rare Brain Disorder," 3. The full report by Hart and Barry Gordon, "Neural Subsystems for Object Knowledge," appears in *Nature,* 3 September 1992.

09. G. W. F. Hegel, "*Philosophy of Spirit,* Introduction," in *Hegel: The Essential Writings,* ed. Frederick G. Weiss, trans. William Wallace (New York: Harper and Row, 1974), 226. Hegel's own sympathies lie unquestionably with the agency of the mind. Further on, Hegel attempts to reconcile the self-constituting act and the self-sufficiency of the mind with its empirical counterpart, the natural organism: "Just as in the living organism generally, everything is already contained, in an ideal manner, in the germ and is brought forth by the germ itself, not by an alien power, so too must all the particular forms of living mind grow out of its Notion as from their germ" ("*Philosophy of Spirit,*" 230).

10. Wilder, "Rare Brain Disorder," 1–3.

11. Temple Grandin, *Thinking in Pictures: And Other Reports from My Life with Autism* (New York: Vintage, 1996), 19.

12. Ibid., 160.

13. Marc Shell, "Marranos (Pigs), or From Coexistence to Toleration," *Critical Inquiry* 17 (1991): 330. For Shell, the rise of bullfighting in Spain and its evolution into a national pastime serves not only "to define the difference between human kind and animal kind" but also "to fix ideologically the difference between national and nonnational" (ibid., 316–19).

14. Max Horkheimer and Theodor W. Adorno, *Dialectic of Enlightenment,* trans. John Cumming (New York: Continuum, 1972), 175. Emmanuel Levinas writes of the metamorphosis that was forced upon him by the gaze of "free" human beings while he was incarcerated in a Nazi prison camp. "But the other men, called free, who had dealings with us or gave us work or orders or even a smile—and the children and women who passed by and sometimes raised their eyes—stripped us of our human skin. We were subhuman, a gang of apes. A small inner murmur, the strength and wretchedness of persecuted people, reminded us of our essence as thinking creatures, but we were no longer part of the world. Our comings and goings, our sorrow and laughter, illness and distractions, the work of our hands and the anguish of our eyes, the letters we received from France and those accepted for our families—all that passed in parenthesis. We were beings entrapped in their species; despite all their vocabulary, beings without language" (Levinas, "The Name of a Dog, or Natural Rights," in *Difficult Freedom: Essays on Judaism,* trans. Seán Hand [Baltimore, Md.: Johns Hopkins University Press, 1990], 153). Levinas's compelling remarks show how the exclusion from free or full humanity inexorably thrusts one toward a discourse of animality: removed from the flow of human existence, one is forced to identify oneself with and as an animal—as a being without language.

15. Horkheimer and Adorno, *Dialectic of Enlightenment,* 245. Nietzsche criticizes the perverse appropriation of the doctrine that separates humanity from animals in his scathing indictment of Wagner, Schopenhauer, and Voltaire. Accusing these three of masking their contempt for other human beings, notably Jews, as kindness to animals, Nietzsche dissects the proximity of the separatist logic to zoophilic behavior. "Wagner is Schopenhauerian when he preaches mercy in our relations with animals. As we know, Schopenhauer's predecessor at this point was Voltaire who may already have mastered the art that we encounter among his successors — to dress up his hatred against certain things and people as mercy for animals" (Friedrich Nietzsche, *The Gay Science,* trans. Walter Kaufmann [New York: Vintage, 1974], 155). To this point, Horkheimer and Adorno add: "The Fascist's passionate interest in animals, nature, and children is rooted in the lust to persecute. The significance of the hand negligently stroking a child's head, or an animal's back, is that it could just as easily destroy them. One victim is fondly stroked shortly before the other is struck down, and the choice made has nothing to do with the victim's guilt. The petting demonstrates that all are equal in the presence of power, that none is a being in its own right" (*Dialectic of Enlightenment,* 253). Accordingly, the otherness of the animal allows one to love the other with the same annihilating force that one excludes it: love and hate are here facilitated by the ontological divide that separates human beings from all others — from animals, children, nature, Jews.

16. Georges Bataille, *The Tears of Eros,* trans. Peter Connor (San Francisco: City Lights, 1989), 35.

17. Ibid.

18. H. Kirchner, "Ein archäologischer Beitrag zur Urgeschichte des Schamanismus," in *Anthropos* 47 (1952).

19. Bataille, *Tears of Eros,* 37.

20. See, for example, Bataille's *Erotism: Death and Sensuality,* trans. Mary Dalwood (San Francisco: City Lights, 1986). In this work, Bataille glosses the traditional designation of the moment of *jouissance* as a "little death" *(le petite morte)* (170). In *The Tears of Eros,* Bataille adds: "If eroticism is viewed in the perspective of desire, independently of the possible birth of a child, it results in a loss, hence the paradoxically valid term 'little death'" (45).

21. U.S. Committee on the Use of Laboratory Animals in Biomedical and Behavioral Research, Commission on Life Sciences National Research Council, Institute of Medicine, *Use of Laboratory Animals in Biomedical and Behavioral Research* (Washington, D.C.: National Academy Press, 1988).

22. This comment was made during a discussion concerning the function of animal figures in philosophy. For a further analysis of the discursive complexity that permeates and impedes the construction of a history of philosophy, see Richard J. Bernstein, *The New Constellation: The Ethical-Political Horizons of Modernity/Postmodernity* (Cambridge: Polity, 1991).

23. Aesop himself has come to be seen in historical accounts as a *monstrous* figure: a deformed former slave and foreigner. Doubts remain as to the accuracy of this portrait, but clearly, in one form or another, Aesop has come to be identified with the bestial figures for which he is famous. See *Fables of Aesop,* trans. S. A. Handford (London: Penguin, 1954). Louis Marin explores the figure of Aesop and his relationship to speaking and eating in a chapter titled "The Fabulous Animal," from *Food for Thought,* trans. Mette Hjort (Baltimore, Md.: Johns Hopkins University Press, 1989), 44–54.

24. Donna J. Haraway, *Simians, Cyborgs, and Women: The Reinvention of Nature* (New York: Routledge, 1991), 11. See also Haraway, *Primate Visions: Gender, Race, and Nature in the World of Modern Science* (New York: Routledge, 1989).

25. Although the question of gender is important to any consideration of the discourse on animality, identity, and being, the present text will not engage the subject, since it forms, in essence, a topology of its own: the issue of gender and human ontology deserves a singular and sustained focus, and cannot be adequately addressed from the margins of another locus. Comments on gender, as well as other relevant concerns that emerge from the figure of the animal—race, cybernetics, infancy, monstrosity, and extraterrestrial being—will be limited to the specific instances in which they arise. Haraway's analyses of zoological research and women's studies perhaps best address the issue of zoomorphology and feminism, and the ways in which the two disciplines intersect and collide. See also Judith Butler, *Gender Trouble: Feminism and the Subversion of Identity* (New York: Routledge, 1990).

26. For a thorough explication and critique of language theory and subjectivity, see Jacques Derrida, *Limited Inc,* ed. Gerald Graff, trans. Samuel Weber (Evanston, Ill.: Northwestern University Press, 1988).

27. See, in particular, Jacques Derrida, *Of Grammatology,* trans. Gayatri Chakravorty Spivak (Baltimore, Md.: Johns Hopkins University Press, 1974); and Derrida, *Writing and Difference,* trans. Alan Bass (Chicago: University of Chicago Press, 1978).

28. Jacques Derrida, "L'animal que donc je suis," presentation, Cerisy-la-Salle, July 1997 (in *L'animal autobiographique,* ed. Marie-Louise Mallet [Paris: Galilée, 1999], 251–301).

29. René Descartes, "Discourse on the Method," in *Descartes: Selected Philosophical Writings,* trans. John Cottingham, Robert Stoothoff and Dugald Murdoch (Cambridge: Cambridge University Press, 1988), 44. Descartes's hostile statements toward animals are notorious and are frequently cited. According to Sarah Kofman, however, Descartes's "cogito" locked him within a machinery that transformed the renowned skeptic into a kind of animal or automaton: "Like a clumsy animal, . . . he [Descartes] remained caught in this trap, and never escaped from it" (Kofman, "Descartes Entrapped," trans. Kathryn Aschheim, in *Who Comes after the Subject?* ed. Eduardo Cadava, Peter Connor, Jean-Luc Nancy [New York: Routledge, 1991], 181).

30. Apropos of Lacan's attempt to recapitulate the metaphysical lineage in the agency of the *objet petit à,* Derrida writes in *"La Facteur de la Vérité"*: "This link is more visible, if not looked upon more highly, in the conglomeration of statements about 'animality,' about the distinction between animal and human language, etc. This discourse on the animal (in general) is no doubt consistent with all the categories and operations of the bi- or tri-partitions of the system. And it condenses no less the system's greatest obscurity. The treatment of animality, as of everything that finds itself in submission by virtue of a hierarchical opposition, has always, in the history of (humanist and phallogocentric) metaphysics, revealed obscurantist resistance" (in *The Post Card: From Socrates to Freud and Beyond,* trans. Alan Bass [Chicago: University of Chicago Press, 1987], 474n). Derrida is referring to passages in which Lacan distinguishes speech from language in the discourse of the other, which is ultimately a discourse of subjectivity. For Lacan, speech marks the human subject as such by "always subjectively includ[ing] its own reply" (Jacques Lacan, "The Function and Field of Speech and Language in Psychoanalysis," in *Écrits: A Selection,* trans. Alan Sheridan [New York: W. W. Norton, 1977], 85). Derrida takes issue with Lacan's system, claiming it reinscribes a residual and circular metaphysics that seeks to limit the universe of discursive exchange to that of human beings.

31. Jacques Derrida, "'Eating Well,' or The Calculation of the Subject: An Interview with Jacques Derrida," trans. Peter Connor and Avital Ronell, in Cadava, Connor, and Nancy, *Who Comes after the Subject?* 116. Derrida gives this compelling response to Jean-Luc Nancy's question: "In the shift that you judge to be necessary, from man to animal —I am expressing myself very quickly and crudely—what happens to language?" (Derrida, "Eating Well," 116).

32. See Sigmund Freud, "Mourning and Melancholia," in *The Standard Edition of the Complete Psychological Works of Sigmund Freud,* ed. and trans. James Strachey, 24 vols. (London: Hogarth Press and the Institute of Psycho-Analysis, 1957), 14:243–58.

33. Ibid., 14:251–52.

34. Michel Foucault, *The Order of Things: An Archaeology of the Human Sciences* (New York: Vintage, 1970).

35. Ibid., 308–9. Foucault writes: "[Man] is a quite recent creature, which the demiurge of knowledge fabricated with its own hands less than two hundred years ago: but he has grown old so quickly that it has been only too easy to imagine that he had been waiting for thousands of years in the darkness for that moment of illumination in which he would finally be known" (ibid., 308).

36. Carl G. Jung, "Approaching the Unconscious," in *Man and His Symbols,* ed. Carl G. Jung (New York: Dell, 1964), 85.

37. Jean-François Lyotard, "Can Thought Go On without a Body?" in *The Inhuman: Reflections on Time,* trans. Geoffrey Bennington and Rachel Bowlby (Stanford, Calif.: Stanford University Press, 1991), 10.

38. Giorgio Agamben, *The Coming Community,* trans. Michael Hardt (Minneapolis: University of Minnesota Press, 1993), 93.

39. Ibid., 90.

40. Ibid., 93. Agamben makes a compelling point concerning human ethics and the transcendence of animal habits or habitats, alluding to the etymological link between *ethos* and the animal den. On the notion of using oneself as the basis to bring oneself forth, or engender oneself, Agamben writes: "Perhaps the only way to understand this free *use of the self,* a way that does not, however treat existence as property, is to think of it as a *habitus,* an *ethos.* Being engendered from one's own manner of being is, in effect, the very definition of habit (this is why the Greeks spoke of a second nature): *That manner is ethical that does not befall us and does not found us but engenders us.* And this being engendered from one's own manner is the only happiness really possible for humans" (ibid., 28–29).

41. Jacques Derrida, "How to Avoid Speaking: Denials," in *Derrida and Negative Theology,* ed. Harold Coward and Toby Foshay, trans. Ken Frieden (Albany: State University of New York Press, 1992), 86–87. Derrida adds, however, that this view is built upon a "naive philosophy of the animal world" and pertains only to the secrecies of human language and consciousness. He points to "the possibility of a preverbal or simply nonverbal secret—linked, for example, to gestures or to mimicry, and even to other codes and more generally to the unconscious" (ibid., 87).

42. Jean-François Lyotard, "The Inarticulate, or The Differend Itself." The text comes from a lecture given at the Whitney Humanities Center at Yale University in 1992. Lyotard defines "passivity" as a condition in which matter—affects, thoughts, sensations—pass through a body without being altered or transformed by subjective forces. Animals and infants, Lyotard claims, are most often identified with this condition.

1. Philosophy and the Animal World

01. Edgar Allan Poe, "The Murders in the Rue Morgue," in *Great Tales and Poems of Edgar Allan Poe* (New York: Washington Square, 1951), 111.

02. Ibid., 112.

03. Ibid., 134.

04. For a further discussion of Aristotle and animality, see Richard Sorabji, *Animal Minds and Human Morals: The Origins of the Western Debate* (Ithaca, N.Y.: Cornell University Press, 1993). According to Sorabji, "a crisis both for the philosophy of mind and for theories of morality" was provoked when Aristotle "denied reason to animals" (ibid., 7).

05. Aristotle, "Politics," in *The Complete Works of Aristotle,* ed. Jonathan Barnes, trans. B. Jowett, 2 vols. (Princeton, N.J.: Princeton University Press, 1984), 2:1988.

06. Poe, "Rue Morgue," 131 (emphasis added).

07. Ibid., 123–24.

08. Jean-Jacques Rousseau, "Essay on the Origin of Languages Which Treats of Melody and Musical Imitation," in *On the Origin of Language,* trans. John H. Morgan (Chicago: University of Chicago Press, 1966), 5. Derrida deconstructs Rousseau's nature and its supplementary language in his seminal *Of Grammatology,* trans. Gayatri Chakravorty Spivak (Baltimore, Md.: Johns Hopkins University Press, 1974).

09. Jacques Derrida, "How to Avoid Speaking: Denials," in *Derrida and Negative Theology,* ed. Harold Coward and Toby Foshay, trans. Ken Frieden (Albany: State University of New York Press, 1992). "Some would say, perhaps imprudently, that only man is capable of speaking, because only he can *not* show what he could show. Of course, an animal may inhibit a movement, can abstain from an incautious gesture, for example in a defensive or offensive predatory strategy, such as in the delimitation of sexual territory or in a mating ritual. One might say, then, that animals can *not* respond to the inquisition or requisition of a stimulus or of a complex of stimuli. According to this somewhat naive philosophy of the animal world, one may nevertheless observe that animals are incapable of keeping or even having a secret,

because they cannot *represent as such,* as an *object* before consciousness, something that they would then forbid themselves from showing" (ibid., 86–87).

10. Ibid., 87.

11. Aristotle, "Politics," 2:1988. Jean-François Lyotard has explicated this passage from Aristotle in his 1992 seminar on "affective phrasing" at Yale University. Lyotard explains that although the signaling of affect is common to both human beings and animals, affects themselves are incommunicable and, as such, remain beyond the confines of discourse. Because pleasure and pain are whole and complete ("achieved," claims Lyotard, citing Aristotle), they do not exist, so to speak, in time.

12. Derrida, *Grammatology,* 166. For further discussion on this topic see Derrida's comments in "The Voice That Keeps Silence," in *Speech and Phenomena: And Other Essays on Husserl's Theory of Signs,* trans. David B. Allison (Evanston, Ill.: Northwestern University Press, 1973), 70–87.

13. Jacques Derrida, "Plato's Pharmacy," in *Dissemination,* trans. Barbara Johnson (Chicago: University of Chicago Press, 1981), 79.

14. René Descartes, "Discourse on the Method," in *Descartes: Selected Philosophical Writings,* trans. John Cottingham, Robert Stoothoff, and Dugald Murdoch (Cambridge: Cambridge University Press, 1988), 45.

15. Ibid.

16. Ibid. With an eye toward psychoanalytic discourse, Peirce offers this critique of Descartes's metaphysics: "Descartes was of the opinion that animals were unconscious automata. He might as well have thought that all men but himself were unconscious" (Charles Sanders Peirce, "Minute Logic," in *Peirce on Signs: Writings on Semiotic by Charles Sanders Peirce,* ed. James Hoopes [Chapel Hill: University of North Carolina Press, 1991], 234).

17. Although Descartes strictly separates human beings from animals over the question of language, he suggests a similarity between the two species with regard to visuality and optics. In his 1637 treatise "Optics," Descartes suggests an experiment in order to confirm that "the objects we look at do imprint quite perfect images of themselves on the back of our eyes." The first stage of the investigation requires the construction of a camera obscura in order to simulate the function of the eye. The second stage calls for the researcher to obtain the eye of a dead person or animal. Descartes initiates the experiment by "taking the eye of a newly dead person (or failing that, the eye of an ox or some other large animal)" ("Optics," in *Descartes: Selected Philosophical Writings,* 63). Descartes concludes the macabre scene: "Now, when you have seen this picture in the eye of a dead animal, and considered its causes, you can-

not doubt that a quite similar picture is formed in the eye of a living person, on the internal membrane for which we substituted the white body—indeed, a much better one is formed there *since the humours in this eye are full of animal spirits*" (ibid., emphasis added).

18. Gottfried Wilhelm Leibniz, "Principles of Nature and Grace, Based on Reason," in *Philosophical Essays,* ed. and trans. Roger Ariew and Daniel Garber (Indianapolis: Hackett, 1989), 209. Leibniz restates this position in "Monadology": "I have therefore, held that if the animal never begins naturally, it does not end naturally, either; and not only will there be no generation, but also no complete destruction, nor any death, strictly speaking" (ibid., 223).

19. Gottfried Wilhelm Leibniz, "A New System of the Nature and Communication of Substances, and of the Union of the Soul and Body," in *Philosophical Essays,* 141.

20. Jean-Luc Nancy, *The Inoperative Community,* ed. and trans. Peter Connor (Minneapolis: University of Minnesota Press, 1991), 13.

21. Leibniz, "Principles of Nature and Grace," 208.

22. Ibid., 209 (emphasis added).

23. Ibid., 208–9.

24. Arthur Schopenhauer, "The Indestructibility of Being," in *Essays and Aphorisms,* ed. and trans. R. J. Hollingdale (New York: Penguin, 1970), 70.

25. Ibid.

26. Ibid., 76. Schopenhauer goes on to claim that this desire to survive, to be aware of one's own continued survival, "arises not from the individuality but from *existence* as such, is intrinsic to everything that *exists* and is indeed the reason *why* it exists, and it is consequently satisfied by existence *as such:* it is this alone to which this desire applies, and not exclusively to some particular existence. That which desires existence so impetuously is only *indirectly* the individual!"

27. Ibid., 71. In *The Gay Science,* Nietzsche extends Schopenhauer's consciousness into the realm of language. Retaining the idea of the sociality of consciousness, Nietzsche insists that consciousness arises from the physiological necessities of communication and not from the metaphysics of language. The distinction is crucial, for it marks one of the transitions from a philosophical discourse to an evolutionary one. Nietzsche writes that "*consciousness has developed only under the pressure of the need for communication;* that from the start it was needed and useful only between human beings (particularly between those who commanded and those who obeyed); and that it also developed in pro-

portion to the degree of this utility. Consciousness is really only a net of communication between human beings; it is only as such that it had to develop; a solitary human being who lived like a beast of prey would not have needed it. That our actions, thoughts, feelings, and movements enter our own consciousness—at least a part of them—that is a result of a 'must' that for a terribly long time lorded it over man. As the most endangered animal, he *needed* help and protection, he needed his peers, he had to learn to express his distress and make himself understood; and for all of this he needed 'consciousness' first of all, he needed to know himself what distressed him, he needed to 'know' how he felt, he needed to 'know' what he thought. For, to say it once more: Man, like every living being, thinks continually without knowing it; the thinking that rises to consciousness is only the smallest part of this—the most superficial and worst part—for only this conscious thinking *takes the form of words, which is to say signs of communication,* and this fact uncovers the origin of consciousness" (*The Gay Science,* trans. Walter Kaufmann [New York: Vintage, 1974], 298–99).

28. Schopenhauer, "Indestructibility of Being," 72.

29. Ibid., 73.

30. Ibid., 74.

31. Jean-Jacques Rousseau, "Discourse on the Origin of Inequality," in *Basic Political Writings of Jean-Jacques Rousseau,* ed. and trans. Donald A. Cress (Indianapolis: Hackett, 1987), 44–45.

32. Ibid., 45. Rousseau refuses to grant the openness of the future to the animal. Unable to perfect itself, the animal cannot partake, according to Rousseau, in the going-to-be of the future. In a statement made obsolete by the theory of evolution, Rousseau writes: "An animal, at the end of a few months, is what it will be all its life; and its species, at the end of a thousand years, is what it was in the first of those thousand years" (ibid.).

33. Ibid., 46.

34. Ibid.

35. Derrida, *Grammatology,* 182.

36. Ibid., 184.

37. Rousseau, "Origin of Inequality," 49.

38. Ibid.

39. Immanuel Kant, "Conjectural Beginning of Human History," in *Kant: On History,* ed. Lewis White Beck, trans. Lewis White Beck, Robert E. Anchor, and Emil L. Fackenheim (New York: Macmillan, 1963), 54.

40. Ibid.

41. Kant is here returning to an Aristotelian formulation in which, as Derrida points out, "only man is capable of *mimesis.*" For a discussion of the mimetic economy that traverses Kantian aesthetics and the animal kingdom, see Derrida, "Economimesis," *Diacritics* 11 (1981): 3–25.

42. G. W. F. Hegel, *Jenenser Realphilosophie,* cited in Giorgio Agamben, *Language and Death: The Place of Negativity,* trans. Karen E. Pinkus with Michael Hardt (Minneapolis: University of Minnesota Press, 1991), 43.

43. Schopenhauer, "Indestructibility of Being," 72–73.

44. Edmund Burke, *A Philosophical Enquiry into the Origin of Our Ideas of the Sublime and Beautiful,* ed. J. T. Boulton (Notre Dame, Ind.: University of Notre Dame Press, 1958), 57.

45. Ibid.

46. Ibid., 84 (emphasis added). Burke adds: "Unless it be the well known voice of some creature, on which we are used to look with contempt." Its unfamiliarity is therefore essential to its evocative value. Precluding the appearance of hysteria, Burke's "great ideas" also signal the hypnoid phenomena that Josef Breuer terms "unconscious ideas" (Josef Breuer and Sigmund Freud, *Studies on Hysteria,* ed. and trans. James Strachey, *SE* 2).

47. Burke, *Sublime and Beautiful,* 84.

48. Hegel, *Jenenser Realphilosophie,* cited in Agamben, *Language and Death,* 45. For a further discussion of the Hegelian voice, see Jacques Derrida, "The Pit and the Pyramid: Introduction to Hegel's Semiology," in *Margins of Philosophy,* trans. Alan Bass (Chicago: University of Chicago Press, 1982), 69–108.

49. Agamben, *Language and Death,* 45.

50. Ibid., 46.

51. G. W. F. Hegel, *Phenomenology of Spirit,* trans. A. V. Miller (Oxford: Oxford University Press, 1977), 51.

52. Alexandre Kojève, *Introduction to the Reading of Hegel: Lectures on the "Phenomenology of Spirit,"* ed. Allan Bloom, trans. James H. Nichols Jr. (Ithaca, N.Y.: Cornell University Press, 1969), 140.

53. Ibid., 141.

54. Ibid.

55. Derrida, "Otobiographies," in *The Ear of the Other,* ed. Christie V. McDonald, trans. Peggy Kamuf and Avital Ronell (New York: Schocken, 1985), 7.

56. Jean-François Lyotard, "The Inarticulate, or The Differend Itself."

57. Ibid.

58. In the "Nicomachean Ethics," Aristotle writes that pleasure "is a whole, and at no time can one find a pleasure whose form will be completed if the pleasure lasts longer. For this reason, too, it is not a movement. . . . it is not possible to move otherwise than in time, but it *is* possible to be pleased; for that which takes place in a moment is a whole" (in *Complete Works*, trans. W. D. Ross, revised by J. D. Urmson, 2:1858).

59. Lyotard, "Inarticulate."

60. Ibid. Hegel also describes the enclosed world of inarticulate phrases that, as Lyotard insists, does not open onto a universe of communication. On the intrusion of the voice of consciousness into the animal's affective muteness, Hegel writes: "The empty voice of the animal acquires a meaning that is infinitely determinate in itself. The pure sound of the voice, the vowel, is differentiated since the organ of the voice presents its articulation as a particular articulation with its differences. This pure sound is interrupted by mute [consonants], the true and proper arrestation of mere resonation" (*Jenenser Realphilosophie,* cited in Agamben, *Language and Death,* 44). Agamben explains that the consonant creates alternation in an attempt to preserve, through sublation, the "mere resonance" of the animal cry: "What is articulated here? Hegel responds: the 'pure sound' of the animal voice, the vowel that is interrupted and arrested through mute consonants. The articulation appears, that is, as a process of differentiation, of interruption and preservation of the animal voice" (*Language and Death,* 44).

61. See Jean-François Lyotard, *The Differend: Phrases in Dispute,* trans. Georges Van Den Abbeele (Minneapolis: University of Minnesota Press, 1988).

62. Lyotard, "Inarticulate." Leibniz also questions the possibility of an empty body. "If there were no souls or something analogous to them, then there would be no I [*Ego*], no monads, no real unities, and therefore there would be no substantial multitudes; indeed there would be nothing in bodies but phantasms" (Leibniz, "From the Letters to Johann Bernoulli," in *Philosophical Essays,* 167).

63. George Boas, "Theriophily," in *Dictionary of the History of Ideas,* ed. Philip P. Wiener, 5 vols. (New York: Scribners, 1973), 4:384–89.

64. Boas recounts the famous episode: "Chrysippus' dog, . . . looking for its master in a wood, comes to a triple fork. He sniffs down two of the branches and finds no scent of his master. He then without sniffing darts down the third branch, thus proving his reasoning powers" ("Theriophily," 384). According to Montaigne, dogs grieve, mourn, and dream as do horses; tortoises and ostriches hatch their eggs with "ejaculative"

glances. And cats, in Montaigne's notes, can fell their prey with lethal and insistent looks (Michel de Montaigne, "Of the Power of the Imagination," in *The Complete Essays of Montaigne*, trans. Donald Frame [Stanford, Calif.: Stanford University Press, 1943], 74–75). Throughout his work Montaigne argues that animals possess various imaginative skills that both align them with and differentiate them from human beings. A version of Montaigne's belief in animal imagination returns in Jakob von Uexküll's twentieth-century studies of the animal *Umwelt*. See in this connection Pierre Alferi, *Le Chemin familier du poisson combatif* (Paris: P.O.L., 1992).

65. Michel de Montaigne, "Apology for Raymond Sebond," in *Complete Essays*, 335.

66. Of the evident similarity between animals and human beings, Montaigne explains: "There is no apparent reason to judge that the beasts do by natural and obligatory instinct the same things that we do by our choice and cleverness. We must infer from like results like faculties, and consequently confess that this same reason, this same method that we have for working, is also that of the animals. Why do we imagine in them this compulsion of nature, we who feel no similar effect?" ("Apology," 336–37).

67. Pliny the Elder, *Natural History: A Selection*, trans. John F. Healy (New York: Penguin, 1991), 74.

68. Ibid.

69. Nietzsche, *On the Genealogy of Morals*, trans. Walter Kaufmann (New York: Random House, 1967), 85. In a different context, Locke and Kant connect the sundering of humanity from its animal past, from nature, to the question of ethics. Decrying the cruelty that human beings regularly exhibit toward their own young, Locke writes: "The Dens of Lions and Nurseries of Wolves know no such Cruelty as this: These Savage Inhabitants of the Desert obey God and Nature in being tender and careful of their Off-spring: They will Hunt, Watch, Fight, and almost Starve for the Preservation of their Young, never part with them, never forsake them till they are able to shift for themselves; And is it the Privilege of Man alone to act more contrary to Nature than the Wild and most Untamed part of the Creation?" (John Locke, *Two Treatises of Government* [Cambridge: Cambridge University Press, 1960], 217). In *The Metaphysics of Morals*, Kant also makes reference to animal virtues: "The *first*, though not the principal, duty of man to himself as an animal being is to *preserve himself* in his animal nature" (Immanuel Kant, *The Metaphysics of Morals*, trans. Mary Gregor

[Cambridge: Cambridge University Press, 1991], 218). Nietzsche insists upon the necessity of overcoming, of surviving that dialectic of melancholia. For Nietzsche, melancholia can be surpassed only when humanity can promise itself futurity, that is, promise itself the right to make promises. He poses the following challenge: "To breed an animal *with the right to make promises*— is not this the paradoxical task that nature has set itself in the case of man? is it not the real problem regarding man?" (*Genealogy of Morals,* 57).

2. Afterthoughts on the Animal ~~World~~

01. Heidegger, "The Origin of the Work of Art," in *Poetry, Language, Thought,* trans. Albert Hofstadter (New York: Harper and Row, 1971), 44–45 (emphasis added). For an extensive reading of Heidegger's philosophy of world, see Philippe Lacoue-Labarthe, *Heidegger, Art, and Politics,* trans. Chris Turner (Cambridge: Basil Blackwell, 1990). See also in this connection Richard J. Bernstein, "Heidegger's Silence? *Ethos* and Technology," in *The New Constellation: The Ethical-Political Horizons of Modernity/Postmodernity* (Cambridge: Polity, 1991), 79–141.

02. Heidegger, "Origin of the Work of Art," 73.

03. Martin Heidegger, "The Thing," in *Poetry, Language, Thought,* 178.

04. Martin Heidegger, "The Nature of Language," in *On the Way to Language,* trans. Peter D. Hertz (New York: Harper and Row, 1971), 107. In *Being and Time,* Heidegger distinguishes between the "biological-ontical" death of "animals and plants" (those deaths measured in "longevity, propagation and growth") and the ontological death of *Dasein.* "The ending of that which lives we have called 'perishing.' Dasein too 'has' its death, of the kind appropriate to anything that lives; and it has it, not in ontical isolation, but as codetermined by its primordial kind of Being" (Heidegger, *Being and Time,* trans. John Macquarrie and Edward Robinson [New York: Harper and Row, 1962], 290–91). Derrida critiques Heidegger's "flash in the sky concerning a link between the *as such* of death and language" in *Aporias.* "Against, or without, Heidegger, one could point to a thousand signs that show that animals also *die.* Although the innumerable structural differences that separate one 'species' from another should make us vigilant about any discourse on animality or bestiality *in general,* one can say that animals have a very significant relation to death, to murder and to war (hence, to borders), to mourning and to hospitality, and so forth, even if they have neither a relation to death nor to the 'name' of death as such, nor, by the same token, to the other as such (Derrida, *Aporias,* trans. Thomas Dutoit [Stanford, Calif.: Stanford University Press, 1993], 75–76).

05. Martin Heidegger, *An Introduction to Metaphysics,* trans. Ralph Manheim (New York: Doubleday, 1961), 37.

06. Martin Heidegger, *The Fundamental Concepts of Metaphysics: World, Finitude, Solitude,* trans. William McNeill and Nicholas Walker (Bloomington: Indiana University Press, 1995), 177.

07. Jacques Derrida, *Of Spirit: Heidegger and the Question,* trans. Geoffrey Bennington and Rachel Bowlby (Chicago: University of Chicago Press, 1989), 49. Concerning the question of degree, or descent, Heidegger insists: "When we ask this question concerning the relation between man and animal we cannot therefore be concerned with deciding whether man is descended from the ape. For we cannot begin to pose this question, let alone answer it, until we clearly appreciate what the distinction between them is and how this distinction should be drawn. And this does not mean finding out how humans and animals are distinguished from one another in this or that particular respect. It means finding out what constitutes the *essence of the animality* of the animal and the *essence of the humanity* of man and through what sorts of questions we can hope to pinpoint the essence of such beings at all" (*Fundamental Concepts of Metaphysics,* 179).

08. Jacques Derrida, "'Eating Well,' or The Calculation of the Subject: An Interview with Jacques Derrida," in *Who Comes after the Subject?* ed. Eduardo Cadava, Peter Connor, and Jean-Luc Nancy, trans. Peter Connor and Avital Ronell (New York: Routledge, 1991), 112.

09. Derrida, *Of Spirit,* 50.

10. Heidegger, *Fundamental Concepts of Metaphysics,* 199. On the apparent paradox, Heidegger claims: "This is contradictory and thus logically impossible. But metaphysics and everything essential has a logic quite different from that of sound common understanding. If these propositions concerning the having and not-having of world in relation to the animal are legitimate, then we must be employing the ideas of world and accessibility of beings in a different sense in each case. In other words, the concept of world has still not been clarified. We cannot as yet see our way forward on account of the obscurity of this concept. Nevertheless we have found the place where such elucidation must begin and have identified the knot which we must first thrive to undo" (ibid.). For Heidegger, then, access to world first requires a navigation through the animal's other world.

11. Derrida, *Of Spirit,* 51.

12. Johann Gottfried Herder, "Essay on the Origin of Language," in *On the Origin of Language,* trans. John H. Morgan and Alexander Gode (Chicago: University of Chicago Press, 1966), 108.

13. Derrida, *Of Spirit,* 53. Derrida quotes the passage in which Heidegger proposes erasure as a means of distinguishing *weltbildend* from *weltarm:* "When we say that the lizard is stretched out on the rock, we should cross through (*durchstreichen*) the word 'rock,' to indicate that while what the lizard is stretched out on is doubtless given him in *some way* (*irgendwie,* italicized), it is not known [or recognized] *as* (*als,* italicized) rock. The crossing-through does not only mean: something else is apprehended, as something else, but: it is above all not accessible as entity (*überhaupt nicht* als Seiendes *zugänglich*)" (52–53).

14. Ibid., 53.

15. Ibid., 52.

16. Derrida, "Eating Well," 111.

17. Martin Heidegger, "What Are Poets For?" in *Poetry, Language, Thought,* 96. For a more sustained examination of Heidegger's thoughts on Rilke, poetry, and animal ontology, see Véronique M. Fóti, *Heidegger and the Poets: Poiesis/Sophia/Techne* (New Jersey: Humanities, 1992).

18. Heidegger, "What Are Poets For?" 99.

19. Ibid., 103.

20. Ibid., 99.

21. Ibid., 108 (emphasis added).

22. Ibid., 134–35. Some years later, Wittgenstein questions the relation between hope and language, between being and humanity's exclusive capacity for the future. "One can imagine an animal angry, frightened, unhappy, happy, startled. But hopeful? And why not? A dog believes his master is at the door. But can he also believe his master will come the day after to-morrow?—And *what* can he not do here?—How do I do it?—How am I supposed to answer this? Can only those hope who can talk? Only those who have mastered the use of a language. That is to say, the phenomena of hope are modes of this complicated form of life" (Ludwig Wittgenstein, *Philosophical Investigations,* trans. G. E. M. Anscombe [New York: Macmillan, 1958], 174).

23. Aristotle, "Metaphysics," in *Complete Works,* trans. W. D. Ross, 2:1552.

24. Heidegger, "What Are Poets For?" 142.

25. Ibid., 110.

26. Rainer Maria Rilke, "Duino Elegies," in *The Selected Poetry of Rainer Maria Rilke,* ed. and trans. Stephen Mitchell (New York: Harper and Row, 1982), 192–97.

27. Friedrich Nietzsche, "On the Uses and Disadvantages of History for Life," in *Untimely Meditations,* trans. R. J. Hollingdale (Cambridge:

Cambridge University Press, 1983), 60–61. In a related thought, Wittgenstein has made the famous remark, "If a lion could talk, we could not understand him" (*Philosophical Investigations,* 223). Richard Macksey glosses this passage in his keynote address that commences the "Structuralist Controversy" in 1966. In "Lions and Squares: Opening Remarks," Macksey writes of Wittgenstein's line: "The philosopher is clearly not talking about 'cracking the code' of lions or dolphins, but of the impossibility of apprehending any language unless we have some access to the speaker's *Lebensform.* Clearly, what is in question here is not the 'form of life' peculiar to zoologists or lion-tamers, who might be expected to know *something* about lions, but of the form of life defined by a lion's view of the world" (in *The Structuralist Controversy: The Languages of Criticism and the Sciences of Man,* ed. Richard Macksey and Eugenio Donato [Baltimore, Md.: Johns Hopkins University Press, 1970], 13–14).

28. In his *Philosophical Investigations,* Wittgenstein continues this line of thinking. Replacing the question of capacity with one of desire or simple pragmatics, he writes: "It is sometimes said that animals do not talk because they lack the mental capacity. And this means: 'they do not think, and that is why they do not talk.' But—they simply do not talk. Or to put it better: they do not use language—if we accept the most primitive forms of language. –Commanding, questioning, recounting, chatting are as much a part of our natural history as walking, eating, drinking, playing" (Wittgenstein, *Philosophical Investigations,* 12). Following Wittgenstein's analysis, another natural history must be written for animals.

29. This logic concerning language and the animal in Nietzsche is derived from Derrida's reading of Nietzsche, "woman," and the politics of castration. In *Spurs,* Derrida explains: "'Woman'—her name made epoch—no more believes in castration's exact opposite, anti-castration, than she does in castration itself" (*Spurs: Nietzsche's Styles,* trans. Barbara Harlow [Chicago: University of Chicago Press, 1979], 61). "Woman," according to Derrida, plays with castration, with the economy to which "she" is not bound.

30. Nietzsche, "Uses and Disadvantages of History for Life," 61.

31. Friedrich Nietzsche, *Ecce Homo,* ed. and trans. Walter Kaufmann (New York: Vintage, 1967), 303. Earlier in *Ecce Homo,* Nietzsche confides that his pregnancy with *Zarathustra* had lasted eighteen months. This "might suggest," Nietzsche writes, "at least to Buddhists, that I am really a female elephant" (ibid., 295).

32. Martin Heidegger, *Nietzsche: The Eternal Recurrence of the Same,* trans. David Farrell Krell, 4 vols. (San Francisco: Harper and Row, 1984), 2:48. Albert Liu has suggested the existence of another contradiction or abyss in Heidegger's recourse to the idiom of "sensuous imagery." Heidegger intimates, Liu argues, that animals speak "out of their natures" and with "sensuous imagery." "Does this constitute a having-language? If only those who have the 'constructive energy' can understand animals, then perhaps, in general, human beings are *language-poor,* even though it is language which gives them world" (Albert Liu, letter to author, 14 January 1999). For Liu, Heidegger's expressive supplement indicates the possibility of a third term in the dialectic of language and affect. "It is interesting that the question revolves around the Kantian faculty of the *Productive Imagination,* which was the crux of Heidegger's interpretation of the third critique in his 1929 debate with Ernst Cassirer at Davos. *Imagination* (and *projection*) could be a third term here in your discussion of the limits of *language* and *affect.* More importantly, perhaps the 'language of sensuous imagery' can be seen as another prefiguration of cinema."

33. Heidegger, *Nietzsche,* 2:49.

34. Ibid., 2:45. In this same passage Heidegger quotes a line that was later expunged from Nietzsche's preface to *Twilight of the Idols:* "*His love of animals*—men have always recognized the solitary by means of this trait." Regarding Nietzsche's notion of an "individuality" that arises from a force in excess of "totality and subjectivity," see Werner Hamacher, "'Disgregation of the Will': Nietzsche on the Individual and Individuality," in *Reconstructing Individualism: Autonomy, Individuality, and the Self in Western Thought,* ed. Thomas C. Heller, Morton Sosna, and David E. Wellbery, trans. Jeffrey S. Librett (Stanford, Calif.: Stanford University Press, 1986), 106–39. In this essay, Hamacher analyzes Nietzsche's concept of individuality as one of "outliving." For Nietzsche, "the individual is nothing other than the unreined, voluptuous self-outliving of life, the ongoing passing away of an excessive being no longer susceptible of being seized in the unity of a historical, social, or logical form. Individuality 'is' outliving. Living without living. 'Living.' The individual does not live. It outlives. Its being is being out and being over, an insubstantial remainder and excess beyond every determinable form of human life. Instead of being a social or psychological form of human existence, the individual—the self-surpassing of type, or genius—is the announcement of what, generally translated as 'superman' or 'overman,' is best translated as 'outman.' *But the individual is this announcement only in the mode of an*

uncanny, dangerous, luxuriating monstrosity, in the form of one who, having outlasted the death of its type, has returned to earth in the form of a living corpse" (Hamacher, "Disgregation of the Will," 119, emphasis added).

35. Heidegger, *Nietzsche,* 2:47. Heidegger's invocation of the "Do Not Disturb" sign provides an interesting glimpse into the living quarters of twentieth-century philosophy. Transient and assailed (disturbed), philosophy appears to have assumed residence in the temporary and anonymous shelters of motels and/or hotels. One imagines in Heidegger's analogy, a figure of philosophy on the run, on the road, pursued (disturbed) rather than in pursuit of.

36. Ibid., 2:45–46. For an analysis of Nietzsche's midday temporalities, see Jacques Derrida, "Otobiographies," in *The Ear of the Other,* ed. Christie V. McDonald, trans. Peggy Kamuf and Avital Ronell (New York: Schocken, 1985), 1–38.

37. Heidegger, *Nietzsche,* 2:47.

38. Ibid., 2:52.

39. Friedrich Nietzsche, *On the Genealogy of Morals,* trans. Walter Kaufmann (New York: Random House, 1967), 61 (emphasis added).

40. Nietzsche's global reconfiguration of morality and its histories is founded upon the necessity for humanity to learn from the animals the act of forgetting and overcoming resentment. Without "this apparatus of repression," humanity cannot, in turn, learn what is most essential to its survival: the ability to promise. With typical vigor, Nietzsche explains: "The man in whom this apparatus of repression is damaged and ceases to function properly may be compared (and more than merely compared) with a dyspeptic—he cannot 'have done' with anything. Now this animal which needs to be forgetful, in which forgetting represents a force, a form of *robust* health, has bred in itself an opposing faculty, a memory, with the aid of which forgetfulness is abrogated in certain cases—namely those cases where promises are made" (Nietzsche, *Genealogy of Morals,* 58). For Nietzsche, the promise, the ability to promise, is the only countermeasure to humanity's history of ressentiment. The ability to promise makes the future possible: without promising, there is no future. The promise, however, is only made possible, can only be made and kept, as an abrogation of forgetting; as a deferral or suspension of the act of forgetting. Thus the capacity to forget must first exist before any promise can be made. This, according to Nietzsche, remains the most important task that humanity faces.

41. Derrida, "Eating Well," 111–12.

3. Evolutions

01. Charles Darwin, *On the Origin of Species* (Cambridge, Mass.: Harvard University Press, 1964), first published in 1859, and *The Descent of Man, and Selection in Relation to Sex* (Princeton, N.J.: Princeton University Press, 1981), published in 1871.

02. John Dewey, "The Influence of Darwin on Philosophy," in *Darwin,* ed. Philip Appleman (New York: Norton, 1970), 308.

03. Sigmund Freud, "The Resistances to Psycho-Analysis," in *The Standard Edition of the Complete Psychological Works of Sigmund Freud,* ed. and trans. James Strachey, 24 vols. (London: Hogarth Press and the Institute of Psycho-Analysis, 1961), 19:221. Hereafter cited as *SE.*

04. Margot Norris, *Beasts of the Modern Imagination: Darwin, Nietzsche, Kafka, Ernst, and Lawrence* (Baltimore, Md.: Johns Hopkins University Press, 1985), 6–7.

05. Henri Bergson, *Creative Evolution,* trans. Arthur Mitchell (New York: Random House, 1944), 359.

06. Dewey, "Influence of Darwin on Philosophy," 305–6.

07. Norris, *Beasts of the Modern Imagination,* 3.

08. Despite Norris's compelling argument, her insistence on a strict genealogical line between Darwin's findings and Nietzsche's philosophy cannot be sustained. Despite her otherwise careful rendering of Nietzsche's thought, Norris misreads the exergue that opens *Ecce Homo.* In an effort to attribute Nietzsche's rhetoric of self-generation and self-giving to a simple autotelism, Norris fails to consider the important role that temporality plays in Nietzsche's construction of identity and destiny. Thus Norris tends to reduce Nietzsche's concept of expenditure—the very foundation of the "eternal recurrence"—to an act of playful, even romantic nihilism. Norris writes of Nietzsche's exergue: "Nietzsche's gratitude to his life is merely an unmotivated discharge of excessive gladness, an emotional overflow without a recipient or a purpose beyond achieving affective relief" (*Beasts of the Modern Imagination,* 83). By contrast, Derrida reads Nietzsche's gift-giving as the sign of an encrypted line of credit that extends into the future, into the promise of a "Nietzsche," or signatory yet to come: "If the life that he lives and tells to himself ('autobiography,' they call it) cannot be *his* life in the first place except as the effect of a secret contract, a credit account which has been opened and encrypted, an indebtedness, an alliance or annulus, then as long as the contract has not been honored—and it cannot be honored except by another, for example, by you—Nietzsche can write that his life is perhaps

a mere prejudice, '*es ist vielleicht bloss ein Vorurteil dass ich lebe*'"
("Otobiographies," in *The Ear of the Other*, ed. Christie V. McDonald,
trans. Peggy Kamuf and Avital Ronell [New York: Schocken, 1985], 9).
In fact, Norris might better argue that Nietzsche's desire, as it is expressed
in *Ecce Homo,* is to phantasmatically inherit himself; to generate himself
by overcoming what is weak—negativity, the dead father, etc.—in his
being. In this sense, Nietzsche's writings portray not so much the author's
attempt to constitute himself as an animal "by transforming his work
into bestial acts and gestures" but rather the attempt to stretch his being,
"through the infinite line of credit," into a species whose existence would
span the range of time itself.

09. Max Horkheimer and Theodor W. Adorno, *Dialectic of Enlightenment,* trans. John Cumming (New York: Continuum, 1972), 6–7.

10. Ibid., 5.

11. Ibid., 3.

12. Theodor Adorno, *Minima Moralia: Reflections from Damaged
Life,* trans. E. F. N. Jephcott (New York: Verso, 1974), 184.

13. Alexandre Kojève, *Introduction to the Reading of Hegel: Lectures
on the "Phenomenology of Spirit,"* ed. Allan Bloom, trans. James H. Nichols
Jr. (Ithaca, N.Y.: Cornell University Press, 1969), 159.

14. In his afterword to the end of history and humanity's "return to
animality," Kojève charts the disappearance of humanity that begins with
the Battle of Jena: "At the period when I wrote the above note (1946),
Man's return to animality did not appear unthinkable to me as a prospect
for the future. But shortly afterwards (1948) I understood that the
Hegelian-Marxist end of History was not yet to come, but was already a
present, here and now. Observing what was taking place around me and
reflecting on what had taken place since the Battle of Jena, I understood
that Hegel was right to see in this battle the end of History properly so-
called. In and by this battle the vanguard of humanity virtually attained
the limit and the aim, that is, the *end,* of Man's historical evolution. What
has happened since then was but an extension in space of the universal
revolutionary force actualized in France by Robespierre-Napoleon. From
the authentically historical point of view, the two world wars with their
retinue of large and small revolutions had only the effect of bringing
backward civilizations of the peripheral provinces into line with the most
advanced (real or virtual) European historical positions. . . . Man's return
to animality appeared no longer a possibility that was yet to come, but as
a certainty that was already present" (*Reading of Hegel,* 160–61).

15. Dewey, "Darwin," 307–8.

16. Ibid., 313–14 (emphasis added).

17. Friedrich Nietzsche, *Twilight of the Idols and The Anti-Christ,* trans. R. J. Hollingdale (New York: Penguin, 1968), 51.

18. In *The Gay Science,* Nietzsche refers to Darwinism as "the last great scientific movement" (trans. Walter Kaufmann [New York: Vintage, 1974], 305). Nietzsche nonetheless links this great science to Hegel: "Without Hegel there could have been no Darwin." Regarding the favorable reception of Darwinism among German intellectuals, Nietzsche attributes this to the "bad habits" that define the German character, the German tendency to value "becoming and development" (ibid., 306). Elsewhere in *The Gay Science,* Nietzsche lambastes "modern natural sciences" for having become "so thoroughly entangled in Spinozistic dogma." Of the complicit sciences, Nietzsche singles out Darwinism: "most recently and worst of all, Darwinism with its incomprehensibly onesided doctrine of the 'struggle for existence'" (ibid., 292). With a reference to Malthus, Nietzsche concludes his uneasy diatribe by returning to the olfactory sense: "The whole of English Darwinism breathes something like the musty air of English overpopulation, like the smell of the distress and overcrowding of small people" (ibid.). Despite Nietzsche's numerous positions on Darwin and Darwinism, the influence of evolutionary theory upon his thought cannot be denied. According to Margot Norris, "Nietzsche misunderstands, rejects, and reappropriates an alienated version of Darwin's most radical thinking" (*Beasts of the Modern Imagination,* 2). See also Nietzsche's attack on Darwin in *Twilight of the Idols,* under the heading "*Anti-Darwin.*" Here, Nietzsche takes issue with Darwin's theory of natural selection and the "survival of the fittest" on psychological grounds. "Darwin forgot the mind (—that is English!): *the weak possess more mind. . . .* To acquire mind one must need mind—one loses it when one no longer needs it. He who possesses strength divests himself of mind" (Nietzsche, *Twilight of the Idols,* 86–87). In this tautology, Nietzsche argues that the strong would gradually lose "mind," which would in turn accumulate in the weak. Having gained mind against the losses of the strong, the weak would eventually revolt against the mindless strong. This scenario is, in fact, precisely the one that Nietzsche portrays in his accounts of Judeo-Christian hegemony in *The Genealogy of Morals, The Anti-Christ,* and *Ecce Homo.*

19. Friedrich Nietzsche, *Ecce Homo,* ed. and trans. Walter Kaufmann (New York: Vintage, 1967), 326. In *Twilight of the Idols,* Nietzsche offers the following assessment of the olfactory sense: "This nose, for example, of which no philosopher has hitherto spoken with respect and gratitude,

is none the less the most delicate tool we have at our command: it can detect minimal differences in movement which even the spectroscope cannot detect" (46). In his critique of the philosophical discourse on the senses, Nietzsche further situates the impasse that Enlightenment philosophy reaches with regard to human prejudices. Smelling, and the animal topos of which it is a metonymy, serves as an emblem then, not only of the encroachment of the sciences upon metaphysics but also of the "degeneration" or "decadence" that has dissociated philosophy from instinct and sensuality. It is, for Nietzsche, the mark of a philosophical collapse.

20. Bergson, *Creative Evolution,* 142.

21. Ibid., 4.

22. Ibid., 3.

23. Ibid., 10.

24. Ibid., 141.

25. Ibid., 159. The difference between ancient and modern science in treating these extracted moments resides, according to Bergson, in the question of privilege and chance: "*Ancient science thinks it knows its object sufficiently when it has noted of it some privileged moments, whereas modern science considers the object at any moment whatsoever*" (ibid., 359). For Bergson, the difference between causality and chance in this instance is less significant than that between immobility and motion.

26. Ibid., 160.

27. Ibid., 126.

28. According to Bergson, intelligence and instinct originate for all animals in the same organism at some distant stage of the evolutionary past. The traces of this past, Bergson states repeatedly throughout *Creative Evolution,* can never be entirely effaced. Thus even the most intelligent animals rely to some extent on instinct as a source of knowledge; conversely, even the most instinctive animals attain some level of intelligence. "Intelligence and instinct, having originally been interpenetrating, retain something of their common origin. Neither is ever found in a pure state. . . . they haunt each other continually" (Bergson, *Creative Evolution,* 149–50).

29. Ibid., 160. Bergson explains: "Throughout the whole extent of the animal kingdom . . . consciousness seems proportionate to the living being's power of choice. It lights up the zone of potentialities that surrounds the act. It fills the interval between what is done and what might be done" (ibid., 197).

30. Ibid., 160.

31. Ibid., 298.

32. Ibid., 158–59.

33. Emmanuel Levinas, *Existence and Existents,* trans. Alphonso Lingus (Dordrecht: Kluwer Academic, 1978), 63.

34. Bergson, *Creative Evolution,* 299.

35. Ibid., 337.

36. Bergson is extremely lucid on the dilemma of virtual nothingness. "Existence appears to me like a conquest over nought. I say to myself that there might be, that indeed there ought to be, nothing, and then I wonder that there is something. Or I represent all reality extended on nothing as on a carpet: at first nothing, and being has come by superaddition to it. Or, yet again, if something has always existed, nothing must always have served as its substratum or receptacle, and is therefore eternally prior. A glass may have always been full, but the liquid it contains nevertheless fills a void. In the same way, being may have always been there, but the nought which is filled, and, as it were, stopped up by it, pre-exists for it none the less, if not in fact at least in right. In short, I cannot get rid of the idea that the full is an embroidery on the canvas of the void, that being is superimposed on nothing, and that in the idea of 'nothing' there is *less* than in that of 'something'" (*Creative Evolution,* 300). For Bergson, this prejudice of metaphysics can only be neutralized by removing the idea of nothing from the path by which something is posited. (Bergson explains the hostility that metaphysics holds for psychological or physical forms of existence: "For the disdain of metaphysics for all reality that endures comes precisely from this, that it reaches being only by passing through 'not-being,' and that an existence which endures seems to it not strong enough to conquer non-existence and itself posit itself" [ibid., 300–301]). Nothing and something must be coextensive within each reality, with neither condition representing a sublation of the other. A movement, an ontological movement, which reinforces the potentials of both something and nothing while hypostatizing neither must enter into the equation. The discovery of this movement lies, according to Bergson, at the heart of evolutionary theory.

37. Ibid., 344. Gilles Deleuze attempts to explain Bergson's difficult arithmetic of being in the introduction to *Matter and Memory* titled *Bergsonism.* Of the differential engine that derives movement from life and duration from matter, Deleuze writes: "It is as if Life were merged into the very movement of differentiation, in ramified series. Movement is undoubtedly explained by the insertion of duration into matter: Duration is differentiated according to the obstacles it meets in matter, according to the materiality through which it passes, according to the

extension that it contracts. But differentiation does not merely have an external cause. Duration is differentiated within itself through an internal explosive force; it is only affirmed and prolonged, it only advances, in branching or ramified series. Duration, to be precise, is called life when it appears in movement" (Gilles Deleuze, *Bergsonism,* trans. Hugh Tomlinson and Barbara Habberjam [New York: Zone, 1991], 94–95).

38. Bergson, *Creative Evolution,* 351.

39. Ibid., 14.

40. Ibid., xxii–xxiii.

41. Ibid., 343.

42. Ibid., 331–32. For a detailed analysis of Bergson's "cinematography" in the field of cinema itself, see Gilles Deleuze, *Cinema 1: The Movement-Image,* trans. Hugh Tomlinson and Barbara Habberjam (Minneapolis: University of Minnesota Press, 1986); and Deleuze, *Cinema 2: The Time-Image,* trans. Hugh Tomlinson and Robert Galeta (Minneapolis: University of Minnesota Press, 1989).

43. Bergson, *Creative Evolution,* 4.

44. Ibid., 354–55.

45. Ibid., 357.

46. Concerning the projection of communities, Lyotard has noted that "psychotics are remarkable because the repressed returns to them from the outside" ("The Inarticulate, or The Differend Itself"). In many ways, this is the path by which animals return to humanity: they come from the outside, in a manner not unlike a psychosis.

47. Sigmund Freud, *Introductory Lectures on Psycho-Analysis, SE* 16:285.

48. Jean Laplanche and J.-B. Pontalis, *The Language of Psycho-Analysis,* trans. Donald Nicholson-Smith (New York: Norton, 1973), 474.

49. Sigmund Freud, "The Unconscious," *SE* 14:167.

50. Zoologist Willy Ley offers the following glimpse into the life and work of the eccentric Jesuit Athanasius Kircher (1602–80): "Father Athanasius Kircher, S. J., was an immensely erudite but strangely careless man, whose books were often ridiculed only a few years after their publication. Still, in almost every one of them something new can be found. He was born in 1602 at Geisa near Eisenbach, lived in Würzburg for some time, then went to Rome and taught mathematics and Hebrew at the College of Rome, until he gave up teaching in 1643. He gave up his post because he wanted to study, specifically archaeology and hieroglyphics. At some time after his retirement he invented the magic lantern. Then

conditions on other planets, animals, and volcanoes successively captured his interest, with three strange books as the result. The interest in other planets produced the strange *Ecstatic Voyage* (*Iter ecstaticum coeleste,* 1656) in which the author is taken on a trip to the known planets by the angel 'Cosmiel.' The conditions on the planets are described according to astrological concepts. Kircher's interest in zoology produced his *Noah's Ark* (Amsterdam, 1675), in which he lists all the animals that were admitted to the Ark 'and therefore did not perish in the Flood.' He even pictured the cages built by Noah for the various kinds of animals. His interest in volcanoes resulted in the two folio volumes of *De mundus subterraneus* (*The Subterranean World,* Amsterdam, 1678) in which he tried to explain the existence of volcanoes by assuming very numerous and very large subterranean caves. These caves were usually filled with water, but some were filled with fire. A few other caves were filled with air only, and these caves were inhabited by dragons—which explained why dragons were so rare. The dragons that had been encountered and slain by heroes were single specimens that had blundered onto the surface of the earth and could not return—for example, because the exit had been collapsed by an earthquake" (Willy Ley, *Dawn of Zoology* [Englewood Cliffs, N.J.: Prentice-Hall, 1968], 202). It is interesting to note that the man credited with introducing the idea of "animal magnetism" should also list among his accomplishments the invention of the magic lantern, a theory linking dinosaur fossils to buried dragons and subterranean volcanoes, and the concept of extinct animal species.

51. Josef Breuer and Sigmund Freud, *Studies on Hysteria, SE* 2.

52. Freud, "The Unconscious," 168–69.

53. Lucille B. Ritvo, *Darwin's Influence on Freud: A Tale of Two Sciences* (New Haven, Conn.: Yale University Press, 1990), 1.

54. See Freud's violent recapitulation of Darwin's narrative of the primal horde in *Totem and Taboo* (*SE* 13:140–46). Freud prefaces his "monstrous" account with this reference to Darwin: "If, now, we bring together the psycho-analytic translation of the totem with the fact of the totem meal and with Darwin's theories of the earliest state of human society, the possibility of a deeper understanding emerges—a glimpse of a hypothesis which may seem fantastic but which offers the advantage of establishing an unsuspected correlation between groups of phenomena that have hitherto been disconnected" (ibid., 141). By psychoanalyzing Darwin's primal horde narrative, Freud forges a speculative link between animals and the earliest states of human social existence that in turn speaks to the very foundation of a human identity. Freud concludes his

analysis by remarking on the ramifications of the "crime" that institutes humanity: "Society was now based on complicity in the common crime; religion was based on the sense of guilt and the remorse attaching to it; while morality was based partly on the exigencies of this society and partly on the penance demanded by the sense of guilt" (ibid., 146).

55. Laplanche and Pontalis, *Language of Psycho-Analysis,* 475.

56. Ibid., 474.

57. Freud, "The Unconscious," 175.

58. Charles Darwin, "N Notebook," in *Darwin on Man: A Psychological Study of Scientific Creativity,* ed. Howard E. Gruber (New York: E. P. Dutton, 1974), together with *Darwin's Early and Unpublished Notebooks* (New York: E. P. Dutton, 1974), 331. Concerning Darwin's displacement of the metaphysical mind, Norris writes: "Darwin collapsed perhaps the cardinal traditional difference between humans and animals by suggesting that the mind is not a fixed spiritual entity but a heuristic form as protean as the body. Not only did it evolve, diachronically, from animal instinct and even plant tropisms . . . , but also viewed synchronically, the mind consists of myriad conscious and unconscious, rational and irrational heuristic behaviors (emotions, curiosity, imagination, memory, reason, self-consciousness, among others) that take their forms not from ideal entities but from the forces, needs, and desires that propel the body in its relation to the world" (*Beasts of the Modern Imagination,* 47).

59. Freud, "The Unconscious," 187.

60. Darwin, cited in Gruber, *Darwin on Man,* 285.

61. Kojève, *Reading of Hegel,* 138.

62. Ritvo, *Darwin's Influence on Freud,* 37.

63. Jacques Lacan, "Of Structure as an Inmixing of an Otherness Prerequisite to Any Subject Whatever," in *The Structuralist Controversy: The Languages of Criticism and the Sciences of Man,* ed. Richard Macksey and Eugenio Donato (Baltimore, Md.: Johns Hopkins University Press, 1970), 193. Concerning the radical implications of Freud's legacies, see Jacques Derrida, "To Speculate—on 'Freud,'" in *The Post Card: From Socrates to Freud and Beyond,* trans. Alan Bass (Chicago: University of Chicago Press, 1987).

64. Freud, "The Unconscious," 169.

65. In his augmentation of evolutionary theory, William Bateson, the founder of modern genetics who also coined the term *genetics* in 1905, supplements "Darwinian orthodoxy" with the rediscovered work of Gregor Mendel. See Bateson, *Problems of Genetics* (New Haven, Conn.: Yale University Press, 1979).

66. Kojève, *Reading of Hegel,* 256–57. The question of time in relation to being gains momentum in the critical thought of this period. Besides Bergson, Heidegger, and Freud, Husserl can also be seen as having addressed the question of temporality with regard to phenomenology and consciousness. In his *Ideas,* Husserl makes this claim of the study of time: "Time is the name for a completely *self-contained sphere of problems* and one of exceptional difficulty" (Edmund Husserl, *Ideas: General Introduction to Pure Phenomenology,* trans. W. R. Boyce Gibson [New York: Macmillan, 1962], 216). And although Freud's entire oeuvre undoubtedly represents a crucial reevaluation of the properties of time and consciousness, perhaps the most influential and controversial contribution in the field of the philosophy of time remains, to this day, Heidegger's *Being and Time.* In it Heidegger states that "the primordial ontological basis for Dasein's existentiality is *temporality*" (Martin Heidegger, *Being and Time,* trans. John Macquarrie and Edward Robinson [New York: Harper and Row, 1962], 277).

4. The Wildside

01. Josef Breuer and Sigmund Freud, *Studies on Hysteria, SE* 2. Breuer and Freud's text appeared in the same year that the Lumière brothers patented and exhibited their cinématographe. For more on psychoanalysis and cinema, see Akira Mizuta Lippit, "Phenomenologies of the Surface: Radiation-Body-Image," in *Collecting Visible Evidence,* ed. Jane Gaines and Michael Renov (Minneapolis: University of Minnesota Press, 1999), 65–83.

02. For a discussion of the preliminal nature of communication, that is, a communication inscribed first in the unconscious before it becomes conscious, see Jacques Derrida, "Freud and the Scene of Writing," in *Writing and Difference,* trans. Alan Bass (Chicago: University of Chicago Press, 1978), 196–231. In this analysis of Freud's "Mystic Writing-Pad," Derrida explains that because dreams, in Freud's conceptualizations, are marked by a primordial textuality, "topographical, temporal, and formal regression in dreams must thus be interpreted, henceforth, as a path back into a landscape of writing. Not a writing which simply transcribes, a stony echo of muted words, but *a lithography before words: metaphonetic, nonlinguistic, alogical*" ("Freud and the Scene of Writing," 207, emphasis added).

03. Breuer and Freud, *Studies on Hysteria,* 12.

04. Ibid., 225.

05. The term *supplement,* to describe the operation of the uncon-scious in Freud's thought, follows Derrida's conceptualization of it. In *Of Grammatology* Derrida argues that the rhetoric of the supplement, far from adhering to the idea of pure surplus, always returns to the primary source of its supplementation and replaces it. Concerning the paradox, Derrida explains: "But the supplement supplements. It adds only to re-place. It intervenes or insinuates itself *in-the-place-of;* if it fills, it is as if one fills a void. If it represents and makes an image, it is by the anterior default of a presence. Compensatory [*suppléant*] and vicarious, the sup-plement is an adjunct, a subaltern instance which *takes-(the)-place* [*tient-lieu*]. As substitute, it is not simply added to the positivity of a presence, it produces no relief, its place is assigned in the structure by the mark of an emptiness. Somewhere, something can be filled up of *itself,* can ac-complish itself, only by allowing itself to be filled through sign and proxy. The sign is always the supplement of the thing itself" (Jacques Derrida, *Of Grammatology,* trans. Gayatri Chakravorty Spivak [Baltimore, Md.: Johns Hopkins University Press, 1974], 145). Although Derrida is here referring to the work of Rousseau, he quickly attributes the rhetoric of the supplement to a psychoanalytical topology. One can hear, in Derrida's deconstruction of Rousseau's concept of nature, the logic of the uncon-scious: "It [Reason] cannot even determine the supplement as its other, as the irrational and the non-natural, for the supplement comes *naturally* to put itself in Nature's place. The supplement is the image and the repre-sentation of Nature. The image is neither in nor out of Nature. The sup-plement is therefore equally dangerous for Reason, the natural health of Reason" (ibid., 149). In this sense, the difference between the splitting of consciousness and the splitting of the mind becomes clearer. Unlike the split consciousness, the unconscious, or split mind, is neither in nor out of consciousness, and therefore, it is more "dangerous." Bringing the con-cept of the supplement to bear directly on the unconscious, Derrida writes: "The indefinite process of supplementarity has always already *in-filtrated* presence, always already inscribed there the space of repetition and the *splitting of the self*" (ibid., 163, emphasis added).

06. Breuer and Freud, *Studies on Hysteria,* 7.

07. Tracing this philosophical axiom to its origin in Epicurus, Kojève offers this gloss: "Epicurus' well-known reasoning is valid only for an an-imal, or for non-dialectical being in general, which can only *suffer* its end without ever being able to prepare it. This being *is* as long as it lives, and it is annihilated after its death. Therefore death does not actually exist *for it,* and one cannot say of it: '*it is dying.*' But man transcends himself in

and by his very existence: in living, he is also beyond his real existence; his future absence is present in his life, and the Epicurean argument cannot blot out this presence of the absence in his existence. Thus, man is mortal *for himself*, and that is why he alone can *die* in the proper sense of the word. For only he can live while knowing that he is going to die. And that is why, in certain cases, he can live in terms of the idea of death, by subordinating to it everything that is dictated to him only by his life (an ascetic life)" (Kojève, *Introduction to the Reading of Hegel: Lectures on the "Phenomenology of Spirit,"* ed. Allan Bloom, trans. James H. Nichols Jr. [Ithaca, N.Y.: Cornell University Press, 1969], 255n).

08. Freud, "The Unconscious," *SE* 14:186.

09. Breuer and Freud, *Studies on Hysteria,* 11.

10. Sandor Ferenczi discusses hypnosis as a means of simulating most unconscious conditions known to psychoanalysis: dreams, love, transference, and even neuroses themselves. According to Ferenczi, hypnosis functions primarily by withdrawing the subject from the world of consciousness. Once withdrawn, the desubjectified "second personality" (for a subject can be said to be one, according to the philosophical definition, only to the extent that it is conscious) is thrust into the world of unconscious phenomena. In Ferenczi's scheme, hypnosis provides a portal to the other, unconscious world. Hypnosis, or animal magnetism, thus provides the means by which one can communicate with this other world. See Sandor Ferenczi, "Introjection and Transference," in *Sex in Psychoanalysis: Contributions to Psychoanalysis* (New York: Robert Brunner, 1950).

11. Breuer and Freud, *Studies on Hysteria,* 12.

12. Ibid., 11.

13. Jean Laplanche and J.-B. Pontalis offer this definition of Freud's use of the term *abreaction (Abreagieren)* with regard to hysteria: "Emotional discharge whereby the subject liberates himself from the affect attached to the memory of a traumatic event in such a way that this affect is not able to become (or to remain) pathogenic. Abreaction may be provoked in the course of psychotherapy, especially under hypnosis, and produce a cathartic effect. It may also come about spontaneously, either a short or long interval after the original trauma" (Jean Laplanche and J.-B. Pontalis, *The Language of Psycho-Analysis,* trans. Donald Nicholson-Smith [New York: Norton, 1973], 1).

14. Breuer and Freud, *Studies on Hysteria,* 12.

15. Ibid., 15.

16. Ibid., 3.

17. Ibid., 17 (emphasis added).

18. Ibid., 12.

19. Freud introduces the idea of deferred action, "*Nachträglichkeit,*" in his 1895 article, "The Project for a Scientific Psychology." In this essay, Freud argues that in hysterics, sexual release takes place "prematurely," that is before consciousness can arrive at the site of excitation and assimilate its occurrence. Accordingly, the usual temporality that follows the logic of cause and effect is suspended and a new ontic dynamic takes its place. Consciousness for hysterics takes place as an aftereffect of preliminary communication, "a posthumous primary affective experience" (*SE* 1:347–59).

20. Breuer and Freud, *Studies on Hysteria,* 193–94 (emphasis added). See in this connection Avital Ronell, *The Telephone Book: Technology—Schizophrenia—Electric Speech* (Lincoln: University of Nebraska Press, 1989).

21. Nicolas Abraham and Maria Torok offer a compelling account of this type of impossible communication, or cryptonymy. Interestingly, one of their figures for this phenomenon is a hybrid human and animal being. "This man, who is at once strange and average, has always lived under the guise of a double identity and has never lacked the resourcefulness needed to preserve it. His friends do not know that for analysts his name is Wolf Man and, as for analysts, they do not know, save for a few, what his real name is. It is as if he has had to maintain two separate worlds that cannot, must not communicate with each other" (Nicholas Abraham and Maria Torok, *The Wolf Man's Magic Word: A Cryptonymy,* trans. Nicholas Rand [Minneapolis: University of Minnesota Press, 1986], 30).

22. Friedrich A. Kittler, *Discourse Networks 1800/1900,* trans. Michael Metteer, with Chris Cullens (Stanford, Calif.: Stanford University Press, 1990), 170.

23. This characterization of unconscious topography appears in the closing paragraph of Freud's "On the History of the Psycho-Analytic Movement" (*SE* 14:66). The entire paragraph, which attempts to rebut the revisions in psychoanalytic theory instigated by Jung, is worth citing here: "Men are strong so long as they represent a strong idea; they become powerless when they oppose it. Psycho-analysis will survive this loss and gain new adherents in place of these. In conclusion, I can only express a wish that the fortune may grant an agreeable upward journey to all those who have found their stay in the underworld of psycho-analysis too uncomfortable for their taste. The rest of us, I hope, will be permitted

without hindrance to carry through to their conclusion our labours in the depths." It is interesting that for Freud the whole process of psychoanalysis is conducted as if in a hypnoid state; "strong men" must succumb to "strong ideas" and the work of psychoanalysis must be continued under the sway of these powerful forces—in the underworld of psychoanalysis.

24. Breuer and Freud, *Studies on Hysteria,* 194.

25. Ibid., 203.

26. Derrida, "Freud and the Scene of Writing," 212.

27. Breuer and Freud, *Studies on Hysteria,* 207 (emphasis added).

28. Freud, *Beyond the Pleasure Principle, SE* 18:39. In his discussion of the death drive, Freud asserts that a higher (conscious) organism's instinctive tendencies appear at odds with its intelligence over the question of death: the organism's instincts push life toward its ultimate "aim," that is, the experience of an ultimate "pleasure" in death, while the organism's intelligence seeks to implement the "reality principle" and prolong its life. According to the death drive, claims Freud, life is only a "*détour*" (ibid.).

29. Breuer and Freud, *Studies on Hysteria,* 256. Several years later (1905), Freud added the following footnote to his analysis of the hysteric Dora. Referring to the theories of hypnosis that he and Breuer had put forth in 1895–96, Freud writes: "I have gone beyond that theory, but I have not abandoned it; that is to say, I do not today consider the theory incorrect, but incomplete. All that I have abandoned is the emphasis laid upon the so-called "hypnoid state," which was supposed to be occasioned in the patient by the trauma, and to be the foundation for all the psychologically abnormal events which followed. If, where a piece of joint work is in question, it is legitimate to make a subsequent division of property, I should like to take this opportunity of stating that the hypothesis of "hypnoid states"—which many reviewers were inclined to regard as the central portion of our work—sprang entirely from the initiative of Breuer. I regard the use of such a term as superfluous and misleading, because it interrupts the continuity of the problem as to the nature of the psychological process accompanying the formation of hysterical symptoms" (Sigmund Freud, "Fragment of an Analysis of a Case of Hysteria," *SE* 7:27n).

30. Breuer and Freud, *Studies on Hysteria,* 249.

31. Ibid., 197.

32. Ibid., 199.

33. Ibid., 200.

34. Ibid.

35. Ibid., 201.

36. Ibid., 228.

37. Sigmund Freud, *Civilization and Its Discontents, SE* 21:71. The idea that all previous stages of the mind are preserved in the unconscious is a direct extrapolation from Darwin's idea that each organism recapitulates the history of its species' evolution during its embryonic stages. In *Beyond the Pleasure Principle,* Freud acknowledges his indebtedness to biology. Comparing the retention of the past in the unconscious to "the facts of embryology," Freud writes: "We see how the germ of a living animal is obliged in the course of its development to recapitulate (even if only in a transient and abbreviated fashion) the structures of all forms from which it has sprung, instead of proceeding quickly by the shortest path to its final shape" (*SE* 18:37).

38. Sigmund Freud, *Introductory Lectures on Psycho-Analysis, SE* 16: 292, cited in Mikkel Borch-Jacobsen, *The Emotional Tie: Psychoanalysis, Mimesis, and Affect,* trans. Douglas Birk et al. (Stanford, Calif.: Stanford University Press, 1992), 39. In this collection of essays, Borch-Jacobsen convincingly charts the movement of psychoanalysis from hypnosis to transference through the function of repetition. In the second section of *Emotional Tie,* titled "From Psychoanalysis to Hypnosis," Borch-Jacobsen states his intention to reclaim the dissolved (but not entirely absent) hypnotic tie from its successor, the transferential tie, by focusing on the aspect of repetition and the uncanny in psychoanalysis. "It is certainly with respect to everything touching on the transference that the 'resurgence of hypnosis' . . . is most spectacular in Freud. And this is hardly surprising, if we reflect that the transference—that strange 'rapport *sans* rapport' set up between patient and analyst—always represented for Freud a kind of blueprint or, better yet, a *repetition* of the 'emotional tie' to others. Therefore it is only natural that the problems, both theoretical and practical, to which this *Gefühlbindung* gave rise should have caused the whole problem of hypnotic 'rapport' to reappear, with the crucial question now being to know how the transferential relationship can finally be distinguished from the hypnotic tie, which analysis initially refused to mobilize in the cure. It is this question that I would like to examine, by attempting to 'repeat' (in Heidegger's but also Freud's possible meaning of this word) that part of history which runs from the discarding of hypnosis up to the definitive isolation of the transference as a distinct problem, and hoping that this journey will finally provide some insight into the 'riddle' of the *Gefühlbindung* to others" (44).

39. Plato, *Timaeus and Critias,* trans. Desmond Lee (New York: Penguin, 1965), 93.

40. Ibid. Edmund Burke, in his investigation of the sublime, finds similar reasons for dismissing the category of smell as incapable of transmitting "great ideas." Linking smells with the properties of taste, he writes: "*Smells,* and *Tastes,* have some share too, in ideas of greatness; but it is a small one, weak in its nature, and confined in its operations. I shall only observe, that no smells or tastes can produce a grand sensation, except excessive bitters, and intolerable stenches" (Burke, *A Philosophical Enquiry into the Origin of Our Ideas of the Sublime and Beautiful,* ed. J. T. Boulton [Notre Dame, Ind.: University of Notre Dame Press, 1958], 85–86). See also Montaigne's contribution to this subject, "Of Smells," in *The Complete Essays of Montaigne,* trans. Donald M. Frame (Stanford, Calif.: Stanford University Press, 1943), 228–29.

41. Vicki Hearne, *Adam's Task: Calling Animals by Name* (New York: Alfred A. Knopf, 1987), 80. For a scientific analysis of the properties of scent see D. Michael Stoddart, *The Scented Ape: The Biology and Culture of Human Odour* (Cambridge: Cambridge University Press, 1990).

42. Hearne, *Adam's Task,* 80.

43. Ibid.

44. Alain Corbin, *The Foul and the Fragrant: Odor and the French Social Imagination,* trans. Miriam L. Kochan, Roy Porter, and Christopher Prendergast (Cambridge, Mass.: Harvard University Press, 1986), 6.

45. On the relation between visuality and the entry of the word *animal* into English, Mary Midgley links the word *animal* to painting. In "Beasts, Brutes, and Monsters," Midgley recounts the word's history: "It is interesting that the Greek word *zographos,* a painter, means one who depicts any living creature, the difference between people and other animals being for this purpose overlooked. This, of course, is how Aristotle and his successors used *zöon* and *animal* in the scientific enquiries which were the source of our modern zoology. Thus, during the Middle Ages the word *animal* crept gradually into scholarly use *as a term of art,* and thence into everyday English" (Mary Midgley, "Beasts, Brutes, and Monsters," in *What Is an Animal?* ed. Tim Ingold [London: Unwin Hyman, 1988], 36, emphasis added).

46. Freud, *Civilization and Its Discontents, SE* 21:99n.

47. Max Horkheimer and Theodor W. Adorno, *Dialectic of Enlightenment,* trans. John Cumming (New York: Continuum, 1972), 184. Horkheimer and Adorno offer the following thoughts on the properties of smell during their discussion of anti-Semitism. According to the authors, the sense of smell facilitates an identification with the other and

causes a longing to become the other, to inhabit the site of the foreign and degraded other. The practice of identification with the other, in this case the Jew, is permitted by the fascist culture as long as the intent or aim of this identification with the other is ultimately to seek out and destroy it. Horkheimer and Adorno conclude: "The civilized individual may only indulge in such pleasure if the prohibition is suspended by rationalization in the service of real or apparent practical ends. The prohibited impulse may be tolerated if there is no doubt that the final aim is its elimination. . . . Anyone who seeks out 'bad' smells, in order to destroy them, may imitate to his heart's content, taking unrationalized pleasure in the experience" (ibid.).

48. Hearne, *Adam's Task*, 80.

49. Corbin, *Foul and the Fragrant*, 7. Derrida also notes that "smell . . . permits the object to dissociate itself into evaporation" ("The Pit and the Pyramid: Introduction to Hegel's Semiology," in *Margins of Philosophy*, trans. Alan Bass [Chicago: University of Chicago Press, 1982], 93n).

50. Corbin, *Foul and the Fragrant*, 8.

51. Freud, *The Complete Letters of Sigmund Freud to Wilhelm Fliess: 1887–1904*, ed. and trans. Jeffrey Moussaieff Masson (Cambridge, Mass.: Harvard University Press, Belknap Press, 1985), 279. Freud's refusal to concede priority to his theory of forgetting finds him indebted to Nietzsche, who had also articulated similar thoughts concerning smell and, in his idiom, the death of God. Nietzsche had predicted that he would not collect his debt (the recognition he was owed by the intellectual world) during his lifetime. Instead, his name would be "re-collected," so to speak, for the first time, in the future. Thus one finds a pressured site building toward Freud's theories of repression: Freud himself, using classic "kettle logic," would continue to deny having read the works of Nietzsche while admitting their relevance to his own. For a brief speculation regarding this aromatic exchange, see Akira Mizuta Lippit, "Crossroads to Nowhere: Utopian Scents," in *Semiotics 1990,* ed. Karen Haworth, John Deely, and Terry Prewitt (Lanham, Md.: University Press of America, 1993), 311–18.

52. Freud, *Complete Letters,* 279. Jacques Derrida has glossed Freud's letter to Fliess in his essay on Kafka's short story of the same title, "Before the Law." In his explication of Freud's discovery of the relationship between smelling and repression, and the morality that this relationship founds, Derrida emphasizes the existence of an absent origin or reference that haunts both the faculty of repression and the sense of smell: "From the outset, therefore, Freud, like others, wanted to write a history of the

law. He was following its traces and told Fliess his own history (his auto-analysis, as he put it), the history of the trail he followed in tracking the law. He smelled out the origin of the law, and for that he had to smell out the sense of smell. He thus set in motion a great narrative, an interminable auto-analysis, in order to relate, to give an account of, the origin of the law, in other words the origin of what, by breaking away from its origin, interrupts the genealogical story. The law, intolerant of its own history, intervenes as an absolutely emergent order, absolute and detached from any origin. It appears as something that does not appear as such in the course of a history. At all events, it cannot be constituted by some history that might give rise to any story. If there were any history, it would neither be presentable nor relatable: *the history of that which never took place.* Freud scented it, he had a nose for this sort of thing, he even had, as he says, a 'presentiment.' And he told Fliess of this, with whom an incredible story of noses was unfolding, lasting until the end of their friendship, which was marked by the sending of a last postcard of two lines" (Jacques Derrida, "Before the Law," in *Acts of Literature,* ed. Derek Attridge, trans. Avital Ronell and Christine Roulston [New York: Routledge, Chapman and Hall, 1992], 194, emphasis added).

53. Freud, *Complete Letters,* 280.

54. Ibid. One senses, in Freud's semi-allegorical account, that the psychoanalyst has begun to turn away from his nasological predecessor and mentor. The memory of priority now forms the basis for disgust and contempt. It is a scent that Fliess would recognize before Freud could reflect on his own evident ambivalence.

55. Ibid., 223 (emphasis added).

56. In *A Thousand Plateaus: Capitalism and Schizophrenia* (trans. Brian Massumi [Minneapolis: University of Minnesota Press, 1987]), Gilles Deleuze and Félix Guattari define the "rhizome" as a collection of interlocking and interacting systems (animal, mechanical, textual, or psychical) or "plateaus." The rhizome cannot be reduced to a singular identity or an autonomous function, since it always exists in conjunction with and in excess of other plateaus and rhizomes.

57. Ibid., 21.

58. Ibid., 163.

59. Brian Goodwin supports this thesis, although in another register, in his essay "Organisms and Minds: The Dialectics of the Animal-Human Interface in Biology" (in Ingold, *What Is an Animal?* 100–109). Working through Whitehead's contributions to the science of cognition, Goodwin makes this claim regarding the rhizomatic activities of minds

and organisms: "There are not things (e.g. thinkers) that generate thoughts; there are processes that generate complementary forms, such as thinkers and thoughts, together with all of the other aspects appropriate to this dynamic constellation of phenomena. So mind is not in the brain, any more than life is in the organism. These are aspects of ordered processes that exist in the dynamic relationship of thinking and acting, cycling and transforming, generated across the moving, fuzzy boundary between inner and outer, subject and object. Life is relational order lived at the interface, where forms are generated" (ibid., 107). One might also remember here, in this connection, Bergson's statement: "To act is to re-adapt oneself" (*Creative Evolution*, trans. Arthur Mitchell [New York: Random House, 1944], 358).

60. Deleuze and Guattari, *Thousand Plateaus*, 4.

61. Thomas A. Sebeok, "'Animal' in Biological and Semiotic Perspective," in *American Signatures: Semiotic Inquiry and Method*, ed. Iris Smith (Norman: University of Oklahoma Press, 1991), 164. See also Sebeok's discussion of animals in literature, "Give Me Another Horse," *American Journal of Semiotics* 8 (1991): 41–52.

62. Gilles Deleuze and Félix Guattari, *Kafka: Toward a Minor Literature,* trans. Dana Polan (Minneapolis: University of Minnesota Press, 1986), 13. See esp. chapter 4, titled "The Components of Expression."

63. Ibid., 13.

64. Deleuze and Guattari, *Thousand Plateaus*, 234.

65. Ibid., 234.

66. Ibid., 249.

67. In his *Theory of Religion*, Georges Bataille writes that the animal is "in the world like water in water." Describing the inability of animals to die, Bataille compares the implications of an animal killing with its human counterpart: "If the animal that has brought down its rival does not apprehend the other's death as does a man behaving triumphantly, this is because its rival had not broken a continuity that the rival's death does not reestablish. This continuity was not called into question, but rather the identity of desires of two beings set one against the other in mortal combat. The apathy that the gaze of the animal expresses after the combat is the sign of an existence that is essentially on a level with the world in which it moves like water in water" (Bataille, *Theory of Religion*, trans. Robert Hurley [New York: Urzone, 1989], 25).

68. Deleuze and Guattari, *Thousand Plateaus*, 239.

69. Ibid.

70. Ibid., 245.

71. Ibid., 238.

72. Sebeok, " 'Animal" in Biological and Semiotic Perspective," 167. Regarding the difference between the deaths of individual human beings and the extinction of entire animal species, Kojève writes: "A man is supposed to be 'the only one of his kind,' by being essentially different from all other men. And at the same time he is supposed to have, in his irreplaceable uniqueness, a positive value even more absolute or universal than that which belongs to a 'species' as such" (*Reading of Hegel*, 235). In Kojève's reasoning, humanity's transcendental singularity actually transforms each individual death into a universal event. The extermination of an entire species, conversely, is, according to Kojève, "almost" a crime. He explains somewhat cryptically in a footnote to the passage cited above: "Thus, for example, it does not seem evil at all to kill or destroy some representative or other of an animal or vegetable species. But the extermination of an entire species is considered almost a crime" (ibid.). The difference between the death of an individual human being, which amounts in fact to a universal event and the extermination of an entire species (is Kojève here referring to the Nazi genocide?), which is very much like the killing of a unique individual, hangs in the balance of this "almost," of this almost of criminality. For further discussions of this subject see Maurice Blanchot, "Literature and the Right to Death," in *The Gaze of Orpheus and Other Literary Essays*, ed. P. Adams Sitney, trans. Lydia Davis (New York: Station Hill, 1981); and Blanchot, *The Writing of the Disaster*, trans. Ann Smock (Lincoln: University of Nebraska Press, 1986).

73. Gilles Deleuze, *Proust and Signs*, trans. Richard Howard (New York: Braziller, 1972). See the last section, titled "The Literary Machine."

74. Derrida, "Plato's Pharmacy," in *Dissemination*, trans. Barbara Johnson (Chicago: University of Chicago Press, 1981), 70.

75. Deleuze and Guattari, *Thousand Plateaus*, 240. Deleuze and Guattari ascribe the mode of becoming by contagion rather than union to nature's true *nature*. "Unnatural participations or nuptials are the true Nature spanning the kingdoms of nature. Propagation by epidemic, by contagion, has nothing to do with filiation by heredity, even if the two themes intermingle and require each other. . . . The difference is that contagion, epidemic, involves terms that are entirely heterogeneous: for example, a human being, an animal, and a bacterium, a virus, a molecule, a microorganism. Or in the case of the truffle, a tree, a fly, and a pig. These combinations are neither genetic nor structural; they are interkingdoms, unnatural participations. *That is the only way Nature operates—against itself*" (ibid., 242, emphasis added).

5. The Literary Animal

01. William Empson, "Alice in Wonderland: The Child as Swain," in *Some Versions of Pastoral* (New York: New Directions, 1974), 254. Empson continues: "The only passage that I am sure involves evolution comes at the beginning of *Wonderland* (the most spontaneous and 'subconscious' part of the books) when Alice gets out of the bath of tears that has magically released her from the underground chamber; it is made clear (for instance about watering places) that the salt water is the sea from which life arose; as a bodily product it is also the amniotic fluid (there are other forces at work here); ontogeny then repeats phylogeny, and a whole Noah's Ark gets out of the sea with her" (ibid., 255). See, in this connection, Neil Hertz, "More Lurid Figures," *Diacritics* 20 (1990): 2–27.

02. Empson argues that Carroll's version of evolution places natural selection and democratic principles at odds. He writes of the "Caucus Race": "It supports Natural Selection (in the offensive way the nineteenth century did) to show the absurdity of democracy, and supports democracy (or at any rate liberty) to show the absurdity of Natural Selection" (Empson, "Alice in Wonderland," 255).

03. In *Totem and Taboo,* Freud points out that children often share a privileged and primitive relationship with animals. In fact, Freud argues, children often feel a stronger identification with animals than they do with adults of their own species. "There is a great deal of resemblance between the relations of children and of primitive men towards animals. Children show no trace of arrogance which urges adult civilized men to draw a hard-and-fast line between their own nature and that of all other animals. Children have no scruples over allowing animals to rank as their full equals. Uninhibited as they are in the avowal of their bodily needs, they no doubt feel themselves more akin to animals than to their elders, who may well be a puzzle to them" (*SE* 13:126–27).

04. Lewis Carroll, *The Annotated Alice: "Alice's Adventures in Wonderland" and "Through the Looking-Glass,"* notes by Martin Gardner (New York: Penguin, 1960), 40–41.

05. Ibid., 129–30.

06. Ibid., 86.

07. Ibid., 82.

08. Ibid.

09. Ibid., 90.

10. Ibid., 95.

11. Ibid., 104.

12. Antonin Artaud describes a moment in a film reminiscent of Carroll's world: "In one of the Marx Brothers' films a man, thinking he is about to take a woman in his arms, ends up with a cow which moos. And through a combination of circumstances too long to relate, at that moment that same moo assumes an intellectual dignity equal to a woman's cry" (Artaud, "The Theatre and Its Double," in *Antonin Artaud: Collected Works,* trans. Victor Corti [London: Calder and Boyars, 1974], 4:30). See in this connection Derrida's extensive writings on Artaud: "The Theater of Cruelty and the Closure of Representation," in *Writing and Difference,* trans. Alan Bass (Chicago: University of Chicago Press, 1978), 232–94; "La Parole soufflée," in *Writing and Difference,* 169–250; and "Forcener le subjectile," in *Artaud: Dessins et Portraits,* Jacques Derrida and Paule Thévenin (Paris: Gallimard, 1986), 55–108.

13. Antonin Artaud, letter to Henri Parisot, in *Lettres de Rodez* (Paris: G.L.M., 1946), cited in Gilles Deleuze, *The Logic of Sense,* ed. Constantin V. Boundas, trans. Mark Lester with Charles Stivale (New York: Columbia University Press, 1990), 84. See also Artaud's translation and text "L'Arve et l'aume, tentative anti-grammaticale contre Lewis Carroll," *L'Arbalète,* no. 12 (1947): 159–84.

14. Antonin Artaud, "To Henri Parisot," in *Antonin Artaud: Selected Writings,* ed. Susan Sontag, trans. Helen Weaver (New York: Farrar, Straus and Giroux, 1976), 448–51. By the end of this letter, Artaud reveals the true source of his anxiety, and not surprisingly it involves fantasies of incorporation. He concludes his diatribe: "'Jabberwocky' is nothing but a sugar-coated and lifeless plagiarism of a work written by me, which has been spirited away so successfully that I myself hardly know what is in it" (ibid., 451).

15. Deleuze, *Logic of Sense,* 89.

16. Ibid., 87. Deleuze continues: "The procedure is this: a word, often of an alimentary nature, appears in capital letters, printed as in a collage which freezes it and strips it of its sense. But the moment that the pinned-down word loses its sense, it bursts into pieces; it is decomposed into syllables, letters, and above all into consonants which act directly upon the body, penetrating and bruising it" (ibid.).

17. Ibid., 91.

18. Jean-François Lyotard, "Can Thought Go On without a Body?" in *The Inhuman: Reflections on Time,* trans. Geoffrey Bennington and Rachel Bowlby (Stanford, Calif.: Stanford University Press, 1991), 13.

19. Artaud, "Theatre and Its Double," 44.

20. Franz Kafka, *The Metamorphosis,* in *The Penal Colony: Stories and Short Pieces,* trans. Willa Muir and Edwin Muir (New York: Schocken, 1948), 70.

21. Ibid., 79.

22. Ibid., 80.

23. Ibid., 86.

24. Ibid., 79–80.

25. Ibid., 88.

26. Ibid., 91–92.

27. Ibid., 100.

28. Gregor's mother, her voice, still asserts the oedipal pull: "On hearing these words from his mother Gregor realized that the lack of all direct human speech for the past two months together with the monotony of family life must have confused his mind. . . . He had indeed been so near the brink of forgetfulness that only the voice of his mother, which he had not heard for so long, had drawn him back from it" (ibid., 102–3).

29. Franz Kafka, "Josephine the Singer, or the Mouse Folk," in *Penal Colony,* 257. For further discussion of Kafka, Josephine, and singing, see Laurence A. Rickels, "Pact Rats," in *The Case of California* (Baltimore, Md.: Johns Hopkins University Press, 1991), 32–39. Of cat music Jean-Claude Lebensztejn writes: "Les musiques de chats mettent en place la contradiction, du moins le paradoye d'une musique anti-musicale." ("The music of cats stages a contradiction, at least the paradox of an anti-musical music.") Lebensztejn, "Miaulique (Fantasie Chromatique)," manuscript 3.

30. Kafka, *Metamorphosis,* 121.

31. Deleuze and Guattari write: "Rich or poor, each language always implies a deterritorialization of the mouth, the tongue, and the teeth. The mouth, tongue, and teeth find their primitive territoriality in food. In giving themselves over to the articulation of sounds, the mouth, tongue, and teeth deterritorialize. Thus, there is a certain disjunction between eating and speaking, and even more, despite all appearances between eating and writing" (Gilles Deleuze and Félix Guattari, *Kafka: Toward a Minor Literature,* trans. Dana Polan [Minneapolis: University of Minnesota Press, 1986], 19–20).

32. Kafka, "Jackals and Arabs," in *Penal Colony,* 150.

33. Deleuze and Guattari, *Kafka,* 5.

34. Kafka, "A Report to an Academy," in *Penal Colony,* 173.

35. Ibid., 176.

36. Ibid., 178.

37. Deleuze and Guattari, *Kafka*, 22.

38. Kafka, "Report to an Academy," 182.

39. Walter Benjamin portrays Kafka choking on the unassimilable law of corporeality: "Because the most forgotten alien land is one's own body, one can understand why Kafka called the cough that erupted from within him 'animal.' It was the most advanced outpost of the great herd" (Benjamin, "Franz Kafka: On the Tenth Anniversary of His Death," in *Illuminations*, ed. Hannah Arendt, trans. Harry Zohn [New York: Schocken, 1969], 132).

40. Jean Laplanche and J.-B. Pontalis, *The Language of Psycho-Analysis*, trans. Donald Nicholson-Smith (New York: Norton, 1973), 229.

41. Ibid., 230.

42. Sigmund Freud, "Mourning and Melancholia," *SE* 14:237–58.

43. Sigmund Freud, *Civilization and Its Discontents, SE* 21:123.

44. Nicolas Abraham and Maria Torok, *The Wolf Man's Magic Word: A Cryptonymy*, trans. Nicholas Rand (Minneapolis: University of Minnesota Press, 1986).

45. Deleuze and Guattari, *Kafka*, 37.

46. Compare, for example, Alice's thoughts as she plummets down the rabbit hole with that of Akutagawa's narrator as he similarly topples headlong down the hole that takes him to Kappaland: "Isn't it strange how, even at the moment of such extreme crisis, our human mind indulges in the most preposterous thoughts?" (Akutagawa Ryunosuke, *Kappa*, trans. Geoffrey Bownas [Rutland, Vt.: Charles E. Tuttle, 1970], 51). Another allusion to Carroll's work can be found in the Kappa who lives his life backward (ibid., 134). In chapter 5 of *Through the Looking-Glass*, Alice and the White Queen discuss the implications of "living backwards" (Carroll, *Annotated Alice*, 245–60).

47. G. H. Healy, introduction to *Kappa*, 40.

48. Jonathan Swift, *Gulliver's Travels and Other Writings*, ed. Miriam Kosh Starkman (New York: Bantam, 1962), 221. Gulliver's shifting body size (from Lilliput to Brobdingnag) can be seen as a prefiguration of Alice's metamorphoses in Wonderland.

49. Akutagawa, *Kappa*, 61–62. In turn the narrator, after returning to the human world and his home in the asylum, states: "For some while after my return from Kappaland, I used to find myself quite unable to stomach the disgusting smell of human beings. Compared with us, the Kappas really are a clean-living race. Again, because I had grown accustomed to seeing Kappa and Kappa only, the human head at first struck me as something terribly weird. Perhaps you may find this rather hard to

understand—but, believe you me, although there may be nothing wrong with human eyes or the human mouth, this protuberance we call a nose is capable, in some mysterious way, of instilling a great deal of dread" (ibid., 137).

50. The notion of a decentered or deconstructed self is an active element of Akutagawa's *shishosetsu*. Karatani describes Akutagawa's literary mode as "a centerless interrelationship of fragments" that relegates the "I" not to the homogeneous space of the cogito but instead to a heterogeneous space, to a "novel without plot" (Karatani Kojin, *Origins of Modern Japanese Literature*, trans. and ed. Brett de Bary [Durham, N.C.: Duke University Press, 1993], 155–61).

51. Coincidentally, Gulliver travels through Japan after leaving the *Struldbruggs* of Luggnagg and plants this literary seed on Japan's soil in the third book of the *Travels:* "There is indeed a perpetual commerce between this kingdom [Luggnagg] and the great empire of Japan, and it is very probable that the Japanese authors may have given some account of the *Struldbruggs;* but my stay in Japan was short, and I was so entirely a stranger to the language, that I was not qualified to make any enquiries" (Swift, *Gulliver's Travels*, 208).

52. In a scene that is best described as uncanny, Swift describes Gulliver's reaction when he realizes that the repulsive Yahoos, whom he had derided as the most "disagreeable" creatures he had yet encountered, are more akin to himself than to the noble, equine Houyhnhnms. Of Gulliver's response, Swift writes: "My horror and astonishment are not to be described when I observed, in this abominable animal, a perfect human figure" (*Gulliver's Travels*, 220).

53. Akutagawa Ryunosuke, *Kamigami no bisho* (Smiles of the Gods), in *Akutagawa Ryunosuke zenshu* (Tokyo: Chikuma Shobo, 1972), 10, cited in Karatani, *Origins of Modern Japanese Literature*, 172. For a discussion of Japan as the exemplary global museum of the other, see Kakuzo Okakura, *The Book of Tea*, ed. Everett F. Bleiler (New York: Dover, 1964).

54. Akutagawa, "Bungeitekina, amari ni bungeitekina" (Literary, all too literary), in *Akutagawa zenshu* (Tokyo: Iwanami Shoten, 1978), 9:57–61, cited in Karatani, *Origins of Modern Japanese Literature*, 141.

55. Karatani, *Origins of Modern Japanese Literature*, 172.

56. Akutagawa, *Kappa*, 67.

57. Foucault notes, "Madness borrowed its face from the mask of the beast" (Michel Foucault, *Madness and Civilization: A History of Insanity in the Age of Reason*, trans. Richard Howard [New York:

Vintage, 1965], 72). During the classical era, Foucault argues, madness was seen as a form of irrationality that rendered human beings as animals. "The animality that rages in madness dispossesses man of what is specifically human in him; not in order to deliver him over to other powers, but simply to establish him at the zero degree of his own nature. For classicism, madness in its ultimate form is man in immediate relation to his animality, without other reference, without any recourse" (ibid., 74). The cure for madness, according to Foucault's analysis, consists of completing the metamorphosis, becoming-animal. "In the reduction to animality, madness finds both its truth and its cure; when the madman has become a beast, this presence of the animal in man, a presence which constituted the scandal of madness, is eliminated: not that the animal is silenced, but man himself is abolished" (ibid., 76).

58. For further representations of Japan and the supernatural see Lafcadio Hearn, *Kwaidan: Stories and Studies of Strange Things* (Rutland, Vt.: Charles E. Tuttle, 1971); and Hearn, *In Ghostly Japan* (Rutland, Vt.: Charles E. Tuttle, 1971).

59. Akutagawa, *Kappa*, 45.

60. Ibid., 57–58.

61. Ibid., 57–59.

62. Ibid., 109.

63. Ibid., 86.

64. Ibid., 50.

65. Ibid., 83.

66. Ibid., 61.

67. Akutagawa Ryunosuke, *Tenkibo*, trans. G. H. Healey (Tokyo: Chikuma Shobo, n.d.), 3:305. Elsewhere, Akutagawa writes: "Heredity, environment, chance—these three govern our fates" (*Shuju no Kotoba*, trans. G. H. Healey [Tokyo: Chikuma Shobo, n.d.], 5:110).

68. Deleuze, *Logic of Sense*, 87.

69. Ibid.

70. Tanizaki Junichiro, "Jozetsu-roku," in *Tanizaki Junichiro zenshu* (Tokyo: Chuokoronsha, 1972–75), 20:108, cited in Karatani, *Origins of Modern Japanese Literature*, 161.

71. Ibid.

72. Akutagawa, "Bungeitekina," 3–80. Cited in Karatani, *Origins of Modern Japanese Literature*, 157.

73. Deleuze, *Logic of Sense*, 88.

6. Animetaphors

01. Sigmund Freud, *The Interpretation of Dreams, SE* 4:131.

02. Ibid., 132. A 1911 footnote credits Ferenczi with a Hungarian source and in 1914, Freud adds a Jewish version of the proverb.

03. Ibid.

04. Freud likens the content of the unconscious to "an aboriginal population in the mind" (Sigmund Freud, "The Unconscious," *SE* 14:195).

05. Sigmund Freud, "The Resistances to Psycho-Analysis," *SE* 19:221.

06. Sigmund Freud, "Fragment of an Analysis of a Case of Hysteria," *SE* 7:48.

07. Sigmund Freud, *The Complete Letters of Sigmund Freud to Wilhelm Fliess: 1887–1904,* ed. and trans. Jeffrey Moussaieff Masson (Cambridge, Mass.: Harvard University Press, Belknap Press, 1985), 223.

08. Jacques Derrida, "Plato's Pharmacy," in *Dissemination,* trans. Barbara Johnson (Chicago: University of Chicago Press, 1981), 79.

09. Giorgio Agamben, *Idea of Prose,* trans. Michael Sullivan and Sam Whitsitt (Albany: State University of New York Press, 1995), 113.

10. Gilles Deleuze and Félix Guattari, *Kafka: Toward a Minor Literature,* trans. Dana Polan (Minneapolis: University of Minnesota Press, 1986), 22.

11. Gilles Deleuze and Félix Guattari, *A Thousand Plateaus: Capitalism and Schizophrenia,* trans. Brian Massumi (Minneapolis: University of Minnesota Press, 1987), 238.

12. Michel de Montaigne, "Of the Power of Imagination," in *The Complete Essays of Montaigne,* trans. Donald Frame (Stanford, Calif.: Stanford University Press, 1958), 75.

13. Theodor Adorno, *Minima Moralia: Reflections from Damaged Life,* trans. E. F. N. Jephcott (London: Verso, 1974), 105 (emphasis added).

14. Alexandre Kojève asserts that morality remains intrinsic to anthropology: "For every morality is an implicit anthropology, and man is speaking of his very being when he judges his actions morally" (*Introduction to the Reading of Hegel: Lectures on the "Phenomenology of Spirit,"* ed. Allan Bloom, trans. James H. Nichols Jr. [Ithaca, N.Y.: Cornell University Press, 1969], 189).

15. René Descartes, "Discourse on the Method," in *Descartes: Selected Philosophic 1l Writings,* trans. John Cottingham, Robert Stoothoff, and Dugald Murdoch (Cambridge: Cambridge University Press, 1988), 20–56.

16. Derrida, "White Mythology: Metaphor in the Text of Philosophy," in *Margins of Philosophy,* trans. Alan Bass (Chicago: University of Chicago Press, 1982), 271.

17. Nicolas Abraham and Maria Torok, "Mourning *or* Melancholia: Introjection *versus* Incorporation," in *The Shell and the Kernel,* ed. and trans. Nicholas Rand (Chicago: University of Chicago Press, 1994), 125–38.

18. Ibid., 132.

19. Martin Heidegger, "The Nature of Language," in *On the Way to Language,* trans. Peter D. Hertz (New York: Harper, 1971), 107. Derrida observes that Heidegger "does not say that the experience of death *as such,* the experience granted to the mortal, of which the animal is incapable, depends upon language" (Derrida, *Aporias,* trans. Thomas Dutoit [Stanford, Calif.: Stanford University Press, 1993], 36).

20. Abraham and Torok, "Mourning *or* Melancholia," 132. See Jacques Derrida's introduction to Abraham and Torok's investigation of the Wolf Man, "*Fors:* The Anglish Words of Nicolas Abraham and Maria Torok," trans. Barbara Johnson, in *The Wolf Man's Magic Word: A Cryptonymy*, Nicolas Abraham and Maria Torok, trans. Nicholas Rand (Minneapolis: University of Minnesota Press, 1986), xi–xlviii.

21. In response to the notion of "animetaphor," presentation, Cerisy-la-Salle, July 1997 (in *"L'Animal autobiographique,* ed. Marie-Louise Mallet [Paris: Galilée, 1999]).

22. Derrida, "White Mythology," 269.

23. Roland Barthes, *Camera Lucida: Reflections on Photography,* trans. Richard Howard (New York: Hill and Wang, 1981), 8.

24. Ibid., 78–79.

25. André Bazin, "The Ontology of the Photographic Image," in *What Is Cinema?* ed. and trans. Hugh Gray (Berkeley: University of California Press, 1967), 1:9.

26. Barthes, *Camera Lucida,* 5.

27. Ibid., 80–81.

28. The second half of *Camera Lucida* begins with the author's search for his dead mother in the form of a photograph. "Now, one November evening shortly after my mother's death, I was going through some photographs. I had no hope of 'finding' her, I expected nothing from these 'photographs of a being before which one recalls less of that being than by merely thinking of him or her' (Proust)" (63). The photograph that Barthes eventually finds does not resemble his mother so much as it conveys the truth of his mother. "There I was alone in the apartment

where she had died, looking at these pictures of my mother, one by one, under the lamp, gradually moving back in time with her, looking for the truth of the face that I had loved. And I found it" (67). Here, the topoi of maternity and photography converge in the phantasm of the luminal umbilicus, the inherent connection between photographic beings: "Something like an essence of the Photograph floated in this particular picture" (73). See also Freud's analysis of Judge Schreber, a paranoiac, who believed that he was being impregnated by rays of light (Sigmund Freud, "Psycho-Analytic Notes on an Autobiographical Account of a Case of Paranoia [Dementia Paranoides]," *SE* 12:1–84).

29. Barthes, *Camera Lucida,* 11.

30. Bazin, "Ontology of the Photographic Image," 9.

31. Barthes, *Camera Lucida,* 96–97.

32. John Berger, "Why Look at Animals?" in *About Looking* (New York: Vintage, 1980), 17.

33. Ibid., 4–5.

34. Ibid., 5.

35. Jacques Lacan, "Of the Gaze as *Objet Petit a,*" in *The Four Fundamental Concepts of Psycho-Analysis,* ed. Jacques-Alain Miller, trans. Alan Sheridan (New York: Norton, 1977), 117.

36. Ibid., 106.

37. Ibid. "Je suis *photo-graphié*" (Jacques Lacan, *Le Séminaire: Les Quatre Concepts fondamentaux de la psychanalyse* [Paris: Éditions du Seuil, 1973], 2:98).

38. Lacan, "Of the Gaze," 118. "Le mauvais œil, c'est le *fascinum,* c'est ce qui a pour effet d'arrêter le mouvement et littéralement de tuer la vie. Au moment où le sujet s'arrête suspendant son geste, il est mortifié. La fonction anti-vie, anti-mouvement, de ce point terminal, c'est le *fascinum,* et c'est précisément une des dimensions où s'exerce directement la puissance du regard" (Lacan, *Le Séminaire,* 11:107).

39. Jean-Luc Nancy, *The Inoperative Community,* ed. and trans. Peter Connor (Minneapolis: University of Minnesota Press, 1991), 6–7.

40. Ibid., 6.

41. Barthes, *Camera Lucida,* 14.

42. Ibid., 13.

43. Ibid., 100.

44. Ibid., 5–6.

45. Bazin, "Ontology of the Photographic Image," 13. Regarding the photographic impasse, Bazin disengages photography from the metaphysics of aesthetics: "Hence the charm of family albums. Those grey or

sepia shadows, phantomlike and almost undecipherable, are no longer traditional family portraits but rather the disturbing presence of lives halted at a set moment in their duration, freed from their destiny; not, however, by the prestige of art but by the power of an impassive mechanical process: for photography does not create eternity, as art does, it embalms time, rescuing it simply from its proper corruption" (ibid., 14).

46. Barthes, *Camera Lucida,* 111.

47. Ibid., 113.

48. Ibid., 116–17.

49. Ibid., 117. Barthes's term is *assagir,* which means more precisely "to subdue." In the present context, however, the translator's choice makes an interesting if unconscious connection between the world of the photograph and that of the animal.

50. Ibid. In the French original: "La société s'emploie à assagir la Photographie, à tempérer la folie qui menace sans cesse d'exploser au visage de qui la regarde" (Roland Barthes, *La Chambre claire: Note sur la photographie* [Paris: Éditions de l'Étoile, Gallimard, Le Seuil, 1980], 180).

51. Barthes, *Camera Lucida,* 119.

52. Walter Benjamin, "A Small History of Photography," in *One Way Street and Other Writings,* trans. Edmund Jephcott and Kingsley Shorter (London: Verso, 1979), 243.

53. Jacques Derrida, *Memoires: for Paul de Man,* trans. Cecile Lindsay, Jonathan Culler, and Eduardo Cadava (New York: Columbia University Press, 1986), 60. Derrida speculates: "What if there were a memory of the present and that far from fitting the present to itself, it divided the instant? What if it inscribed or revealed difference in the very presence of the present, and thus, by the same token, the possibility of being repeated in representation?" The photographic temporality that Derrida describes can be read as the temporal dimension that animals inhabit—a radically persistent presence that nonetheless refuses to adhere to the *logos* of the present.

54. Francis Bacon, in *The Brutality of Fact: Interviews with Francis Bacon,* ed. David Sylvester (Oxford: Alden Press, 1975), 23.

55. Kojève, *Reading of Hegel,* 244n. One need not be able to "recognize" a loved object, Kojève explains, for one to continue loving it. One loves "given-Being *(Sein)*" and not "Action *(Tun)*" or "Product *(Werk)*." Thus, he asserts, following Goethe: "One loves a man not because of what he *does* but for what he *is,* that is why one can love a dead man . . . that is also why one can love an animal, without being able to 'recognize' the animal" (ibid.).

56. Bacon, *Brutality of Fact,* 46.

57. Citing Lalande, Laplanche and Pontalis note that identification determines an "act whereby an individual becomes identical with another or two beings become identical with each other" (Jean Laplanche and J.-B. Pontalis, *The Language of Psycho-Analysis,* trans. Donald Nicholson-Smith [New York: Norton, 1973], 205).

58. Bacon, *Brutality of Fact*, 30.

59. Richard von Krafft-Ebing, *Psychopathia Sexualis,* trans. F. J. Rebman (New York: Physicians and Surgeons Book Company, 1925), 125 (emphasis added).

60. Derrida, "'Eating Well,' or The Calculation of the Subject: An Interview with Jacques Derrida," in *Who Comes after the Subject?* ed. Eduardo Cadava, Peter Connor, and Jean-Luc Nancy, trans. Peter Connor and Avital Ronell (New York: Routledge, 1991), 112.

61. Adorno, *Minima Moralia,* 105.

62. Derrida, "Eating Well," 96.

63. Ibid., 114.

64. Barthes, *Camera Lucida,* 96.

65. Derrida, "Eating Well," 114.

66. Ibid., 111.

67. In thanking his translator, Karl von Frisch makes this comment regarding intracommunicational systems that exist between human beings and bees: "Suppose German and English bees were living together in the same hive, and one of the Germans found a lot of nectar: its English companions would easily understand what it had to say about the distance and direction of the find. Human language is not so perfect" (*The Dancing Bees: An Account of the Life and Senses of the Honey Bee,* trans. Dora Ilse [New York: Harcourt, Brace and Company, 1953], ii).

68. Eadweard Muybridge, *Animals in Motion,* ed. Lewis S. Brown (New York: Dover, 1957); and Muybridge, *The Human Figure in Motion* (New York: Dover, 1955). Both works are derived from Muybridge's complete portfolio of photographs, *Animal Locomotion,* which was published in 1887. The most thorough analyses of "chronophotography," from Muybridge to Etienne-Jules Marey, have been conducted by Michel Frizot. See, for example, Michel Frizot, *La Chronophotographie* (Beaune, France: Association des Amis de Marey et Ministère de la Culture, 1984).

69. Christian Metz, *The Imaginary Signifier: Psychoanalysis and the Cinema,* trans. Celia Britton, Annwyl Williams, Ben Brewster, and Alfred Guzzetti (Bloomington: Indiana University Press, 1982), 43.

70. Ibid., 44.

71. Cited in Vicki Hearne, *Bandit: Dossier of a Dangerous Dog* (New York: HarperCollins, 1991), 58.

72. A horsepower was calculated at 33,000 foot-pounds per minute in England; a French "cheval-vapeur" was estimated at the ability of a horse to lift seventy-five kilograms one meter in one second. See Richard Lewinsohn, *Animals, Men, and Myths,* trans. Harper and Brothers (New York: Harper and Brothers, 1954). Lewinsohn explains: "After James Watt had built his steam engine, he wanted to find out how much work his machine could accomplish. The most impressive way of measuring work done was by comparing the engine's output with that of a horse. Physiological experiments revealed that a horse could work constantly at the rate of 22,000 foot-pounds per minute. This figure was arbitrarily increased to 33,000 foot-pounds per minute and called a 'horsepower'" (ibid., 273). At the instant of its conception, then, the engine was already imagined as an equine crypt.

73. Attempting to impede the consolidation of competing AC (alternating current) distributing systems and advance his own DC (direct current) generators, Thomas Edison and his then assistant Charles Batchelor regularly demonstrated the execution of animals with high-voltage alternating current. "The big laboratory at West Orange was the principal source of 'scientific' evidence purportedly exposing all those who were making and selling a-c systems to the public. There, on any day in 1887, one might have found Edison and his assistants occupied in certain cruel and lugubrious experiments: the electrocution of stray cats and dogs by means of high-tension currents. In the presence of newspaper reporters and other invited guests, Edison and Batchelor would edge a little dog onto a sheet of tin to which were attached wires from an a-c generator supplying current at 1,000 volts. . . . The feline and canine pets of the West Orange neighborhood . . . were executed in such numbers that the local animal population stood in danger of being decimated" (Matthew Josephson, *Edison: A Biography* [New York: John Wiley and Sons, 1959], 347). Edison's particularly brutal massacre of West Orange's animal population suggests an intensity of purpose: to prove his point regarding the dangers of alternating current, Edison seemed willing to eliminate an entire population. A phantasmatic exchange can perhaps be seen in Edison's repetition compulsion: animals for electricity, life for power. One might speculate that animals, in Edison's laboratories, were reducible to pure force, animus, electricity. Josephson describes an incident in which Edison's assistant Batchelor accidentally received the animal's voltage: "In one of those sadistic 'experiments,' Batchelor, while

trying to hold a puppy in the 'chair,' by accident received a fearful shock himself and 'had the awful memory of body and soul being wrenched asunder. . . . the sensations of an immense rough file thrust through the quivering fibers of the body.' Though badly shaken up, he recovered in a day or two, it was said, 'with no visible injury, *except in the memory of the victim*'" (*Edison*, 347). The episode highlights the strange connection between the space of animals, electricity, and psychic multiplication.

74. Avital Ronell has connected Bell's research on sheep to the advent of the telephone in *The Telephone Book: Technology —Schizophrenia— Electric Speech* (Lincoln: University of Nebraska Press, 1989). Troubled by the relative weakness of the sheep's reproductive system, Bell attempted to increase the number of their nipples. "For Alexander Graham Bell the sheep take up a significance of affective investment of the same intensity as the telephone. He must multiply nipples, keep the connection going; they need to be kept from perishing" (ibid., 338).

75. The animal achieves a vital superiority in Austrian physicist Erwin Schrödinger's 1925 "black box" demonstration of quantum mechanics. A cat is placed in an experimental crypt along with a decaying radioactive nucleus, a trigger mechanism, and a cyanide capsule. "After one minute," writes commentator-scientist Paul Davies, "there is a fifty per cent chance that the nucleus has decayed. The device is switched off automatically at this stage. Is the cat dead or alive?" According to the "overlapping waves" that represent different possible states of both the cat and its poison, the animal rests in its quantum casket simultaneously dead and alive. Davies concludes his commentary by psychoanalyzing the cat: "It seems that the cat goes into [a] curious state of schizophrenia . . . and its fate is only determined when the experimenter opens the box and peers in to check on the cat's health. However, as he can choose to delay this final step as long as he pleases, the cat must continue to endure its suspended animation, until either finally dispatched from its purgatory, or resurrected to a full life by the obliging but whimsical curiosity of the experimenter" (Paul Davies, *Other Worlds: Space, Superspace, and the Quantum Universe* [New York: Simon and Schuster, 1980], 131). In Davies's description, one returns to the strange metaphysics of Schrödinger's dead and alive cat, which allows for the conceptualization of alternative, parallel worlds. Technology emerged as the memorial and aesthetic of an extinct animality. Ironically, within the technological frame, animals became subjects. Animal substance became the very possibility of the new technological environment. Schrödinger writes: "If we consider our earthly environment, it consists almost exclusively of the

living or dead bodies of plants and animals" (Erwin Schrödinger, *My View of the World,* trans. Cecily Hastings [Woodbridge, Conn.: Ox Bow, 1983], 41).

76. Georges Bataille, *The Accursed Share,* trans. Robert Hurley (New York: Zone, 1991), vols. 2 and 3, 216.

77. Thomas A. Sebeok, "'Animal' in Biological and Semiotic Perspective," in *American Signatures: Semiotic Inquiry and Method,* ed. Iris Smith (Norman: University of Oklahoma Press, 1991), 159.

78. Of the secret words that attest to the Wolf Man's subjectivity and crypt, Abraham and Torok assert: "What distinguishes a verbal exclusion of this kind from neurotic repression is precisely that it renders verbalization impossible" (*Wolf Man's Magic Word,* 21). See also Nicolas Abraham and Maria Torok, *L'Écorce et le noyau* (Paris: Flammarion, 1987).

79. Derrida, "*Fors,*" xix.

80. Gottfried Wilhelm Leibniz, "Principles of Nature and Grace, Based on Reason," in *Philosophical Essays,* ed. and trans. Roger Ariew and Daniel Garber (Indianapolis: Hackett, 1989), 209.

81. Derrida, "*Fors,*" xix.

82. Moving from Bertram Lewin's hypotheses on the dream screen, Jean-Louis Baudry argues that the cinematic screen doubles the maternal breast and forms, for the viewer, a type of surrogate maternity that simultaneously triggers regression and an "artificial psychosis." "Cinema, like dream, would seem to correspond to a temporary form of regression, but whereas dream, according to Freud, is merely a 'normal hallucinatory psychosis,' cinema offers an artificial psychosis without offering the dreamer the possibility of exercising any kind of immediate control" (Jean-Louis Baudry, "The Apparatus: Metapsychological Approaches to the Impression of Reality in the Cinema," in *Narrative, Apparatus, Ideology: A Film Theory Reader,* ed. Philip Rosen, trans. Jean Andrews and Bertrand Augst [New York: Columbia University Press, 1986], 315). The image of a nurturing film brings the apparatus closer to the threshold of animality, at least to mammalian animals. In the same anthology, see also Jean-Louis Baudry, "Ideological Effects of the Basic Cinematographic Apparatus," trans. Alan Williams, 286–98.

83. Derrida, "*Fors,*" xiv.

84. "*I dreamt that it was night and that I was lying in my bed. (My bed stood with its foot towards the window; in front of the window there was a row of old walnut trees. I know it was winter when I had the dream, and night-time.) Suddenly the window opened of its own accord, and I was terrified to see that some white wolves were sitting on the big walnut tree in front*

of the window. There were six or seven of them. The wolves were quite white, and looked more like foxes or sheep-dogs, for they had big tails like foxes and they had their ears pricked like dogs when they are attending to something. In great terror, evidently of being eaten up by the wolves, I screamed and woke up" (cited in Sigmund Freud, "From the History of an Infantile Neurosis," *SE* 17:29).

85. Abraham and Torok, *Wolf Man's Magic Word,* 33.

86. Ibid., 18.

87. Ibid., 33. See also Abraham and Torok's chapter "The False 'False Witness' and the Rank Affair," in *Wolf Man's Magic Word,* 52–54.

88. Sandor Ferenczi, "Introjection and Transference," in *Sex in Psychoanalysis: Contributions to Psychoanalysis* (New York: Robert Brunner, 1950), 36.

89. Laplanche and Pontalis, *Language of Psycho-Analysis,* 457.

90. Sigmund Freud, *The Interpretation of Dreams, SE* 5:553.

91. Ibid., 553 (emphasis added).

92. Sergei Eisenstein, "The Fourth Dimension in Cinema," in *S. M. Eisenstein: Selected Works: Writings, 1922–34,* ed. and trans. Richard Taylor (Bloomington: Indiana University Press, 1988), 1:192.

93. Ibid., 183.

94. Dziga Vertov, "We: Variant of a Manifesto," in *Kino-Eye: The Writings of Dziga Vertov,* ed. Annette Michelson, trans. Kevin O'Brien (Berkeley: University of California Press, 1984), 8.

95. Ibid., 191.

96. Jacques Derrida, "Freud and the Scene of Writing," in *Writing and Difference,* trans. Alan Bass (Chicago: University of Chicago Press, 1978), 211.

97. Ibid., 228.

Bibliography

Abraham, Nicolas, and Maria Torok. *L'Écorce et le Noyau*. Paris: Flammarion, 1987.

———. "Mourning *or* Melancholia: Introjection *versus* Incorporation. In *The Shell and the Kernel,* ed. and trans. Nicholas T. Rand. Vol. 1, 125–38. Chicago: University of Chicago Press, 1994.

———. *The Wolf Man's Magic Word: A Cryptonymy*. Trans. Nicholas Rand. Minneapolis: University of Minnesota Press, 1986.

Adorno, Theodor. *Minima Moralia: Reflections from Damaged Life*. Trans. E. F. N. Jephcott. New York: Verso, 1974.

Aesop. *Fables of Aesop*. Trans. S. A. Handford. London: Penguin, 1954.

Agamben, Giorgio. *The Coming Community*. Trans. Michael Hardt. Minneapolis: University of Minnesota Press, 1993.

———. *Idea of Prose*. Trans. Michael Sullivan and Sam Whitsitt. Albany: State University of New York, 1995.

———. *Language and Death: The Place of Negativity*. Trans. Karen E. Pinkus with Michael Hardt. Minneapolis: University of Minnesota Press, 1991.

Akutagawa, Ryunosuke. "Bungeitekina, amari ni bungeitekina." *Akutagawa zenshu*. Vol. 9, 57–61. Tokyo: Iwanami Shoten, 1978.

———. *Kamigami no bisho* (Smiles of the Gods). In *Akutagawa Ryunosuke zenshu*. Tokyo: Chikuma Shobo, 1972.

———. *Kappa*. Trans. Geoffrey Bownas. Rutland, Vt.: Charles E. Tuttle, 1970.

———. *Shuju no Kotoba*. Trans. G. H. Healy. Tokyo: Chikuma Shobo, n.d.

———. *Tenkibo*. Trans. G. H. Healy. Tokyo: Chikuma Shobo, n.d.

Alferi, Pierre. *Le Chemin familier du poisson combatif*. Paris: P.O.L., 1992.

Aristotle. *The Complete Works of Aristotle*. Ed. Jonathan Barnes. 2 vols. Princeton, N.J.: Princeton University Press, 1984.

———. "De Interpretatione." In *Complete Works*, 1:25–38.

———. "Metaphysics." In *Complete Works*, 2:1552–728.

———. "Nicomachean Ethics." In *Complete Works*, 2:1729–1867.

———. "Politics." In *Complete Works*, 2:1986–2129.

Artaud, Antonin. "L'Arve et l'aume, tentative anti-grammaticale contre Lewis Carroll." *L'Arbalète* no. 12 (1947): 159–84.

———. "The Theatre and Its Double." In *Antonin Artaud: Collected Works,* trans. Victor Corti. Vol. 4, 1–110. London: Calder and Boyars, 1974.

———. "To Henri Parisot." In *Antonin Artaud: Selected Writings,* ed. Susan Sontag, trans. Helen Weaver, 448–51. New York: Farrar, Straus and Giroux, 1976.

Bacon, Francis. *The Brutality of Fact: Interviews with Francis Bacon.* Ed. David Sylvester. Oxford: Alden Press, 1975.

Barthes, Roland. *Camera Lucida: Reflections on Photography.* Trans. Richard Howard. New York: Hill and Wang, 1981.

———. *La Chambre claire: Note sur la photographie.* Paris: Éditions de l'Étoile, Gallimard, Le Seuil, 1980.

Bataille, Georges. *The Accursed Share.* Trans. Robert Hurley. Vols. 2, 3. New York: Zone, 1991.

———. *Erotism: Death and Sensuality.* Trans. Mary Dalwood. San Francisco: City Lights, 1986.

———. *The Tears of Eros.* Trans. Peter Connor. San Francisco: City Lights, 1989.

———. *Theory of Religion.* Trans. Robert Hurley. New York: Urzone, 1989.

Bateson, William. *Problems of Genetics.* New Haven, Conn.: Yale University Press, 1979.

Baudry, Jean-Louis. "The Apparatus: Metapsychological Approaches to the Impression of Reality in the Cinema." In *Narrative, Apparatus, Ideology: A Film Theory Reader,* ed. Philip Rosen, trans. Jean Andrews and Bertrand Augst, 299–318. New York: Columbia University Press, 1986.

———. "Ideological Effects of the Basic Cinematographic Apparatus." In *Narrative, Apparatus, Ideology: A Film Theory Reader,* ed. Philip Rosen, trans. Alan Williams, 286–98. New York: Columbia University Press, 1986.

Bazin, André. "The Ontology of the Photographic Image." In *What Is Cinema?* ed. and trans. Hugh Gray. Vol. 1, 9–16. Berkeley: University of California Press, 1967.

Benjamin, Walter. "Franz Kafka: On the Tenth Anniversary of His Death." In *Illuminations,* ed. Hannah Arendt, trans. Harry Zohn, 111–40. New York: Schocken, 1969.

———. "A Small History of Photography." In *One Way Street and Other Writings,* trans. Edmund Jephcott and Kingsley Shorter, 240–57. London: Verso, 1979.

Berger, John. "Why Look at Animals?" In *About Looking,* 3–30. New York: Vintage, 1980.

Bergson, Henri. *Creative Evolution.* Trans. Arthur Mitchell. New York: Random House, 1944.

Bernstein, Richard J. "Heidegger's Silence? *Ethos* and Technology." In *New Constellation,* 79–141.

———. *The New Constellation: The Ethical-Political Horizons of Modernity/Postmodernity.* Cambridge: Polity, 1991.

Blanchot, Maurice. "Literature and the Right to Death." In *The Gaze of Orpheus and Other Literary Essays,* ed. P. Adams Sitney, trans. Lydia Davis, 21–62. New York: Station Hill, 1981.

———. *The Writing of the Disaster.* Trans. Ann Smock. Lincoln: University of Nebraska Press, 1986.

Boas, George. "Theriophily." In *Dictionary of the History of Ideas,* ed. Philip P. Wiener, 4:384–89. New York: Scribners, 1973.

Borch-Jacobsen, Mikkel. *The Emotional Tie: Psychoanalysis, Mimesis, and Affect.* Trans. Douglas Birk et al. Stanford, Calif.: Stanford University Press, 1992.

Breuer, Josef, and Sigmund Freud. *Studies on Hysteria.* Vol. 2 of *The Standard Edition of the Complete Psychological Works of Sigmund Freud.* Ed. and trans. James Strachey. 24 vols. London: Hogarth and the Institute of Psycho-Analysis, 1961.

Burke, Edmund. *A Philosophical Enquiry into the Origin of Our Ideas of the Sublime and Beautiful.* Ed. J. T. Boulton. Notre Dame, Ind.: University of Notre Dame Press, 1958.

Butler, Judith. *Gender Trouble: Feminism and the Subversion of Identity.* New York: Routledge, 1990.

Carroll, Lewis. *The Annotated Alice: "Alice's Adventures in Wonderland" and "Through the Looking-Glass."* New York: Penguin, 1960.

Clark, David. "On Being 'The Last Kantian in Nazi Germany': Dwelling with Animals after Levinas." In *Animal Acts: Configuring the Human in Western History,* ed. Jennifer Ham and Matthew Senior, 165–98. New York: Routledge, 1997.

Corbin, Alain. *The Foul and the Fragrant: Odor and the French Social Imagination.* Trans. Miriam L. Kochan, Roy Porter, and Christopher Prendergast. Cambridge, Mass.: Harvard University Press, 1986.

Darwin, Charles. *Darwin's Early and Unpublished Notebooks.* New York: E. A. Dutton, 1974.

———. *The Descent of Man, and Selection in Relation to Sex.* Princeton, N.J.: Princeton University Press, 1981.

———. "N Notebook." In *Darwin on Man: A Psychological Study of Scientific Creativity,* ed. Howard E. Gruber. New York: E. P. Dutton, 1974.

——. *On the Origin of Species.* Cambridge, Mass.: Harvard University Press, 1964.

Davies, Paul. *Other Worlds: Space, Superspace, and the Quantum Universe.* New York: Simon and Schuster, 1980.

Deleuze, Gilles. *Bergsonism.* Trans. Hugh Tomlinson and Barbara Habberjam. New York: Zone, 1991.

——. *Cinema 1: The Movement-Image.* Trans. Hugh Tomlinson and Barbara Habberjam. Minneapolis: University of Minnesota Press, 1986.

——. *Cinema 2: The Time-Image.* Trans. Hugh Tomlinson and Robert Galeta. Minneapolis: University of Minnesota Press, 1989.

——. *The Logic of Sense.* Ed. Constantin V. Boundas. Trans. Mark Lester with Charles Stivale. New York: Columbia University Press, 1990.

——. *Proust and Signs.* Trans. Richard Howard. New York: Braziller, 1972.

Deleuze, Gilles, and Guattari, Félix. *Kafka: Toward a Minor Literature.* Trans. Dana Polan. Minneapolis: University of Minnesota Press, 1986.

——. *A Thousand Plateaus: Capitalism and Schizophrenia.* Trans. Brian Massumi. Minneapolis: University of Minnesota Press, 1987.

Derrida, Jacques. "L'animal que donc je suis." In *L'animal autobiographique,* ed. Marie-Louise Mallet, 251–301. Paris: Galilée, 1999.

——. *Aporias.* Trans. Thomas Dutoit. Stanford, Calif.: Stanford University Press, 1993.

——. "Before the Law." In *Acts of Literature,* ed. Derek Attridge, trans. Avital Ronell and Christine Roulston, 221–52. New York: Routledge, Chapman and Hall, 1992.

——. "'Eating Well,' or The Calculation of the Subject: An Interview with Jacques Derrida." In *Who Comes after the Subject?* ed. Eduardo Cadava, Peter Connor, and Jean-Luc Nancy, trans. Peter Connor and Avital Ronell, 96–119. New York: Routledge, 1991.

——. "Economimesis." *Diacritics* 11 (1981): 3–25.

——. "La Facteur de la Vérité." In *The Post Card: From Socrates to Freud and Beyond,* trans. Alan Bass, 411–96. Chicago: University of Chicago Press, 1987.

——. "Forcener le subjectile." In *Artaud: Dessins et Portraits,* 55–108. Paris: Gallimard, 1986.

——. "*Fors:* The Anglish Words of Nicolas Abraham and Maria Torok," trans. Barbara Johnson, in *The Wolf Man's Magic Word: A Cryptonomy,* Nicolas Abraham and Maria Torok, trans. Nicholas Rand (Minneapolis: University of Minnesota Press, 1986), xi–xlviii.

———. "Freud and the Scene of Writing." In *Writing and Difference,* 196–231.

———. "How to Avoid Speaking: Denials." In *Derrida and Negative Theology,* ed. Harold Coward and Toby Foshay, trans. Ken Frieden, 73–142. Albany: State University of New York Press, 1992.

———. *Limited Inc.* Ed. Gerald Graff. Trans. Samuel Weber. Evanston, Ill.: Northwestern University Press, 1988.

———. *Memoires for Paul de Man.* Trans. Cecile Lindsay, Jonathan Culler, and Eduardo Cadava. New York: Columbia University Press, 1986.

———. *Of Grammatology.* Trans. Gayatri Chakravorty Spivak. Baltimore, Md.: Johns Hopkins University Press, 1974.

———. *Of Spirit: Heidegger and the Question.* Trans. Geoffrey Bennington and Rachel Bowlby. Chicago: University of Chicago Press, 1989.

———. "Otobiographies." In *The Ear of the Other,* ed. Christie V. McDonald, trans. Peggy Kamuf and Avital Ronell, 1–38. New York: Schocken, 1985.

———. "La Parole soufflée." In *Writing and Difference,* 169–250.

———. "The Pit and the Pyramid: Introduction to Hegel's Semiology." In *Margins of Philosophy,* trans. Alan Bass, 69–108. Chicago: University of Chicago Press, 1982.

———. "Plato's Pharmacy." In *Dissemination,* trans. Barbara Johnson, 61–172. Chicago: University of Chicago Press, 1981.

———. *Spurs: Nietzsche's Styles.* Trans. Barbara Harlow. Chicago: University of Chicago Press, 1979.

———. "The Theater of Cruelty and the Closure of Representation." In *Writing and Difference,* 232–94.

———. "To Speculate—on 'Freud.'" In *The Post Card: From Socrates to Freud and Beyond,* trans. Alan Bass, 257–410. Chicago: University of Chicago Press, 1987.

———. "The Voice That Keeps Silence." In *Speech and Phenomenon: And Other Essays On Husserl's Theory of Signs,* trans. David B. Allison, 70–87. Evanston, Ill.: Northwestern University Press, 1973.

———. "White Mythology: Metaphor in the Text of Philosophy." In *Margins of Philosophy,* trans. Alan Bass, 207–71. Chicago: University of Chicago Press, 1982.

———. *Writing and Difference,* trans. Alan Bass. Chicago: University of Chicago Press, 1978.

Descartes, René. "Discourse on the Method." In *Descartes: Selected Philosophical Writings,* trans. John Cottingham, Robert Stoothoff, and Dugald Murdoch, 20–56. Cambridge: Cambridge University Press, 1988.

———. "Optics." In *Descartes: Selected Philosophical Writings,* trans. John Cottingham, Robert Stoothoff, and Dugald Murdoch, 57–72. Cambridge: Cambridge University Press, 1988.

Dewey, John. "The Influence of Darwin on Philosophy." In *Darwin,* ed. Philip Appleman, 305–13. New York: Norton, 1970.

Eisenstein, Sergei. "The Fourth Dimension in Cinema." In *S. M. Eisenstein: Selected Works: Writings, 1922–34,* ed. and trans. Richard Taylor, Vol. 1, 181–94. Bloomington: Indiana University Press, 1988.

Empson, William. "Alice in Wonderland: The Child as Swain." In *Some Versions of Pastoral.* New York: New Directions, 1974.

Ferenczi, Sandor. "Introjection and Transference." In *Sex in Psychoanalysis: Contributions to Psychoanalysis,* 35–93. New York: Robert Brunner, 1950.

Fóti, Véronique M. *Heidegger and the Poets: Poiesis/Sophia/Techne.* N.J.: Humanities, 1992.

Foucault, Michel. *Madness and Civilization: A History of Insanity in the Age of Reason.* Trans. Richard Howard. New York: Vintage, 1965.

———. *The Order of Things: An Archaeology of the Human Sciences.* New York: Vintage, 1970.

Freud, Sigmund. *Beyond the Pleasure Principle.* In *Standard Edition,* 18:1–64.

———. *Civilization and Its Discontents.* In *Standard Edition,* 21:57–146.

———. *The Complete Letters of Sigmund Freud to Wilhelm Fliess: 1887–1904.* Ed. and trans. Jeffrey Moussaieff Masson. Cambridge, Mass.: Harvard University Press, Belknap Press, 1985.

———. "Fragment of an Analysis of a Case of Hysteria." In *Standard Edition,* 7:1–122.

———. "From the History of an Infantile Neurosis." In *Standard Edition,* 17:1–122.

———. "Group Psychology and the Analysis of the Ego." In *Standard Edition,* 18:65–144.

———. *The Interpretation of Dreams.* In *Standard Edition,* vols. 4, 5.

———. *Introductory Lectures on Psycho-Analysis.* In *Standard Edition,* vols. 15, 16.

———. "Mourning and Melancholia." In *Standard Edition,* 14:237–58.

———. "The Project for a Scientific Psychology." In *Standard Edition,* 1:281–387.

———. "Psycho-Analytic Notes on an Autobiographical Account of a Case of Paranoia (Dementia Paranoides)." In *Standard Edition,* 12:1–84.

———. "The Resistances to Psycho-Analysis." In *Standard Edition,* 19:213–22.

———. *The Standard Edition of the Complete Psychological Works of Sigmund Freud.* Ed. and trans. James Strachey. 24 vols. London: Hogarth Press and the Institute of Psycho-Analysis, 1961.

———. *Totem and Taboo.* In *Standard Edition,* 13:1–161.

———. "The Unconscious." In *Standard Edition,* 14:159–204.

Fried, Michael. *Courbet's Realism.* Chicago: University of Chicago Press, 1990.

Frisch, Karl von. *The Dancing Bees: An Account of the Life and Senses of the Honey Bee.* Trans. Dora Ilse. New York: Harcourt, Brace and Company, 1953.

Frizot, Michel. *La Chronophotographie.* Beaune, France: Association des Amis de Marey et Ministère de la Culture, 1984.

Goodwin, Brian. "Organisms and Minds: The Dialectics of the Animal-Human Interface in Biology." In *What Is an Animal?* ed. Tim Ingold, 100–109. London: Unwin Hyman, 1988.

Grandin, Temple. *Thinking in Pictures: And Other Reports from My Life with Autism.* New York: Vintage, 1996.

Hamacher, Werner. "'Disgregation of the Will': Nietzsche on the Individual and Individuality." In *Reconstructing Individualism: Autonomy, Individuality, and the Self in Western Thought,* ed. Thomas C. Heller, Morton Sosna, and David E. Wellbery, trans. Jeffrey S. Librett, 106–39. Stanford, Calif.: Stanford University Press, 1986.

Haraway, Donna J. *Primate Visions: Gender, Race, and Nature in the World of Modern Science.* New York: Routledge, 1989.

———. *Simians, Cyborgs, and Women: The Reinvention of Nature.* New York: Routledge, 1991.

Hart, John Jr., and Barry Gordon. "Neural Subsystems for Object Knowledge," *Nature* 3 September 1992: 60–64.

Hearn, Lafcadio. *In Ghostly Japan.* Rutland, Vt.: Charles E. Tuttle, 1971.

———. *Kwaidan: Stories and Studies of Strange Things.* Rutland, Vt.: Charles E. Tuttle, 1971.

Hearne, Vicki. *Adam's Task: Calling Animals by Name.* New York: Alfred A. Knopf, 1987.

———. *Bandit: Dossier of a Dangerous Dog.* New York: HarperCollins, 1991.

————. *Nervous Horses*. Austin: University of Texas Press, 1980.

Hegel, G. W. F. *Phenomenology of Spirit*. Trans. A. V. Miller. Oxford: Oxford University Press, 1977.

————. *"Philosophy of Spirit*, Introduction." In *Hegel: The Essential Writings*, ed. Frederick G. Weiss, trans. William Wallace, 190–252. New York: Harper and Row, 1974.

Heidegger, Martin. *Being and Time*. Trans. John Macquarrie and Edward Robinson. New York: Harper and Row, 1962.

————. *The Fundamental Concepts of Metaphysics: World, Finitude, Solitude*. Trans. William McNeill and Nicholas Walker. Bloomington: Indiana University Press, 1995.

————. *An Introduction to Metaphysics*. Trans. Ralph Manheim. New York: Doubleday, 1961.

————. "The Nature of Language." In *On the Way to Language*, trans. Peter D. Hertz, 57–110. New York: Harper and Row, 1971.

————. *Nietzsche: The Eternal Recurrence of the Same*. Trans. David Farrell Krell. 4 vols. San Francisco: Harper and Row, 1984.

————. "The Origin of the Work of Art." In *Poetry, Language, Thought*, 15–88.

————. *Poetry, Language, Thought*. Trans. Albert Hofstadter. New York: Harper and Row, 1971.

————. "The Thing." In *Poetry, Language, Thought*, 163–86.

————. "What Are Poets For?" In *Poetry, Language, Thought*, 89–142.

Herder, Johann Gottfried. "Essay on the Origin of Language." In *On the Origin of Language*, trans. John H. Morgan and Alexander Gode. Chicago: University of Chicago Press, 1966.

————. "More Lurid Figures." *Diacritics* 20(1990): 2–27.

Horkheimer, Max, and Theodor W. Adorno. *Dialectic of Enlightenment*. Trans. John Cumming. New York: Continuum, 1972.

Husserl, Edmund. *Ideas: General Introduction to Pure Phenomenology*. Trans. W. R. Boyce Gibson. New York: Macmillan, 1962.

Josephson, Matthew. *Edison: A Biography*. New York: John Wiley and Sons, 1959.

Jung, Carl G. "Approaching the Unconscious." In *Man and His Symbols*, ed. Carl G. Jung, 1–94. New York: Dell, 1964.

Kafka, Franz. "Jackals and Arabs." In *Penal Colony*, 150–54.

————. "Josephine the Singer, or the Mouse Folk." In *Penal Colony*, 256–78.

————. *The Metamorphosis*. In *Penal Colony*, 67–134.

————. *The Penal Colony: Stories and Short Pieces,* trans. Willa Muir and Edwin Muir. New York: Schocken, 1961.

————. "A Report to an Academy." In *Penal Colony,* 173–83.

Kant, Immanuel. "Conjectural Beginning of Human History." In *Kant: On History,* ed. Lewis White Beck, trans. Lewis White Beck, Robert E. Anchor, and Emil L. Fackenheim, 53–68. New York: Macmillan, 1963.

————. *The Metaphysics of Morals.* Trans. Mary Gregor. Cambridge: Cambridge University Press, 1991.

Karatani, Kojin. *Origins of Modern Japanese Literature.* Trans. and ed. Brett de Bary. Durham, N.C.: Duke University Press, 1993.

Kirchner, H. "Ein archäologischer Beitrag zur Urgeschichte des Schamanismus." *Anthropos* 47 (1952).

Kittler, Friedrich A. *Discourse Networks 1800/1900.* Trans. Michael Metteer with Chris Cullens. Stanford, Calif.: Stanford University Press, 1990.

Kofman, Sarah. "Descartes Entrapped." In *Who Comes After the Subject?* ed. Eduardo Cadava, Peter Connor, Jean-Luc Nancy, trans. Kathryn Aschheim, 178–97. New York: Routledge, 1991.

Kojève, Alexandre. *Introduction to the Reading of Hegel: Lectures on the "Phenomenology of Spirit."* Ed. Allan Bloom. Trans. James H. Nichols Jr. Ithaca, N.Y.: Cornell University Press, 1969.

Krafft-Ebing, Richard von. *Psychopathia Sexualis.* Trans. F. J. Rebman. New York: Physicians and Surgeons Book Company, 1925.

Lacan, Jacques. *Écrits.* Paris: Éditions du Seuil, 1970.

————. *Le Séminaire: Les Quatre Concepts fondamentaux de la psychoanalyse.* Vol. 11 (xi). Paris: Éditions du Seuil, 1973.

————. "Of Structure as an Inmixing of an Otherness Prerequisite to Any Subject Whatever." In *The Structuralist Controversy: The Languages of Criticism and the Sciences of Man,* ed. Richard Macksey and Eugenio Donato, 186–200. Baltimore, Md.: Johns Hopkins University Press, 1970.

————. "Of the Gaze as *Objet Petit a.*" In *The Four Fundamental Concepts of Psycho-Analysis,* ed. Jacques-Alain Miller, trans. Alan Sheridan, 67–122. New York: Norton, 1977.

Lacoue-Labarthe, Philippe. *Heidegger, Art, and Politics.* Trans. Chris Turner. Cambridge: Basil Blackwell, 1990.

Laplanche, Jean. *Life and Death in Psychoanalysis.* Trans. Jeffrey Mehlman. Baltimore, Md.: Johns Hopkins University Press, 1976.

Laplanche, Jean, and Pontalis, J.-B. *The Language of Psycho-Analysis.* Trans. Donald Nicholson-Smith. New York: Norton, 1973.

Lebensztejn, Jean-Claude. "Miaulique (Fantasie chromatique)." Manuscript, 1996.

Leibniz, Gottfried Wilhelm. "From the Letters to Johann Bernoulli." In *Philosophical Essays,* 167–70.

———. "A New System of the Nature and Communication of Substances, and of the Union of the Soul and Body." In *Philosophical Essays,* 138–44.

———. *Philosophical Essays.* Ed. and trans. Roger Ariew and Daniel Garber. Indianapolis, Ind.: Hackett, 1989.

———. "Principles of Nature and Grace, Based on Reason." In *Philosophical Essays,* 206–12.

———. "The Principles of Philosophy, or the Monadology." In *Philosophical Essays,* 213–24.

Levinas, Emmanuel. *Existence and Existents.* Trans. Alphonso Lingus. Dordrecht: Kluwer Academic, 1978.

———. "The Name of a Dog, or Natural Rights." In *Difficult Freedom: Essays on Judaism,* trans. Seán Hand, 151–53. Baltimore, Md.: Johns Hopkins University Press, 1990.

Lewinsohn, Richard. *Animals, Men, and Myths.* Trans. Harper and Brothers. New York: Harper and Brothers, 1954.

Ley, Willy. *Dawn of Zoology.* Englewood Cliffs, N.J.: Prentice-Hall, 1968.

Lippit, Akira Mizuta. "Crossroads to Nowhere: Utopian Scents." In *Semiotics 1990,* ed. Karen Haworth, John Deely, and Terry Prewitt, 311–18. New York: University Press of America, 1993.

———. "Phenomenologies of the Surface: Radiation-Body-Image." In *Collecting Visible Evidence,* ed. Jane Gaines and Michael Renov, 65–83. Minneapolis: University of Minnesota Press, 1999.

Liu, Albert. Letter to author, 14 January 1999.

Locke, John. *Two Treatises of Government.* Cambridge: Cambridge University Press, 1960.

Lyotard, Jean-François. "Can Thought Go On without a Body?" In *The Inhuman: Reflections on Time,* trans. Geoffrey Bennington and Rachel Bowlby, 8–23. Stanford, Calif.: Stanford University Press, 1991.

———. *The Differend: Phrases in Dispute.* Trans. Georges Van Den Abbeele. Minneapolis: University of Minnesota Press, 1988.

———. "The Inarticulate, or The Differend Itself." Lecture, Whitney Humanities Center, Yale University, 1992.

Macksey, Richard. "Lions and Squares: Opening Remarks." In Macksey and Donato, *Structuralist Controversy,* 1–14.

Macksey, Richard, and Eugenio Donato, eds. *The Structuralist Controversy: The Languages of Criticism and the Sciences of Man.* Baltimore, Md.: Johns Hopkins University Press, 1970.

Marin, Louis. "The Fabulous Animal." In *Food for Thought,* trans. Mette Hjort, 44–54. Baltimore, Md.: Johns Hopkins University Press, 1989.

Metz, Christian. *The Imaginary Signifier: Psychoanalysis and the Cinema.* Trans. Celia Britton, Annwyl Williams, Ben Brewster, and Alfred Guzzetti. Bloomington: Indiana University Press, 1982.

Midgley, Mary. "Beasts, Brutes, and Monsters." In *What Is An Animal?* ed. Tim Ingold, 35–46. London: Unwin Hyman, 1988.

Montaigne, Michel de. "Apology for Raymond Sebond." In *Complete Essays,* 318–457.

———. *The Complete Essays of Montaigne.* Trans. Donald Frame. Stanford, Calif.: Stanford University Press, 1958.

———. "Of Smells." In *Complete Essays,* 228–29.

———. "Of the Power of the Imagination." In *Complete Essays,* 68–75.

Muybridge, Eadweard. *Animals in Motion.* Ed. Lewis S. Brown. New York: Dover, 1957.

———. *The Human Figure in Motion.* New York: Dover, 1955.

Nancy, Jean-Luc. *The Inoperative Community.* Ed. and trans. Peter Connor. Minneapolis: University of Minnesota Press, 1991.

Nietzsche, Friedrich. *Ecce Homo.* Ed. and trans. Walter Kaufmann. New York: Vintage, 1967.

———. *The Gay Science.* Trans. Walter Kaufmann. New York: Vintage, 1974.

———. *On the Genealogy of Morals.* Trans. Walter Kaufmann. New York: Random House, 1967.

———. "On the Uses and Disadvantages of History for Life." In *Untimely Meditations,* trans. R. J. Hollingdale, 57–123. Cambridge: Cambridge University Press, 1983.

———. *Thus Spoke Zarathustra: A Book for None and All.* Trans. Walter Kaufmann. New York: Penguin, 1954.

———. *Twilight of the Idols and The Anti-Christ.* Trans. R. J. Hollingdale. New York: Penguin, 1968.

Norris, Margot. *Beasts of the Modern Imagination: Darwin, Nietzsche, Kafka, Ernst, and Lawrence.* Baltimore, Md.: Johns Hopkins University Press, 1985.

Okakura, Kakuzo. *The Book of Tea*. Ed. Everett F. Bleiler. New York: Dover, 1964.

Peirce, Charles Sanders. "Minute Logic." In *Peirce on Signs: Writings on Semiotic by Charles Sanders Peirce,* ed. James Hoopes, 231–38. Chapel Hill: University of North Carolina Press, 1991.

Plato. *Timaeus and Critias*. Trans. Desmond Lee. New York: Penguin, 1965.

Pliny the Elder. *Natural History: A Selection*. Trans. John F. Healy. New York: Penguin, 1991.

Poe, Edgar Allan. "The Murders in the Rue Morgue." In *Great Tales and Poems of Edgar Allan Poe*. New York: Washington Square, 1951.

Rickels, Laurence A. "Pact Rats." In *The Case of California*. Baltimore, Md.: Johns Hopkins University Press, 1991.

Rilke, Rainer Maria. "Duino Elegies." In *The Selected Poetry of Rainer Maria Rilke,* ed. and trans. Stephen Mitchell, 151–226. New York: Harper and Row, 1982.

Ritvo, Lucille B. *Darwin's Influence on Freud: A Tale of Two Sciences*. New Haven, Conn.: Yale University Press, 1990.

Ronell, Avital. *The Telephone Book: Technology—Schizophrenia—Electric Speech*. Lincoln: University of Nebraska Press, 1989.

Rousseau, Jean-Jacques. "Discourse on the Origin of Inequality." In *Basic Political Writings of Jean-Jacques Rousseau,* ed. and trans. Donald A. Cress, 25–110. Indianapolis: Hackett, 1987.

———. "Essay on the Origin of Languages Which Treats of Melody and Musical Imitation." In *On the Origin of Language*. Trans. John H. Morgan. Chicago: University of Chicago Press, 1966.

Schopenhauer, Arthur. "The Indestructibility of Being." In *Essays and Aphorisms,* ed. and trans. R. J. Hollingdale. New York: Penguin, 1970.

Schrödinger, Erwin. *My View of the World*. Trans. Cecily Hastings. Woodbridge, Conn.: Ox Bow, 1983.

———. *What Is Life? The Physical Aspect of the Living Cell*. Cambridge: Cambridge University Press, 1967.

Sebeok, Thomas A. "'Animal' in Biological and Semiotic Perspective." In *American Signatures: Semiotic Inquiry and Method,* ed. Iris Smith, 159–73. Norman: University of Oklahoma Press, 1991.

———. "Give Me Another Horse." *American Journal of Semiotics* 8 (1991): 41–52.

Shell, Marc. "Marranos (Pigs), or From Coexistence to Toleration." *Critical Inquiry* 17.2 (1991): 306–35.

Sorabji, Richard. *Animal Minds and Human Morals: The Origins of the Western Debate*. Ithaca, N.Y.: Cornell University Press, 1993.

Stoddart, D. Michael. *The Scented Ape: The Biology and Culture of Human Odour*. Cambridge: Cambridge University Press, 1990.

Swift, Jonathan. *Gulliver's Travels and Other Writings*. Ed. Miriam Kosh Starkman. New York: Bantam, 1962.

Tanizaki, Junichiro. "Jozetsu-roku." In *Tanizaki Junichiro Zenshu*. Vol. 20. Tokyo: Chuokoronsha, 1972–75.

U.S. Committee on the Use of Laboratory Animals in Biomedical and Behavioral Research, Commission on Life Sciences National Research Council, Institute of Medicine. *Use of Laboratory Animals in Biomedical and Behavioral Research*. Washington, D.C.: National Academy Press, 1988.

Vertov, Dziga. "We: Variant of a Manifesto." In *Kino-Eye: The Writings of Dziga Vertov,* ed. Annette Michelson, trans. Kevin O'Brien. Berkeley: University of California Press, 1984.

Wilder, Rachel. "Rare Brain Disorder Sheds Light on How We Think." *Johns Hopkins Gazette,* 14 September 1992: 1, 3.

Wittgenstein, Ludwig. *Philosophical Investigations*. Trans. G. E. M. Anscombe. New York: Macmillan, 1958.

Index

267

Akira Mizuta Lippit is professor of comparative literature, East Asian languages and cultures, and cinema at the University of Southern California. He is author of *Atomic Light (Shadow Optics)* (Minnesota, 2005).